Publishers for Mass Entertainment in Nineteenth Century America

Publishers for Mass Entertainment in Nineteenth Century America

**Edited by
Madeleine B. Stern**

G. K. Hall & Co.   Boston, Massachusetts

Library of Congress Cataloging in Publication Data

Stern, Madeleine Bettina, 1912-
  Publishers for mass entertainment in nineteenth
century America.

  Includes index.
  1. Popular literature—Publishing—United States—
History—19th century. 2. Publishers and publishing—
United States—History—19th century. I. Title.
Z473.S8575   070.5'0973   80-17692
ISBN 0-8161-8471-2

Contents

Introduction   ix

Acknowledgments   xxi

1   John B. Alden   1

2   W. L. Allison and Company   9

3   Altemus & Co.   11

4   D. Appleton & Company   17

5   Maturin Murray Ballou   27

6   Beadle & Co.   35

7   Irwin P. Beadle   51

8   Belford, Clarke & Company   59

9   A. L. Burt Company 65

10   Carey & Lea   73

11   G. W. Carleton   81

12   T. R. Dawley   89'

13   Robert M. DeWitt   93

14   DeWolfe, Fiske, & Company   97

15   Dick & Fitzgerald   101

16   Donnelley, Loyd & Co.   115

Contents

17   Donohue & Henneberry   119

18   Elliott, Thomes & Talbot   123

19   Samuel French   131

20   Gleason's Publishing Hall   137

21   An Introductory Review of Harper Highlights   147

22   Harper & Bros.   151

23   Henry Holt and Company   157

24   Hurst and Company   167

25   M. J. Ivers and Company   173

26   Laird and Lee   177

27   The Frank Leslie Publishing House   181

28   A. K. Loring   191

29   John W. Lovell   199

30   Lovell, Coryell & Company   211

31   F. M. Lupton Publishing Company   215

32   George Munro   221

33   Norman L. Munro   225

34   T. B. Peterson & Brothers   229

35   Pictorial Printing Company   237

36   Pollard & Moss   241

37   Porter & Coates   245

Contents

38   Louis Prang & Co.   251

39   James Redpath   261

40   Roberts Brothers   267

41   Street & Smith   277

42   Frank Tousey   295

43   Sinclair Tousey   303

44   United States Book Company   307

45   Wiley and Putnam   311

46   R. W. Worthington & Company   317

     Author-Title Index   323

Introduction

Of all the literary revolutions that have occurred over
the centuries, none is more fascinating than the upheaval
in reading habits triggered by nineteenth-century American publishers who produced and distributed cheap books
for the millions. Many of those publishers have been
forgotten; their imprints have become their epitaphs.
Yet their influence has been incalculable. They cre-
ated--and then proceeded to supply--an all but unlim-
ited demand for entertaining and instructive reading
matter in portable format at low prices. They upheld
the belief that the reader had the right (as Marie E.
Korey states in her study of John B. Alden) to "easier
access to good books," that "'the best literature of
the world [should and could be] placed within the reach
of millions to whom it was before unattainable.'" The
multitudinous series and so-called libraries of books
projected by those publishers constituted for the masses of nineteenth-century American readers the motion
picture, radio, and television of our day. Many
nineteenth-century American publishers built their
houses upon the thesis that the millions had the right
to affordable literature, and in so doing they not only
launched a literary revolution but produced books that
still reflect the reading tastes of their age. Those
publishing houses--and the literary revolution they
generated--form the focus of this volume.

There has long been a need for such a work. Histories of the publishing trade, analyses of literary
movements, even surveys of the paperback industry and
the cheap book do not fulfill its purpose: to provide
an encylopedic assemblage of detailed information not
readily available elsewhere concerning those publishing
houses that shaped popular literary taste in nineteenth-
century America.

ix

Introduction

The forty-five firms represented were selected on
the basis of their relative contribution to mass entertainment. A few, such as Appleton, Harper, and Holt,
devoted only part of their resources to that field; the
majority, including Beadle, Street & Smith, Frank Tousey,
and many lesser houses, confined themselves to applying
the principle: cheap books for the millions. Some of
the houses, such as Redpath and the United States Book
Company, flourished only a few years; others--for example Appleton, Samuel French, Holt, Hurst--endured a
century or more. Like James Redpath, some published
only a few titles; others produced vast quantities:
"Book-A-Day Lovell," for example, or John B. Alden, who
claimed to have "published some 2,000 tons of good literature" and to produce "4,000 books a day." Some publishers, such as Dick & Fitzgerald, became millionaires;
others, such as Loring, went bankrupt. Some publishers
were motivated by high ideals. Summarizing Appleton's
"role in satisfying the popular tastes of new and avid
nineteenth-century readers in a rapidly expanding, literate nation," Frank E. Comparato writes that "it was
mass publishing with a grand purpose." Others, such as
Hurst, lent their imprints to books not only cheaply
priced but cheaply produced.

Whatever the variations among the forty-five selected publishers, they had one thing in common. They
all combined money-making with the popularization of
entertainment and instruction. Having helped a nation
to read and enjoy reading, they demanded a share of the
profits accruing from that process. Like the Appletons,
for example, they "could not watch America's growing
mass reading market without feeling themselves entitled
to a part of the business." Like Carey & Lea, they
"involved themselves in . . . publishing ventures that
proved to be important in the rise of the American book
industry, of significance to American readership, and of
profit to themselves." As Lawrence Parke Murphy puts it
succinctly in his sketch of Altemus & Co., the firm exerted "its influence by combining money-making with the
popularization of culture."

Such popularization was made possible primarily by
the publication and widespread distribution of inexpensive

Introduction

books; and so this volume--with its encyclopedic histories of publishing houses, their founders, their development, their purposes, and their achievements--is also
a survey of the cheap book and its effect upon American
literary taste. Early in the century, as Joel Myerson
puts it in his account of Wiley and Putnam, "reprints of
English and continental authors formed nearly all of a
publisher's list." In those days the Philadelphia publisher had a strategic location from which to distribute
his foreign reprints. As David Kaser writes in his study
of Carey & Lea, an important factor that gave the firm
dominance was "Philadelphia's geographical proximity to
the South and its situation at the head of the wagon
road over the mountains to Pittsburgh and thence down
the Ohio to the western country. Advantageous delivery
schedules and freight costs thus gave Philadelphia a
trading monopoly over western markets." Within two
decades, however, the picture shifted. As Kaser puts
it, "By the late 1830s . . . much was changing that
would impact upon American publishing. . . . The technology of printing was changing, paving the way for
cheap publishing in the years just ahead. The Erie
Canal had been opened, giving New York the ability to
compete equitably with Philadelphia for the rapidly
growing western markets."

Boston too competed. From that city, Gleason's
Publishing Hall and Maturin M. Ballou sent forth the
story papers in which, in a sense, one major type of
cheap book had its beginning. In such periodicals as
The Flag of Our Union, Gleason's Pictorial Drawing Room
Companion, and Ballou's Dollar Monthly were run colorful
serials of sensational adventures, heavily plotted cliff-
hangers of pirates and buccaneers, revolution, the border, and the West. Of all comparable periodicals none
was more popular than Street & Smith's New York Weekly,
which was launched in the 1850s and in which, as Ralph D.
Gardner writes, "were romances of kidnapped English heiresses, noble schoolteachers, and courageous working
girls." "The publishers knew what readers wanted:
maidens pursued--but never quite caught--by villains;
poor lads who overcame enormous obstacles to win fame
and fortune." The narratives featured in those story

xi

papers would soon reemerge in a different guise as the
dime novel, the cheap fiction, a new indigenous American
literature. Indeed, many later publications of the New
York firm of Frank Leslie still suggest to the eye "a
transition stage between periodical and book."

Of the many varieties of cheap book that figure in
this volume, perhaps the most interesting is the one
known as the dime novel. The concept of producing a
novel similar to or reprinted from the story paper serials, casing it in gaudily illustrated paper covers, pric-
ing it at a dime, and publishing it in a numbered series,
belongs to the House of Beadle, whose Dime Novel No. 1--
Malaeska: the Indian Wife of the White Hunter by Ann S.
Stephens--appeared in 1860. In time the Dime Library
would be followed by the Half-Dime Library (opening with
Deadwood Dick, the Prince of the Road), the Beadle Boy's
Library, the Fireside Library, the Waverly Library--
names that have a nostalgic ring today.

The series concept was not new. As early as 1831,
for example, the House of Harper had published its Library of Select Novels which, according to Anna Lou
Ashby, "antedated by four decades the 'library' period
of cheap book production." Wiley's Library of American
Books of the 1840s included in its roster of authors
Hawthorne, Melville, and Poe. The Beadle series, however, along with a multitude of series of cheap books
produced by competing publishers, had a distinctive flavor. Ralph D. Gardner calls the dime novel "perhaps the
first uniquely American form of literature," and asserts
that Street & Smith "made national heroes of Buffalo
Bill and Nick Carter. . . . Readers were enthralled by
story heroes whose names have become American colloquialisms." Stories based upon colonial America and the American Revolution, the Mexican War and the winning of the
American West, stories peopled with painted Indians and
forty-niners, trappers and Texas rangers, joined romances
concerned with English barons or Turkish slaves and did
indeed inject a strong American flavor into the concoc-
tion that was the dime novel.

The authors of dime novels and other cheap series
were often as colorful as their heroes. Ralph D.
Gardner traces the careers of such writers as Edward

Introduction

Zane Carroll Judson, who began life by running away to
sea and ended it by writing, under the pseudonym Ned
Buntline, the stories that made the hunter and army
scout William F. Cody famous as Buffalo Bill. In between he fought in the Seminole War, the Mexican War,
and the Civil War, killed a man in a duel, spent some
time in prison, and traveled the frontier with Texas
Jack, Wild Bill Hickok, and William F. Cody. The author
of stories about Pawnee Bill and General Custer--Colonel
Prentiss Ingraham--went Judson a few steps (and battles)
better. Before heading West he fought not only in the
Civil War but with Juarez in Mexico, in the Austrian
army, in Africa, Asia, and Cuba.

One of the most popular authors of "tales of impoverished lads who, with luck and pluck, strove and
succeeded until they achieved fame and fortune" was
Horatio Alger, Jr. According to Ralph D. Gardner, Alger
"lived in the Newsboys Lodging House in New York, dashed
westward with the homesteaders, traveled alone through
wild Indian country, visited lawless mining camps in the
California Sierras, and sailed around Cape Horn in a
four-masted schooner." Alger's rags-to-riches stories
sold in the millions after they appeared--or reappeared--
in the 10-cent format.

Other types of mass market books, whether published
in series or as individual volumes, whether cased in paper or in cloth, whether priced at a dime or a dollar,
also made a powerful impact. One of the most popular
novels of the 1860s was St. Elmo by Augusta Evans Wilson,
published by G. W. Carleton, a story in which "the heroine, a model of virtue and erudition, reforms a man of
the world and marries him." According to the historian
of best-sellers, Frank Luther Mott, "children were named
'St. Elmo'; towns, streets, hotels were christened with
the magic name," and the novel had "a sale of a million
copies." It was St. Elmo's publisher, Carleton, who also
"catered to mass entertainment by the publication of
books of humor," the writings of "Artemus Ward," "Josh
Billings," and "Private Miles O'Reilly," books that exposed "the absurdities of American life by such devices
as graphic caricature, execrable spelling, and gross
exaggeration," books whose gentle but pointed satire was

relished by a nation learning to laugh at itself. And
for a nation that spent much of its life at home, another publishing house, Dick & Fitzgerald, became large-
scale specialists in books for home entertainment:
recitation, dialogue, and jokebooks, songsters and guides
to dancing, books of tableaux, shadow pantomimes, and
charades.

Sentimental romances, sensational thrillers, adventure stories, society novels, humor, and parlor entertainments could reach a mass readership only if they
were produced in wholesale and priced cheaply. Advancing technology applied to processes of binding, printing,
composition, and stereotyping helped make mass production
and cheap prices possible. In order to entertain the
masses such books also required adequate methods of distribution. Some firms, such as Dick & Fitzgerald, operated primarily as mail-order houses, shipping cheap
books across the country from a post office box number.
Appleton sold its Webster spellers "'in cases of seventy-
two dozen,'" to be "'bought by all the large dry-goods
houses and supply stores and furnished by them to every
cross-roads store in the country.'" By and large, the
majority of publishers of cheap series reached the masses of readers through the work of Sinclair Tousey. His
American News Company was, as Nathaniel H. Puffer states,
"primarily the distributor for all publications of dozens of publishers" and "was in the forefront of wholesale
newspaper and periodical distribution in New York and
the country at large."

Thanks to improvements in technology and distribution, opportunity for the mass production and sale of
cheap books was wide open. Ralph Gardner describes the
competition: " . . . publishers early joined the rush
to provide . . . exciting, action-filled, inexpensive
literature to men who were laying railroad tracks across
the continent, to Union soldiers who carried them in
knapsacks to battlefield in the South, to people who
worked on farms or in teeming cities"--in short, to the
masses.

Actually, imitation and keen competition had characterized the publishing trade long before Beadle's innovation. Early in the century, as David Kaser explains,

Introduction

"the reprinting of English novelists in this country
was entirely a matter of piracy. . . . In 1814 . . .
Sir Walter Scott's <u>Waverley</u> had appeared in Edinburgh,
and its unprecedented marketability bred fierce competition among American reprinters. . . . By the time
H. C. Carey & I. Lea went into business in their own
name in 1822, the reprint industry was in chaos, with
small fortunes being made and lost on as little as one
day's priority into the market of a particular edition
of a Waverley novel." Or, as Anna Lou Ashby comments
in her account of Harper, "One major factor in
nineteenth-century publishing was the lack of an international copyright law. As a result, many American
publishers were able to publish and sell books very
cheaply; consequently, competition was keen. After the
ships arrived carrying proof of the newest English fiction, the first publisher to get the books on the street
made the sales." Without an international copyright law,
piracy was the order of the day and the American market
was flooded with cheap reprints.

Imitators of the dime novel were as rampant, as
aggressive, and as reckless as the reprinters and pirates of foreign titles. Among the earliest Beadle competitors was the firm of Elliott, Thomes & Talbot, which
dished up in its periodical and its Ten Cent Novelettes
the pseudonymous thrillers of Louisa May Alcott, tales
that brought the sensational delights of "opium addiction, disguises, violent deaths, and Gothic devices" to
a country recovering from Civil War. In time, one publisher after another joined the ranks of Beadle imitators
until their wares reached farm and city street, railroad
kiosk and paddle steamer, camp and fireside, until inexpensive series literally papered the nation. Such mass
merchandising played a part in the shaping of American
literary taste.

As the century rolled on, taste changed. The history of the dime novel itself epitomizes the nation's
evolving appetite. The series of the 1860s were literally dog-eared and thumbed out of existence, devoured by
avid readers until the strikingly illustrated paper-
covered survivals have become collectors' items. By the
1880s and 1890s, some readers began to distrust the dime

xv

novel and to deplore its wide appeal. The Honorable
Abel Goddard, member of the New York Assembly, introduced into that body a bill declaring that "Any person
who shall sell, loan, or give to any minor under sixteen . . . any dime novel . . . without first obtaining
the written consent of the parent or guardian of such
minor, shall be deemed guilty of a misdemeanor, punish-
able by imprisonment or by a fine not exceeding $50."
Although the peak had passed, publishers--notably
Street & Smith, which joined the competition late--con-
tinued to flood the country through the turn of the century with dime and nickel libraries. Today Webster
defines dime novel, not entirely accurately, as "orig.,
a novel, usually sensational, sold for a dime; hence,
any cheap, lurid novel." Collectors and literary historians are in this instance wiser than the lexicographer. Like many nineteenth-century American readers,
they recognize the genre for what it is--a historical
romance based upon a nation's history.

The colorful adventure story cased in graphically
illustrated paper covers, priced at a dime, and published in a series, was only one variety of cheap book
produced in quantity during the century. Many other
titles punctuate these pages, from paper-covered reprints of standard literature to "cheap and nasty"
twelvemos. David S. Edelstein describes one type of
fairly inexpensive book when he quotes the Holt advertisement for its Leisure Hour Series of the 1870s: "A
collection of Works whose character is light and entertaining, though not trivial. While they are handy for
the pocket or the satchel, they are not, either in contents or appearance, unworthy of a place on library
shelves." While the volumes in Holt's Leisure Hour
Series were priced at $1.00 or $1.25, John B. Alden was
able to offer Shakespeare's plays in "neat paper-covered
volumes" at what Marie E. Korey calls "the unbelievable
price of 3 cents each." Altemus's motto, "the best is
the cheapest," did not necessarily work in reverse. A
bevy of publishers, competing for a mass market during
the later years of the century, placed their imprints
upon books whose cloth bindings deceptively concealed
the third-rate paper and inferior typography within.

Introduction

Indeed, such was the reckless competition among publishers of cheap books that by 1890, in an effort to
put an end to it and to control "the entire output of
cheap literature in the United States," John W. Lovell
organized the giant combine known during its short life
as the United States Book Company. The coup de grace
to the cheap book as the masses of nineteenth-century
American readers knew it was delivered by two events:
passage of the international copyright law in 1891,
which put an end to reckless piracy, and the Panic of
1893, which depressed the publishing industry along
with business in general.

Before its demise the phenomenon known as the
cheap book had run a colorful course, and its extraordinary history is reflected in this work, which mir-
rors many aspects of trade history. Not only are the
chaotic effects of the lack of international copyright
revealed, but also the workings of that curious practice known as "courtesy of the trade." This crops up
in the histories of numerous publishers--Holt, Appleton,
Carey & Lea--and is described by David Kaser as a custom
"which allowed that any publisher who announced a title
should have exclusive rights to it until his edition was
sold off." A publisher, in other words, could claim
prior rights to a foreign import and his claim would be
respected by the majority of his colleagues.

The impact of censorship upon the publisher is
also discernible here, as the Secretary of the Society
for the Suppression of Vice, Anthony Comstock, tangles
with purveyors of the printed word. As Nathaniel H.
Puffer states in his study of Frank Tousey, "Comstock
and his group regularly attacked publishers, authors,
booksellers, and newsdealers in an attempt to stop what
they thought unwholesome literature." As a result of
Comstock's interference, R. W. Worthington was threatened with arrest when he attempted to distribute Balzac
and Payne's translation of the Arabian Nights, and Frank
Tousey, having been jailed and pushed into bankruptcy
for publication of his Brookside Library with its reprints of Zola and Daudet, was arrested by Comstock for
publishing stories of London court life.

Introduction

Of all the aspects of trade history reflected in these pages, perhaps the most interesting is the relationship between publisher and author. Fact after fact emerges regarding royalty arrangements and fees paid for serials. Publisher A. K. Loring of Boston, the first major publisher of Alger, takes on the role of critic and counselor when he outlines his literary credo in a remarkable letter to Louisa May Alcott. "I judge a book by the impression it makes and leaves in my mind," he writes, "by the _feelings_ solely as I am no scholar.-- A story that touches and moves me, I can make others read and believe in.--What I like is conciseness in introducing the characters, getting them upon the stage and into action as quickly as possible. . . . Stories of the _heart_ are what live in the memory and when you move the reader to tears you have won them [sic] to you forever." Who could describe more aptly the action-packed romances that were geared for a mass market?

Ormond Smith of the firm of Street & Smith is caught in the act of presenting to author William G. Patten ("Burt L. Standish") a detailed outline for "a series of stories . . . in all of which will appear one prominent character surrounded by suitable satellites. The essential idea . . . is to interest readers in the career of a young man at a boarding school. . . . After the first twelve numbers, the hero is obliged to leave the academy. . . . A little love element would not be amiss. . . . When the hero is once projected on his travels there is an infinite variety to choose from. . . . After we run through twenty or thirty numbers of this, we would bring him back and have him go to college--say, Yale University; thence we could take him on his travels again to the South Seas or any-where." As a result of this publisher participation, Frank Merriwell was born.

Publisher participation was not always welcome or beneficent to authors. As Timothy K. Conley reminds us, "After he had acquired the plates to the 1860 edition of _Leaves of Grass_, Worthington wrote to Whitman and offered him an immediate payment of $250.00 for the rights to the edition. Whitman refused, but nonetheless Worthington ran off copies. In November 1880 Whitman

xviii

received a copy of the pirated edition and began proceedings against 'Holy Dick,' as Whitman called him,
to prevent the sale of those 'languid, surreptitious
copies.' Although Whitman later denied receiving any
royalties, he apparently was sent $143.50 by Worthington,
who felt that these payments entitled him to print hardbound copies."

Such is the nature of publishing that its annals
perforce disclose facts about books and authors as well
as trade practices. To the discerning eye these studies
of individual publishing houses also reflect the age in
which they flourished. The industrial revolution makes
an inescapable impact upon publishers and their lists.
Stories that proceed from "'chilling deed' to 'daring
rescue,' from 'forlorn hope' to 'joyous reunion,'" as
Peter Benson explains in his article on Gleason, were
"called 'steam literature' because they were printed on
the new rotary steam presses." Similarly, many titles
in Frank Leslie's series of cheap reprints "were designed
as railroad literature--books to be read on the railroad. . . . Between 1876 and 1877, when railroad expansion was at a height, [Leslie] tripled his book production
of the preceding years, catering to the developing mass
market for cheap reprints to read aboard trains."

The wars of the century created not only new literature but new markets for books. The panics of the
century all had their impact upon the publishing trade
until the last--that of 1893--helped end the cheap book
for mass distribution. Like the development of rotary
presses and the mushrooming of railroads, those wars and
panics are threaded through the pages of this volume.
The taste of the age is there too, as well as its style
of entertainment, for it was a taste created in no small
measure by those publishers of society novels, sentimental romances, and adventure stories who became mass mer-
chandisers of popular literature.

Madeleine B. Stern

Acknowledgments

The editor is most grateful to Jean Peters, librarian of the Frederic G. Melcher Library of R. R. Bowker Company, for making available to contributors the scrapbooks forming the Adolf Growoll Collection. American Book Trade History; to Rollo G. Silver, whose notes on publishers, deposited at the Grolier Club, provided a fruitful source of information, and to Robert Nikirk, librarian of the Grolier Club, for making those notes available to contributors. Neither the Growoll scrapbooks nor Mr. Silver's notes have been cited in the references following each article, although they have been used by the majority of contributors. The references also omit long runs of Publishers' Weekly, biographical sketches in the Dictionary of American Biography, and city directories--all of which have provided considerable information to contributors.

The editor is also deeply indebted to Edward T. LeBlanc, publisher of the Dime Novel Round-Up, who generously supplied contributors with numbers of that periodical as well as with illustrations for the volume.

Finally, the editor wishes to express her gratitude to the distinguished roster of scholar-contributors whose work has been indispensable to this volume: Dr. Anna Lou Ashby, Arents Collection, New York Public Library; Dr. Peter Benson, Visiting Research Fellow, Humanities, The Rockefeller Foundation; Cass Canfield, Harper & Row, Publishers, Inc.; Jacob L. Chernofsky, Editor, AB Bookman's Weekly; Dr. William Clarkin, Professor of Library Science, School of Library and Information Science, State University of New York at Albany; Frank E. Comparato; Dr. Timothy K. Conley, Department of English, Pennsylvania State University; Ross Craufurd; Dr. David S. Edelstein, Professor of Education, Western Connecticut State College; Ralph D. Gardner; Jack Golden; Dr. Michael B. Goodman; Chandler B. Grannis,

Acknowledgments

former Editor-in-Chief, Publishers' Weekly; Professor
David Kaser, Graduate Library School, Indiana University;
Marie E. Korey, Curator of Printed Books, Library Com-
pany of Philadelphia; A. Dean Larsen, Harold B. Lee Li-
brary, Brigham Young University; William B. Liebmann,
Curator, Herbert H. Lehman Papers, Columbia University;
Lawrence Parke Murphy, Keeper of Rare Books, New York
Public Library; Professor Joel Myerson, Department of
English, University of South Carolina; Irene P. Norell,
Associate Professor, Division of Library Science, San
Jose State University; Nathaniel H. Puffer, Assistant
Director, University of Delaware Library; Daniel G.
Siegel, President, M & S Rare Books, Inc., and M & S
Press, Inc.; Madeleine B. Stern, Leona Rostenberg -
Rare Books; Roger E. Stoddard, Associate Librarian, The
Houghton Library, Harvard University; Dr. Marie Olesen
Urbanski, Associate Professor, Department of English,
University of Maine, Orono.

1   John B. Alden

John B. Alden (1879-1908), the American Book Exchange,
and the Useful Knowledge Publishing Company attempted to
revolutionize publishing by providing good literature,
both fiction and nonfiction, at the lowest possible
prices. As president of the American Book Exchange,
Alden commenced publishing at 55 Beekman Place, New York,
in 1879. The firm moved to the Tribune Building at 154
Nassau Street in 1880 and again in 1881 to 764 Broadway.
With the bankruptcy and subsequent collapse of the American Book Exchange in December 1881, Alden formed the
Useful Knowledge Publishing Company at 18 Vesey Street
in 1882. He published books under the imprints of
John B. Alden, Alden Book Company, and Alden Publishing
Company at 18 Vesey Street in 1883 and at 393 Pearl
Street from 1884 to 1892. From 1892 to 1894 his business was located at 57 Rose Street, where in 1893 he
also established the Elzevir Publishing Company. In
1895 John B. Alden Publisher moved to 12 Vandewater
Street; two years later to 440 Pearl Street; and finally
in 1900 to 84 Bible House (Ninth Street and Fourth Avenue), where from 1905 to his retirement in 1908 he was
president of Alden Brothers Publishers.

Major Works: Among the major standard and classical works published by Alden were Chambers's Cyclopaedia of English Literature, The Library of Universal
Knowledge, Alden's Cyclopedia of Universal Literature,
the Elzevir Library, Library Magazine, Good Literature,
and the collected works of Dickens, Ruskin, Scott, and
Shakespeare.

John Berry Alden was born in Mount Pleasant, Iowa,
in 1847 and died in Neshanic, New Jersey, in 1924. He
began his career as editor of Bright Side Stories: Gems
of Beauty in Prose, Poetry and Picture (1871), What Next?
Favorite Poems, for Boys and Girls (1873), and Hearth and
Home (1874-1875). Alden came to New York from Chicago

1

with a supply of some fifty secondhand books and capital of $70.00, and established in 1874 a secondhand book business called the American Book Exchange. His plan was to exchange books with his customers, charging a small fee for each volume sold or exchanged. Within a few years he was ready to expand his horizons. Noticing the success of the paper-covered Seaside Library and other cheap quarto libraries, Alden decided there was an unlimited market for good literature bound in a handier size than the quarto and sold at very low prices. He formed a stock company, sold shares, and with a capital of $30,000 began publishing in 1879.

Alden made series of standard authors the specialty of the American Book Exchange. His Acme and Aldus libraries, small duodecimos (3.5 by 5.5 inches) printed from electrotype plates, were issued in cloth at 35 to 50 cents and in half russia at $1.00. The Acme Library of Standard Biography contained Macaulay's Frederick the Great and William Pitt; Lamartine's Mary Queen of Scots, Life of Oliver Cromwell, and Life of Christopher Columbus; Carlyle's Life of Robert Burns, and others. Plutarch's Lives of Illustrious Men; Gibbon's History of the Decline and Fall of the Roman Empire; Macaulay's History of England; and Rollin's Ancient History were represented in the Library of History. The Acme Library of Modern Classics included Goldsmith's The Vicar of Wakefield; Johnson's Rasselas; and St. Pierre's Paul and Virginia. Bunyan's Pilgrim's Progress; Arabian Nights; Defoe's Robinson Crusoe; and Swift's Gulliver's Travels were part of the series of Juvenile Classics. The complete works of Chaucer, Dante, Shakespeare, Milton, Byron, Burns, Browning, Poe, Shelley, Tennyson and others made up the forty-five-volume Library of Poetry. The Library of Choice Fiction included the works of Scott, Dickens, Cooper, Hawthorne, Irving, George Eliot, and Thackeray.

Early in 1879 Alden advertised the Acme edition of Robert Chambers's Cyclopaedia of English Literature in four volumes. He subsequently announced his plan to publish The Library of Universal Knowledge, a reprint of the last Edinburgh and London edition of William and Robert Chambers's Encyclopaedia with copious additions

2

by American editors. The twenty-volume set, containing
over 1,600 pages, sold at $10.00 clothbound, $15.00 in
half morocco, and $20.00 in half russia. Specimen vol-
umes were offered for examination and early subscribers
were promised special discounts. It was, Alden declared
in The American Bookseller of 2 February 1880, "an enterprise so extraordinary that its success, beyond all prec-
edent in book publishing, may be fairly claimed to
inaugurate a Literary Revolution."

In 1879 Alden also commenced publishing a Library
Magazine of Select Foreign Literature as a monthly at
10 cents a number or $1.00 a year. Modeled on Littell's
Living Age and Eclectic Magazine but adopting a more
serious tone, Library Magazine carried choice selections, excluding fiction and light literature, from
English and continental journals. With the July 1880
number, Alden began a policy of issuing bound volumes
only, with bimonthly numbers. American topics were included in December 1880 and the title changed to Library
Magazine of American and Foreign Thought. In the fall
of 1880 Alden added Good Literature, A Literary Eclectic
Weekly, edited by Charles Francis Richardson, to the
American Book Exchange publications. Both journals suffered when the American Book Exchange went bankrupt in
December 1881. Good Literature was suspended from 26
November 1881 to 4 March 1882, when Alden revived it.
He continued to publish it until it merged in 1884 into
the Critic: an Illustrated Monthly Review of Literature,
Art and Life. After a hiatus of a year, Library Magazine reappeared in 1883 as Choice Literature. With the
first number of the new series, Alden returned to his
original policy of including only English and continental literature. In 1885 the title reverted to Library
Magazine and was retained until the publication's demise
in 1888.

Alden's advertisements and "Revolution Pamphlets,"
which he produced by the hundreds, extolled the virtues
of his "Literary Revolution." The guiding principles of
the American Book Exchange--to adopt low prices, to sell
in large quantity, and to sell directly to buyers, thus
eliminating the bookseller's commission--had popular
appeal but were guaranteed to antagonize both publishers

3

and booksellers. The trade journals were filled with
commentary on the "Literary Revolution." On 15 March
1880 The American Bookseller gave its opinion of Alden's
method of dealing directly with the public and concluded
that his venture would never destroy or even greatly
damage the book trade. In fact, within a few months
Alden had to admit that the booksellers could be of use
to him. But his terms to the trade were still restric-
tive. His discount to dealers was not very high and he
required cash with the order. He also insisted that the
American Book Exchange would sell to only one bookseller
in any city, except in cities of over 100,000.

Publishers had even less affection for the leader
of the "Literary Revolution." Alden's prices drasti-
cally undercut the expensive publishers. His editions
of Shakespeare's plays were published separately in neat
paper-covered volumes and sold at the unbelievable price
of 3 cents each. It was also his custom to compare the
prices of his publications with those of other publishers. Publishers' Weekly refused an advertisement from
Alden's firm and defended its decision in the 7 August
1880 issue, stating that the advertisement conveyed
false impressions favorable only to the "Revolution."

Authors fared no better than publishers or booksellers. Though many Alden publications were standard
works on which no American publisher paid royalties,
Alden's firm made no provision for the payment of royalties on any of its publications. Alden stated on many
occasions that he did not favor the royalty system,
adding that authors received payment enough with the increased circulation he gave their works. Alden did,
however, favor an international copyright and claimed
that the "Literary Revolution," by enforcing the con-
sequences of noncopyright on the expensive book publishers, would stir them to support the international
copyright movement.

Alden took the attacks of the trade in stride and
continued to churn out books at an incredible rate. By
the summer of 1880 he claimed he had published some
2,000 tons of good literature in 120 separate volumes
and was producing 4,000 books a day. He employed 500
men and women on a regular basis and was adding new

4

equipment to increase his output. He decided to distribute 10,000 additional shares of stock at $10.00 a
share so that others could participate in his good
fortune. Details of his plan, which promised to double investment within a year, were advertised in leading magazines including many religious journals. His
scheme prompted an analysis of the "Literary Revolution"
by a Chicago trade journal, Bookseller and Stationer,
which was reprinted in Publishers' Weekly 2 April 1881.
The article depicted Alden as a confidence man and
questioned his motives for "sharing" his profits. Nevertheless, his arguments and the quality of the literature he produced were enough to convince a large number
of people to become investors.

Despite the infusion of new money the American
Book Exchange was not destined to last. Alden had been
doing a very large business on very small capital and
was selling his books at less than the cost of production. His profits were dependent upon mass production
and sales, but the vast audience he envisioned for his
publications never materialized on a scale large enough
to save his enterprise. On 3 December 1881 Publishers'
Weekly reported that a receiver has been appointed for
the American Book Exchange, which had been carried for
months by creditors. Thousands of small investors lost
their money because the accounts were in a state of
utter chaos.

The failure of the American Book Exchange did not
destroy Alden's desire to provide good literature at
cheap prices. The same article in Publishers' Weekly
that reported his bankruptcy announced the formation of
a new concern, his Useful Knowledge Publishing Company.
As manager of this company in 1882, and, after 1883, of
John B. Alden, Alden Book Company, and Alden Publishing
Company, he sold many of the books he had formerly published. Good Literature and Library Magazine (with its
title changed to Choice Literature) reappeared after a
brief hiatus. In 1883 Alden began publishing the Elzevir
Library and produced selections from it in 1884 in a series called Elzevir Classics. By 1885 he was again making his presence felt in the cheap book business. In
January 1885 he announced the publication of two new

5

magazines, <u>Juvenile Gems</u>, a weekly intended for young people, and <u>The Novelist</u>. In the same year he issued the first volume of <u>Alden's Cyclopedia of Universal Literature</u>, a twenty-volume set completed in 1891. His edition of Ruskin's <u>Works</u> was heralded as a triumph of cheap book publishing. His relationship with the book trade had also improved by this time. Alden supported the movement for an international copyright law and was offering his books to dealers at liberal discounts. On 25 December 1886 Alden announced in <u>Publishers' Weekly</u> his intention to withdraw from the wholesale book business and to sell only at retail thereafter. When John W. Lovell proposed his scheme for a book trust to stabilize prices and eliminate the competition among the cheap reprint publishers, Alden was initially opposed. He did, however, turn over many of his publications to the United States Book Company when it was incorporated in July 1890.

Alden continued to publish until his retirement in 1908, but he never created quite the same furor in the publishing world as he had with the American Book Exchange. He considered himself the defender of the rights of readers to have easier access to good books, declaring proudly in <u>Publishers' Weekly</u> of 21 March 1885 that "the best literature of the world has by my efforts been placed within the reach of millions to whom it was before unattainable." His journals, particularly <u>Library Magazine</u>, fostered a taste for foreign literature. When Alden died in December 1924 both <u>The New York Times</u> and <u>Publishers' Weekly</u> acknowledged the role he played in establishing popularly priced editions of good literature.

Marie E. Korey

References

Ralph Admari, "The Literary Revolution," <u>The American Book Collector</u>, 6 (1935): 138-40.

John B. Alden

Raymond H. Shove, <u>Cheap Book Production in the United States, 1870 to 1891</u> (Urbana: University of Illinois Library, 1937).

2   W. L. Allison and Company

W. L. Allison and Company (1869-1890) was a comparatively late entry into the cheap library field. The
firm began in July 1869 as successor of T. O'Kane and
Company of New York. During the 1880s, when it was
most active in the cheap library field, it was located
at 93 Chambers Street, New York. In 1890 its plates
were sold to the United States Book Company, the giant
combine organized by John W. Lovell.

Major Series: Arundale Edition.

William L. Allison was born in Orange County,
New York; he died 4 March 1893. Before becoming a publisher of books, Allison edited the Newburg Gazette and
published the Working Farmer. Among the more notable
sets and reference works bearing the Allison imprint
are Chambers's Cyclopaedia, the works of Shakespeare,
Schmucker's Arctic Explorations and Discoveries During
the Nineteenth Century, as well as Allison's Webster's
Counting-House Dictionary of the English Language and
an electrical dictionary.

In order to attract a mass market Allison produced
cheap books during the 1880s. According to Shove, the
firm was an "important" New York publisher of cheap
clothbound books during the latter part of the 1880s.
Allison's Arundale Edition consisted of cheap twelvemos
of standard books priced at $1.00 but actually sold in
dry goods stores for only 25 cents. The list price was
not the only deceptive feature of these books. Bound in
cloth casings which concealed the inferior paper and
typography within, Allison books were the type that
earned the ignominious description of "cheap and nasty"
twelvemos.

In 1890, seeking to corner the market with his
United States Book Company, John W. Lovell purchased
Allison's plates. Thus what Shove describes as

9

W. L. Allison and Company

Allison's "competing editions of standard low priced
. . . twelvemos" were henceforth controlled by Lovell's
combine.

During the 1880s especially W. L. Allison was
one of the companies that produced deceptively priced
books of shoddy manufacture, flooding the market with
inferior products.

A. Dean Larsen

References

American Booksellers' Guide, 1 (1 August 1869): 19.

Publishers' Weekly, 43 (11 March 1893): 425.

Raymond H. Shove, Cheap Book Production in the United
    States, 1870 to 1891 (Urbana: University of
    Illinois Library, 1937).

3   Altemus & Co.

Altemus & Co. (1842-1936), bookbinders, gradually became
publishers, first of Bibles and then of inexpensive reprints in elaborately decorated hardcovers, using the
imprint "Henry Altemus Company." The first recorded
address was at Fourth and Race in Philadelphia, where
the firm remained until its large manufacturing plant
was built at Fourth and Cherry during the early 1880s,
the latter address used on its catalogs until 1914. A
separate editorial office was operating by 1874 at
806 Market, and by 1890 it had moved to 28 South 4th.
In 1914 it was at 1326 Vine and finally in 1935 at 24
South Orianno.

    Noted for its advanced machinery, the company
became one of the largest binders in the United States,
employing 150 people in the 1860s and supplying orders
from all parts of the country. In 1886 Altemus could
manufacture 5,000 books a day and bind not only its own
products but those of other publishers. The fancy covers were inexpensive machine-produced copies or imitations of the better handbound books of Europe and
America. Altemus had used elaborate bindings when it
became one of the first and largest manufacturers of
photograph albums. Similar covers were used on their
Bibles, another large venture, and finally in 1889 the
firm produced inexpensive but elaborately bound reprints
of famous books. Later there were a few original works.
During the twentieth century the firm became a publisher
solely of inexpensive juvenile titles.

    Joseph T. Altemus (died 1851) supposedly started
binding books in 1790. The "Henry Altemus Company"
sideline began in 1842, perhaps through the purchase of
a publishing business by Joseph's sons Henry and Samuel,
but there was no separation between the publishing and
the bookbinding. The company was a family business
throughout its existence, and the most influential

11

member, as far as publishing is concerned, was the
third-generation son, Henry Altemus, Jr. (born in
1833, died in Philadelphia 19 October 1906). According to an obituary in Publishers' Weekly (27 October
1906), he was noted as "a man of wide culture," who
"spoke both French and German fluently," and who "had
travelled extensively." It was his taste that evidently dominated the choice of bindings and the selection of famous authors to be reprinted. On his death,
the firm was taken over by his four sons, Howard,
Robert, Henry, Jr., and Roland. At some point, probably
in 1900, Henry Altemus Company was separated from Altemus
& Company, the publishing business being incorporated
under the former name and the manufacturing plant under
the latter, both firms remaining under family control.
The publishing business ceased in 1936.

The elaborate Altemus catalog of 1884, red cover
with gold printing, contains pictures of Bibles for
"Family, Pulpit and Reference," all in special covers
of great variety, some of them imitations of famous
bindings. Judging by the large size and unusual luxury
of the catalog, the firm's Bibles must have been popular
and profitable. In 1889 the catalog added four non-
Bible items: Milton's Paradise Lost, Dante's Inferno
and Purgatory and Paradise, and Coleridge's The Rime of
the Ancient Mariner, all with Gustave Doré illustrations
and all bound in fancy hardcovers. Each year thereafter
the Bible list decreased and the literature list increased until by 1897 the Bibles were omitted, an "illustrated catalogue of Bibles supplied on application."
Meanwhile the list of reprints had grown to some 250
titles, each available in a variety of bindings. In
1892 the Altemus Library series had begun with works by
Ruskin, Bacon, Thomas a Kempis, Oliver Goldsmith, Charles
and Mary Lamb, Hawthorne, and Emerson, selling for 75
cents in cloth binding, $1.50 in half crushed Levant,
and $1.75 in half genuine English calf. The next year
the Laurel Series was added, consisting of boxed, two-
volume sets of famous authors, $1.00 to $4.00 per set,
depending upon the bindings.

The Altemus Vademecum series began in 1894, master-
pieces of English literature for 25 cents to 75 cents,

depending upon binding. In 1895 the new series was
Altemus' Representative Poets, the works of Longfellow,
Scott, Tennyson, Bryant, Byron, Poe, and Moore, 75
cents to $4.00 according to binding. There was also
the Altemus' Devotional Series: Thomas a Kempis, Henry
Drummond, Phillips Brooks, Henry Ward Beecher, each 35
cents, and for the first time, the Altemus' Young People's Library: Robinson Crusoe, Alice's Adventures in
Wonderland, Pilgrims' Progress, 50 cents each. Added
too were pocket foreign language dictionaries ($1.00),
picture books (50 cents to $1.00), birthday date books
($1.25 to $2.00), and "how-to" books, The Care of Children ($1.00), Women's Work in the House (50 cents).

    By 1897 the motto of the firm was "the best is the
cheapest," accompanied by an open book with the words
"and there was light." That year the firm was the first
to pirate Quo Vadis, which sold at $1.25 in an edition
that moved at the rate of 10,000 copies a week. In 1899
another big money-maker, In His Steps, became a standard
item. By 1902 the children's books had increased, a
trend that was to continue until, in 1912, the firm's
list was almost completely juveniles with only a few of
the old classical reprints for adults. By 1921 the
motto of the company had changed to "The Right Books
for Boys and Girls," and in the 1928 catalog the juvenile list completely filled the sixty-two pages of the
firm's catalog, all of them bound in covers that were
distinctive but considerably less elaborate than some
of the earlier publications. From that time on, the
list remained almost the same until the firm ceased in
1936.

    The Altemus books were intended primarily as pre-
sentation editions, with original sales efforts mainly
directed toward the Christmas trade. The books were
also used as household ornaments, and one could select
the bindings that would look best in the parlor. In
1895, for example, one could order Carlyle's Sartor
Resartus in a choice of five different bindings, the
least expensive (cloth-covered boards stamped in a design of gold, silver, and colors) for 75 cents, and the
most expensive (full calf with inlaid sides) for $4.00.
The contents of the volumes often were not as fancy;

13

the printing plates were sometimes worn and the ink
smudged. The printing was usually easy to read but
not distinctive. The quality of the writing, however,
was often extremely high, and the titles in the catalogs remind one of the reading lists for today's college courses in nineteenth-century literature.

There are no publishing statistics, but the
Altemus business was evidently prosperous, and Altemus
publications can still be found in small towns throughout the country, indicating that the distribution was
large. The books probably were sold by traveling
salesmen or mail-order houses, these towns being too
small to have had anything but general food and dry
goods stores. The well-thumbed Altemus books one
finds in secondhand stores are indications that at
least some people did read the gifts they received, and
by so doing were often exposed to the best of authors,
who in this way sometimes reached their largest audiences. The original editions of Emerson's Essays, for
example, had slow sales, but when the copyright ran out
and reprint publishers such as Altemus produced them,
the sales were so large that the Essays became best-
sellers. The elaborate bindings themselves perhaps increased the appeal of book reading; the Art Nouveau
designs on the covers were especially enjoyable. Thus
did the Altemus Company exert its influence by combining
money-making with the popularization of culture.

Lawrence Parke Murphy

References

Edwin T. Freedley, Philadelphia and Its Manufacturers
    (Philadelphia: Young, 1867).

"Obituary Notes," Publishers' Weekly, 70 (27 October
    1906): 1155.

Altemus & Co.

Frank E. Comparato, <u>Books for the Millions: A History of the Men whose Methods and Machines Packaged the Printed Word</u> (Harrisburg: Stackpole, 1972).

Interior view of Appleton's Book Store about 1855.
(From *Imprints on History* by Madeleine B. Stern)

4 D. Appleton & Company

D. Appleton & Company (c. 1825-1933), although not primarily a publisher of cheap series, used its large manufacturing facilities to introduce important technological
innovations in bookmaking and new sales and marketing
techniques to reach an American mass audience.

Daniel Appleton (1785-1849) started in business
about 1813 as a dry goods merchant in Haverhill, Massachusetts, where he was born. He moved to Boston and
then in 1825 to New York, where he first added books to
his inventory. With help from bookbinder Jonathan
Leavitt, his brother-in-law, the book business soon outdistanced other departments. Abandoning dry goods,
Appleton in 1830 moved his original shop from Exchange
Place to Beekman Street, then (in 1838) to lower Broadway. In 1854 the company established its headquarters
at 346 Broadway (which burned down in 1867); it then
moved to 443-445 Broadway, 95 Grand Street, 549-551
Broadway, 1-5 Bond Street, and in 1894 to 72 Fifth
Avenue.

Upon the founder's retirement in 1848 five sons
ultimately ran the firm: William H. (1814-1899),
John A. (1817-1881), George S. (1821-1878), Daniel S.
(1824-1890), and Samuel F. (1826-1883). While their
father's publishing had been somewhat ephemeral, the
sons methodically divided chores among themselves--
John, for example, handling finances, Daniel manufacturing, and George (after a short independent career) specializing in "art" books. The brothers developed all
the usual branches of publishing and (until 1881) book
wholesaling as well, handling the works of other firms,
both domestic and foreign. Although one of the largest
in the United States, this family enterprise failed in
1900 and was reorganized.

D. Appleton & Company

Major Mass Authors: Grace Aguilar, Hall Caine,
James Fenimore Cooper, Charles Dickens, Louisa Mühlbach,
Christian Reid (Frances C. Tiernan), Walter Scott.

With a host of important British writers in its
ranks by way of "trade courtesy," as well as newly emerging native authors, including leaders on both sides of
the Civil War and distinguished American historians,
D. Appleton & Company prospered. It also had a large
textbook department, and juvenile, medical, foreign language (especially Spanish), and technical and engineer-
ing divisions. This large volume of work quickly
demonstrated that, to ensure quality and steady production, the Appletons would need their own factory. A
bindery was completed in 1854, a printing plant a year
later, and composition and stereotyping followed shortly
thereafter. In 1867 the scattered shops were consolidated at a new factory at 201-219 Kent Avenue, Williams-
burg, Brooklyn, designed by master craftsman William
Matthews.

Hand binder Matthews (1822-1896) had come to America in 1843. When his 1853 Crystal Palace exhibit came
to the Appletons' attention they promptly hired him to
run their works. Despite his superb hand techniques
Matthews installed every modern machine that would turn
out books with dispatch. In 1868 he bought exclusive
rights to David Smyth's first book sewer (Appleton's
fifteen machines were the only thread-sewing devices in
existence until 1879). He next (1874) took the wire
stitcher of Ellicott Averell, possibly the first workable machine stapler. Both sewer and stitcher were excellent for magazines, pamphlets, and schoolbooks: they
did a day's hand work (2,000 books) in an hour. As an
experimenter with adhesive binding as well (his 1853 exhibit masterpiece had a rubber spine) he lent encourage-
ment, willy-nilly, to all three cheap binding processes.
The Brooklyn plant's 175-girl bindery was almost completely mechanized, using steam folders and board cut-
ters. Despite this mass production, Appleton publishing
programs were far from cheap and tawdry.

In 1857 the firm began The American Cyclopedia,
and with a revised edition it kept a large editorial
staff working until 1876. Modeled somewhat on Chambers's

Cyclopedia (Edinburgh), it grew to become the largest
original work published in America. Charles A. Dana
and George Ripley (then both at the New York Tribune)
were its editors, marshaling 364 contributors to furnish
some 13,000 printed pages in sixteen volumes. Marketed
by house-to-house canvassing and by subscription installments, the $80.00 set--and a supplement, American Annual
Cyclopedia--sold by the tens of thousands, for a total
of over three million volumes. This was mass publishing,
but of the highest literary and bookmaking quality.

Appleton's proudest illustrated art publications
were Picturesque America, Picturesque Europe, and Picturesque Palestine, which set a standard for the industry. Oliver B. Bunce, an editor on Appletons' Journal,
conceived the first of these sumptuous travel books and
George S. Appleton recognized the public's enormous interest in the vast country spanning from ocean to ocean--
and in the Old World as well. William Cullen Bryant was
listed as editor (for greater sales), and at almost
eighty years old he reportedly read every word of the
proofs.

Illustrated with full-page steel-plate engravings
printed for the first time on a steam-powered gravure
press (again involving exclusive use, here employing the
invention of Robert Neale developed with Appleton funds)
as well as hundreds of wood engravings, Picturesque America: Or, The Land We Live In (1872-1874) cost $138,000
to prepare. It was marketed by subscription in forty-
eight monthly parts at 50 cents each (later bound into
two volumes). Nearly a million sets were sold.

For the similar Picturesque Europe (1875-1879)
Bayard Taylor was editor. A quarter of a million dollars was budgeted for production, and--with heavy "romantic" treatment--it succeeded handsomely. It was
later bound as three volumes. Then followed Picturesque
Palestine, Sinai, and Egypt (two volumes), edited variously by Henry C. Potter, bishop of New York, and an
explorer, "Colonel" Wilson, apparently to attract both
religious and antiquarian readers. Such marketing
strategies were never ignored.

For the 1876 Philadelphia Centennial William
Matthews hand-bound copies of these books with such

care and taste they were displayed and discussed for
decades. The three (commercially) bound works ultimately sold a total of 600,000 copies, and the invalu-
able subscription lists were reemployed for the dozens
of increasingly impressive travel and art books that
followed. One set, The World's Great Books, forty
volumes, was priced at $300.00; Artistic Country Seats,
$125.00 and Artistic Interiors, $300.00--per copy.
"Caution and enterprise" were the company's watchwords,
however, and the busy Appletons at the same time did
not forget their common readers.

The opening of the 1854 Broadway shop had been
the brothers' formal commitment to book sales--and
local competition. Gleason's Magazine (24 June 1854)
visited the "principal sales room," and was much impressed: ". . . The purchaser will buy his book as
cheaply or (with the extension of the business) cheaper
than ever, and will have his property besides in the
convenience and elegance [14 Corinthian columns imitat-
ing "Sienna" marble] about him. . . ." After a decade
of publishing their own works, however, the Appletons
were less concerned with counter sales. When it started
the weekly Appletons' Journal of Literature, Science,
and Art, the firm (in the 3 April 1869 issue) described
its more lofty accomplishments: "The Publishing House
by which the present Journal is issued has been extensively engaged, for nearly half a century, in the work
of promoting general education, and diffusing information among the people of the United States, through the
medium of valuable books, in all the leading departments
of knowledge. . . ." Within a few years, as the industrial revolution made itself felt in the nation's market-
place, the erudite publishers expressed no objection to
cheap clothing and household articles for the poor. How
they would react to cheap literature was quite another
matter.

The Appletons certainly could not watch America's
growing mass reading market without feeling themselves
entitled to a part of the business. With a full comple-
ment of texts they had, after all, long helped to teach
the nation to read. With its outstanding manufacturing
facilities D. Appleton & Company was already capable of

many production economies. As early as 1854 it had a
variety of inexpensive publications (starting at 6 1/4
cents), apparently religious tracts and schoolbooks.
Noah Webster's "Blue-back" <u>Elementary Spelling Book</u>
(acquired 1855) was so successful it was kept on one
large press for decades; by 1890 it had sold 35 million
copies. William H. Appleton reminisced (<u>Publishers'
Weekly</u>, 1 May 1880) about the "Blue-backs": "We sell
them in cases of seventy-two dozen, and they are bought
by all the large dry-goods houses and supply stores and
furnished by them to every cross-roads store in the
country." In the 1850s too the firm began its "Popular
Library of Best Authors," in cloth at 50 cents each,
although in those days half a dollar was not a "cheap"
price. Appleton mass production nevertheless soon furnished a model for ambitious trade publishers who had
even greater economies in mind.

After the Civil War the sheer volume of publishing
in large houses demanded some orderly grouping of titles
for practical marketing and distribution. Appleton had
found that issuing large works in fascicle would amelio-
rate their cost and provoke sustained interest, thus
providing some income well before they were finished.
Under such conditions no publishing scheme was beyond
even the common--mass--audience; sales among the country's new readers were almost addictive. Books both in
fascicle and in series (or sets) relied heavily on subscription; installments were sent (in the absence of
bookstores) through the mails with second-class (periodical) postage to the remotest hamlets of America.

With a sizable acquisitions program and workable
sales formulas, few titles, whether popular or technical,
escaped serialization by content or format. Major
Appleton series or libraries grew yearly by the dozens:
Library of Choice Novels (begun 1870?), sixty titles by
1883; paper, 25 cents to $1.00; Appletons' Illustrated
Library of Romance (1872), twenty-seven titles by 1878;
paper $1.00, cloth $1.50; Appletons' Library of American
Fiction (1872), twenty-three titles by 1893; paper 75
cents, cloth $1.25; International Science Series (1873),
almost one hundred titles; cloth, $1.50 to $2.00;
Appletons' New Handy-Volume Series (1878), seventy

D. Appleton & Company

volumes by 1883; paper, 20 to 40 cents; International Education Series (1886), sixty volumes, cloth, $1.00 to $2.00.

No less popular were Miniature English Classics, twenty-eight titles, $10.50 per set; Appletons' Twenty-five Cent Series, twenty-six titles, paper; Appletons' Students' Library, thirty-four volumes, cloth, $20.00 per set; Library of [Natural] Wonders, many titles; Appletons' Home Books, twelve titles, 60 cents; Appletons' Summer Series, eight titles; Happy Child's Library, eighteen titles; Miniature Classical Library, twenty-eight volumes, 38 cents; Collection of Foreign Authors, seventeen volumes, paper 25 cents, cloth 60 cents; Popular Science Library, cloth, $1.00; Library of Valuable Information, cloth, and so on. Despite their low prices, these and still other series were produced with more than usual care, although in so telling Publishers' Weekly (1 May 1880) Appleton badly confused his markets: "I don't believe that people, when they buy a book for fifty cents, have any idea of the capital invested to bring it down at that price. For example, it cost us $138,000 to publish 'Picturesque America,' and that without adding the cost of printing. . . ." Nevertheless, the firm so enjoyed its popular and general sales it readily jettisoned its fussy textbook line in 1890 to form a trust (American Book Company), while at almost the same time it refused vehemently to surrender its "cheap" properties to a similar scheme.

For authors' collected works in sets the situation was much the same. When Charles Dickens visited America (1867-1868) the literary furor was immense. Despite their support of trade courtesy and copyright, the Appletons felt they had to publish something--and grandly issued Dickens's complete works. Ticknor & Fields, the author's approved American publishers, reported to Dickens that the Appleton edition of The Mystery of Edwin Drood alone had done "incalculable damage," but by 1869 Appleton was offering (postpaid) an eighteen-volume set of Dickens and twenty-five volumes of Scott--forty-three volumes in all--for $10.00. Karl Marx's authorized edition of Das Kapital sold for $12.00, but Appleton similarly brought out one for $3.00.

D. Appleton & Company

Yet the great classics were virtually in the public domain, if not actually so. The complete Dickens
was (by 1873) available in half a dozen Appleton editions, cheapest of which were the Handy Volume Edition,
fourteen volumes, cloth, 75 cents ($10.50 boxed); the
New Household Edition ("the best cheap edition"--
Appleton's 1873 catalog), nineteen volumes, paper, 15
to 35 cents. The works of James Fenimore Cooper,
thirty-two volumes, paper 75 cents, cloth $1.25; Louisa
Mühlbach's historical novels, twenty titles, paper $1.00,
cloth $1.25; Scott's Waverley Novels, in a twenty-five-
volume "Popular Edition . . . pronounced 'A Miracle of
Cheapness'" (Appleton's 1873 catalog), paper, were 25
cents each. But such productions at Appleton were only
aberrations. As firm members had long worked toward
effective trade self-regulation (since 1855), and then
toward international copyright (since 1887), they knew
that such reckless publishing could not--must not--last.

In later introducing a relatively cheap--but rea-
soned, and somewhat protected--series, Appletons' Town
and Country Library (1888) in cloth at $1.00, paper 50
cents, the company was returning to more sober conditions. The series nevertheless reached 312 titles and
included novels by Hall Caine, S. Baring-Gould, Justin
McCarthy, Grant Allen, Edna Lyall (Donavan), George
Gissing, Gilbert Parker, Edgerton Castle, Anthony Hope,
Leonard Merrick, William J. Locke, E. F. Benson (Dodo),
and Joseph Conrad. Many titles were written especially
for this collection.

Toward 1890, as John W. Lovell's ambitious plan to
monopolize the entire cheap market became clear to the
trade, only a few "respectable" publishers had not suc-
cumbed to the scheme. Raymond Shove (in Cheap Book Production in the United States) quotes a reporter who
noted no Harper or Appleton titles on Lovell's list.
"No," Lovell replied. "They would not join the trust
unless they had to. [But t]hey can't live outside. . . ."
The cheap libraries ended with the 1891 copyright law
and the depression of 1893, but Lovell was strangely
right: Appleton and Harper, despite their moral victories, soon toppled.

D. Appleton & Company

D. Appleton & Company failed at the end of the century, to the great consternation of the whole publishing industry. Its expensive travel and art books, its installment and subscription programs, and its more erudite periodicals had depleted its cash reserves at a crucial time, and it was forced into receivership in 1900. A year later the Trow Printing Company of Manhattan bought the Appleton factory in Brooklyn--now said to be among the world's largest--and got with it an agreement to handle all of Appleton's work. Also in 1901 the firm announced that its entire backlist of 4,000 titles was available by subscription to readers who wanted to form a quality library through modest weekly payments. Thus the company returned to the business of publishing and slowly recovered.

Noting that until 1933, when it merged with The Century Company, D. Appleton & Company had published over 15,000 titles, editor Samuel Chew, in the firm's anniversary volume Fruit Among the Leaves, commended the industrious brothers: "The Appletons had always shared with other great publishing houses the sense that their business was in the nature of a public trust and that they must at times bring out works of weighty significance involving large outlays of money without an absolute assurance of remuneration. . . ." The company's role in satisfying the popular tastes of new and avid nineteenth-century readers in a rapidly expanding, literate nation did not involve works of weighty significance, nor indeed had it provided great remuneration; but in the name of "public trust" it put massive quantities of good literature into waiting hands and receptive minds. Like the "Blue-back" speller itself it was mass publishing with a grand purpose.

Frank E. Comparato

24

D. Appleton & Company

References

William Matthews, <u>Modern Bookbinding Practically Con-</u>
<u>sidered: A Lecture (March 25, 1885)</u> (New York:
Grolier Club, 1889).

"Daniel Appleton." <u>Appletons' Cyclopedia of American</u>
<u>Biography</u>, I (1891):   84.

Grant Overton, <u>Portrait of a Publisher and the First</u>
<u>Hundred Years of the House of Appleton, 1825-</u>
<u>1925</u> (New York: D. Appleton & Co., 1925).

Raymond H. Shove, <u>Cheap Book Production in the United</u>
<u>States, 1870 to 1891</u> (Urbana: University of
Illinois Library, 1937).

Samuel C. Chew, ed., <u>Fruit Among the Leaves: An Anni-</u>
<u>versary Anthology</u> (New York: Appleton-Century-
Crofts, 1950).

Hellmut Lehmann-Haupt, <u>The Book in America: A History</u>
<u>of the Making and Selling of Books in the United</u>
<u>States</u>, 2nd ed. (New York: R. R. Bowker Company,
1951).

Donald Sheehan, <u>This Was Publishing: A Chronicle of</u>
<u>the Book Trade in the Gilded Age</u> (Bloomington:
Indiana University Press, 1952).

Frank E. Comparato, <u>Books for the Millions: A History</u>
<u>of the Men whose Methods and Machines Packaged</u>
<u>the Printed Word</u> (Harrisburg: Stackpole, 1972).

5 Maturin Murray Ballou

Maturin Murray Ballou (1845-1893), writer, editor, and
publisher of periodicals, novels, weekly novelettes,
and travel books, specialized in seafaring tales, stories about the American Revolution, didactic sketches,
and stories set in exotic locales. At various stages
of his nearly fifty-year career, Ballou's periodicals
and novelettes competed with The Olive Branch (Boston),
The New World (New York), Graham's Magazine, Bonner's
New York Ledger, Street's New York Weekly, and Beadle's
Dime Novels. His firm published a half-dozen periodicals and hundreds of single titles. It began in Boston
as Gleason's Publishing Hall, under Frederick Gleason's
proprietorship, at 1 1/2 Tremont Row; moved to Court
Street, at the corner of Tremont, in 1847; to the Museum
Building, 24 and 26 Tremont, in 1850; and to 100 Tremont
Street, at the corner of Bromfield, in 1852. After
Gleason's "retirement" in 1854, the firm remained at
100 Tremont for a time, under the name of its new proprietor, Ballou, before relinquishing that address to
Gleason's newly-formed company. Ballou's offices were
then at 22 Winter Street. After he sold out to Elliott,
Thomes & Talbot in 1863, Ballou's business address was
33 School Street, room 54.

 Major Authors: Horatio Alger, Jr., T. S. Arthur,
Maturin Murray Ballou, Osgood Bradbury, Sylvanus Cobb,
Jr., A. J. Duganne, J. H. Ingraham, Justin Jones,
E. Z. C. Judson, Edgar Allan Poe, Ben Perley Poore,
Mrs. Lydia H. Sigourney, Mrs. Ann S. Stephens.

 Maturin M. Ballou was born in 1820 into an austere
Massachusetts family of Universalist scholars and di-
vines, and died in 1895. His first journalistic experiences, in his teens, were with his cousin Hosea Ballou's
religious magazines, where he developed his talent for
writing travel sketches and for editorial management;
he also contributed to The Olive Branch, a Boston family

27

story paper. Ill health had forced Ballou to leave
Harvard University before completing his studies, and
to begin a series of travels abroad that were to become a lifelong obsession. Ballou's travels were to
supply material for a long career as a writer of popular literature. Eventually, like Nathaniel Hawthorne
in Salem, Ballou found work in Boston at the custom-
house, where he served as deputy navy agent (an employment that supplied him with a wealth of practical
information for the nautical adventure stories in which
he later specialized).

At the age of twenty-five, together with Frederick
Gleason, then a struggling job printer, Ballou conceived
the idea of producing, for mass distribution, simple
melodramatic adventure stories about naval warfare and
piracy. Written by Ballou under his pseudonym "Lieutenant Murray," the first three offerings, Fanny Campbell;
or the Female Pirate Captain, Red Rupert; or the American
Buccaneer, and The Naval Officer; or the Pirate's Cave,
were phenomenally successful. Fanny Campbell alone sold
80,000 copies within the first few months. Encouraged
by their early success, Gleason and Ballou continued the
series with new authors (all of whom were to find great
success writing for popular publishers) such as J. H.
Ingraham, Justin Jones [Harry Hazel], and Mrs. Ann
Stephens. In 1845 Ballou joined Gleason in establishing the new publishing house, variously called Gleason's
Publishing Hall and the United States Publishing Company,
to publish shilling novelettes and distribute them effi-
ciently to a mass audience. In January 1846, Gleason as
publisher and Ballou as editor founded The Flag of Our
Union, a "bedsheet-sized" weekly family paper that would
capitalize on this newly-established mass market for
sensational adventure stories and didactic sketches.
One measure of the success of their periodical, in
those days of questionable circulation claims, was the
host of imitators that sprang up almost immediately.
In Boston alone, they included the American Union, the
Flag of the Free, the Line of Battle Ship, the Star
Spangled Banner, the True Flag, Uncle Sam, the Yankee,
the Yankee Nation, and the Yankee Privateer.

28

Maturin Murray Ballou

Gleason's Publishing Hall prospered under Ballou's editorial management, and in 1851 the two proprietors determined to try yet another ambitious venture. Ballou had taken on a new employee, a recently-arrived Englishman named Henry Carter, who was later to make a name for himself in American publishing as Frank Leslie. Gleason's Pictorial Drawing Room Companion, a weekly avowedly imitative of the Illustrated London News for which Leslie had worked, was concocted by Ballou and Leslie in May 1851. In undertaking this new venture, Gleason and Ballou again had identified an entirely new market. One of the earliest profusely illustrated weeklies in the country, the Pictorial specialized in woodcuts depicting new buildings, foreign scenes, public figures, martial encampments, and nautical scenes.

The Pictorial generally featured a single serial per issue, several shorter fictions, an editorial miscellany, a few poems, and a few brief "news items" of the sensational variety, which served as filler. Many articles were no more than extended captions to Leslie's engravings, which often were completed first. Sylvanus Cobb's journals, for example, contain entries such as "Received a letter from Mr. Gleason with several pictures from which to write a sea story," or, "Received a picture from Mr. Gleason for a Revolutionary story." The illustrations were dominated by single scenes of climactic adventure, captioned with a lurid quotation from the story; but Ballou and the Pictorial's other authors also relied heavily on a carefully described setting--usually of some faraway, exotic, or bygone place--and some of the illustrations might easily have appeared in travel books. In fact, the first three or four paragraphs of a Ballou story might have been reprinted as impressionistic travel or American "local color" sketches.

By 1854 Ballou was confident enough in his success to begin to maneuver his business partner, Gleason, out of the firm. Leslie had left the previous year to work for Barnum and Beach's Illustrated News of New York, and when Gleason pulled the rug out from under him by buying that periodical (which was struggling in spite of a circulation of 70,000), Leslie stayed in New York to begin

the first of the long series of periodicals that bore
his adopted name. Ballou used equally aggressive tac-
tics with Gleason, threatening to open two rival weeklies
in Boston if he wasn't allowed to buy Gleason's share of
their mutual enterprise. Gleason capitulated, declaring
in the Pictorial that he had "realized an ample competency" and now wished to "retire from business
altogether."

Ballou now faced strong competition from Robert
Bonner's New York Ledger. Like Gleason, Bonner bragged
of enormous premiums and prizes paid to contributors.
In 1855 when Bonner announced that he had paid $400.00
for a four-column story by Fanny Fern, Ballou, in the
Flag, characterized that figure as "information intended
for the Marines, we suppose." Bonner wasted no time in
avenging the slur on his honesty, launching a frontal
assault on Ballou's paper in his own advertising columns.
The Flag, he said, was overpriced, unpopular, small-time,
and "burdened with a debt of $150,000."

There must have been some truth to Bonner's alle-
gations because the Flag, by anyone's reckoning, did
not keep pace with the Ledger's booming circulation
(which had reached 150,000 in 1856 to about half that--
averaging the various claims and counterclaims--for the
Flag; later the Ledger's circulation reached a steady
400,000, to lead all the popular magazines). Ballou re-
taliated in January 1855 by founding America's first
monthly devoted largely to fiction, Ballou's Dollar
Monthly, a hundred-page quarto widely advertised as
"the cheapest paper in the world." Its mainstay was
Sylvanus Cobb, Jr., a prolific writer of formula adventure stories and didactic sketches who had been one of
Gleason's earliest contributors. Writing under an array
of pseudonyms, Cobb contributed a large percentage of
the new material in Ballou's Dollar Monthly, whose pages
were often filled out with reprints from the Flag. Cobb
was joined on the staff of the Monthly by his younger
imitator, Horatio Alger, Jr., who, like Cobb, exalted
the homely American virtues. In the first issue's editorial department, Ballou announced: "No more convenient collection of reading matter for perusal in the
cars or by the fireside could be devised, and it is

30

intended to make it a welcome visitor anywhere." That
Ballou's Dollar Monthly was such a welcome visitor
(circulation grew steadily) was as much due to its con-
soling moralism as to its melodramatic adventure.

Bonner dealt Ballou a severe blow in 1856, however, soon after the founding of the new monthly, when
he lured away Sylvanus Cobb, Jr., installing Cobb immediately as the new mainstay of the Ledger. Cobb's
first effort at the Ledger, "The Gunmaker of Moscow,"
was an enormous success, becoming one of the best-known
of all of the popular serials. Another fixture at
Gleason's, E. Z. C. Judson [Ned Buntline], also left,
lured away by Street's New York Weekly, where he was
transformed from a writer of nautical romances resem-
bling Ballou's to America's first celebrated writer of
popular western adventure stories.

Oddly enough, it was not the Flag or the Dollar
Monthly that suffered most from these depredations, but
the Pictorial, which had to cope with the additional
threat posed by Frank Leslie's and the House of Harper's
new ventures. After Gleason's departure Francis A.
Durivage had been installed as assistant editor, better
paper was used, and a new building erected; but circulation lagged. In 1855 Ballou tried the unheard-of expe-
dient of inserting advertisements, but he stopped when
readers protested. By 1857 the situation had become
desperate.

The Dollar Monthly, inexplicably, was doing well.
A good businessman, Ballou used the capital earned by
the Monthly to expand into another market. Once again
he established a periodical genre entirely new to the
American scene, the Weekly Novelette, which is said to
have suggested the concept of the dime novel to Erastus
Beadle. Begun in April 1857, the Weekly Novelette specialized in four- or five-part fictions of sensational
adventure, many of them reprints from the Flag or the
Pictorial. Ballou never quite settled on an appropriate
format, trying for a time to convert the series, which
had sold at 4 cents per issue, to a weekly magazine with
departments like those in the Flag, at $2.00 per year.
Later he sold bound volumes, each containing four or

five issues (one complete novelette). Only thirteen
numbers of the weekly magazine were published.

At this point, Ballou's career had passed its
zenith. He was to continue in publishing for another
thirty years, but without approximating his early success. Ballou, with Gleason, established the major
genres of American pulp fiction; others, including
Bonner, made enormous profits from Ballou's innovations.
Ballou, with Frank Leslie, brought the illustrated
weekly to America; Leslie got rich. Ballou's early
series with Gleason and his later Weekly Novelette
made popular fiction available for the first time in
cheap editions for mass audiences; the dime novel publishers, Beadle among them, reaped huge sums. Ballou
and Gleason discovered many of the leading authors of
popular fiction: Alger, T. S. Arthur, Cobb, Ingraham,
and Judson among them; they made Ballou money, but
their biggest successes came later, for other publishing houses. Even the magazines themselves survived to
make significant sums for other publishers, who capitalized on the names that Gleason and Ballou had made
famous.

After 1857 Street's New York Weekly, Bonner's
Ledger, Frank Leslie's and the Harpers' weeklies made
increasing inroads into the Pictorial's readership.
Ballou tried reducing the price to $2.50 in 1858, but
was not able to boost circulation significantly. He
suspended publication in December 1859, announcing in
the final editorial section that 451 issues of the
Pictorial had cost $767,000--$423,000 for paper, $161,000
for drawing and engraving, and only $28,000 for contrib-
utors. At that rate, the Pictorial could not afford to
allow its circulation to dip much below 50,000 per issue.

The expense figures clear up another matter regarding the history of Ballou's publishing house as well,
the question of why so many of Ballou's best-known
writers left him for other publishing firms. Gleason's
and Ballou's prize announcements had made sensations in
their day--and had been greeted with widespread skepti-
cism by competitors. There is no way to ascertain
whether they were genuine--whether, for instance, $1,000
was really awarded to the author of the best novelette

in the 1848 prize competition. It is known, however, that Edgar Allan Poe, late in his life, was offered only $15.00 for an article and, from the figures announced in the final issue, that the Pictorial paid only an average of $62.00 per issue for copy. At that rate, Ballou probably paid about $100.00 for a complete novelette, and the reason for authorial defection was probably simply financial. Bonner, Street, and Beadle, with more capital, could offer higher rates. Bonner paid Cobb $200.00 each for eight installments of "The Gunmaker of Moscow."

Ballou tried for a time to continue the Pictorial in a more modest way as The Welcome Guest (another "mammoth" weekly miscellany). That venture also failed, however, contributing to the series of setbacks that finally forced him in 1863 to sell his publishing house--typically to a new company established by one of his and Gleason's own protégés, Newton Talbot, founder with James R. Elliott and William Henry Thomes of Elliott, Thomes & Talbot. Although he was never to attain his former eminence, Ballou was not through as a publisher. In 1872 he took another enormous gamble, founding what was to become one of America's best-known newspapers, the Boston Globe, which was taken over in 1874 by General Charles H. Taylor. Ballou soon had two new periodicals going, however, the Boston Budget and Ballou's Magazine. The latter, a 15-cent miscellany, lasted until 1893; the former outlived its founder, finally suspending publication in 1918.

Nor was publishing Ballou's only interest. He continued to write and edit, churning out a dozen travel books, such as Due South; or Cuba, Past and Present (1885) and Footprints of Travel; or Journeyings in Many Lands (1889), and a half-dozen reference books, among them Notable Thoughts About Women (1882) and Edge Tools of Speech (1886). He lectured and wrote dozens of plays, none ever staged and only one or two ever published. He also had a number of other business and financial interests, one of the most important of which was the building of the huge St. James Hotel for working people in South Boston. He continued to travel, circumnavigating

33

the globe in 1882. Ballou died 27 March 1895 in Cairo, Egypt, while on yet another foreign tour.

Ballou's publications and the audience he cultivated reflect American taste for romantic adventure, the violence of bloody nautical and martial encounters, and the ethical ideals of virtuous maidens and hardworking young men. Is not Mark Twain's Tom Sawyer essentially an ironic idyll about boys who have accepted the story-paper ethos as their own? Indeed, does not the runaway Tom adopt the name of a character from a Gleason serial ("The Black Avenger of the Spanish Main") first published in The Flag of Our Union in 1847? Maturin Murray Ballou helped publicize the self-confident idealism and optimism of the story-paper heroes and heroines whose inspiring adventures were devoured by a mass American audience for three decades after the Civil War.

Peter Benson

References

Ralph Admari, "Ballou, the Father of the Dime Novel," The American Book Collector, 4 (September-October 1933): 121-29.

Henry Nash Smith, Virgin Land (Cambridge: Harvard University Press, 1950).

Mary Noel, Villains Galore . . . The Heyday of the Popular Story Weekly (New York: Macmillan, 1954).

Madeleine B. Stern, Imprints on History: Book Publishers and American Frontiers (Bloomington: Indiana University Press, 1956; reprinted, New York: AMS Press, 1975).

Frank Luther Mott, A History of American Magazines, Vol. 2 (Cambridge: Harvard University Press, 1957).

6 Beadle & Co.

Beadle & Co. (1851-1898), one of various names for the same firm, was the first to issue novels in numbered series for a set price of 10 cents. The firm also published story papers and magazines, handbooks, songbooks, biographies, baseball books, dialogues (dramatic sketches), speakers (orations), and miscellaneous pamphlets, a total of some 3,500 titles in over 5,500 editions, most of which sold for 5 or 10 cents.

The business began in 1851 as Beadle & Vanduzee, 6 West Seneca Street, Buffalo, with partners Erastus F. Beadle and Benjamin C. Vanduzee. When the latter dropped out in 1853, the name became Beadle & Brother to include Erastus's younger brother Irwin, who left temporarily in 1854, after which the name was E. F. Beadle, first at 11 West Seneca and then at 199 Main Street. When Robert Adams joined in 1856 the company became Beadle & Adams at 227 Main Street, the address of Irwin Beadle's news depot and bookstore. In 1858 Erastus Beadle, Robert Adams, and Irwin Beadle moved to 333 Broadway, New York, keeping the Beadle & Adams name but using also the imprint Irwin P. Beadle. In 1859 the three moved to 137 William Street, New York, the street where the Beadle firm was to remain at various house numbers: in 1860 at number 141, 1862 number 118, 1868 number 98, and 1896 number 92. In May 1860 the name changed to Irwin P. Beadle & Co., and in October to Beadle & Co. In 1862 Irwin left the firm and with George Munro established a separate company, Irwin P. Beadle & Co., while his brother Erastus and Robert Adams kept the name Beadle & Co. In 1872 the name changed back to Beadle & Adams, which it remained until the firm ceased in 1898. The Adams in this last change referred to William and David Adams, brothers of Robert, who had died in 1866. The assets of the company were purchased by M. J. Ivers & Co. in 1898.

(Courtesy Rare Book Division, The New York Public Library; Astor, Lenox and Tilden Foundations)

Beadle & Co.

Beadle's American Sixpenny Publishing House, 44
Paternoster Row, London, was the English branch of the
firm, which began in 1861 and closed in 1866 when the
rights to reprinting Beadle publications were purchased
by George Routledge and Sons. Frank Starr & Co., publishers of dime novels, was established in late 1868 or
early 1869 as a subsidiary company at 41 Platt Street,
New York, the side entrance to 98 William Street, the
Beadle location. Adams, Victor & Co., 98 William Street,
and after 1896 at 92 William Street, the Beadle addresses,
was begun by the firm in 1872 and continued for a short
time after M. J. Ivers & Co., bought the Beadle assets.
The name was used on some clothbound books selling for
$1.25 to $1.50, and in 1877 it appeared on a short series of 10- and 20-cent reprints of famous classics.
The name Adams & Co. was also used, but as far as is
known, only as the publisher of the periodical The Young
New Yorker, which ran from 1878 to 1879.

Major Authors: Augustus Comstock ("Roger
Starbuck"), Mary A. Denison, Edward S. Ellis, Prentiss
Ingraham, E. Z. C. Judson, Ann S. Stephens, Metta V.
Victor, Edward L. Wheeler.

Erastus Flavel Beadle was born in Pierstown, New
York, 11 September 1821, one of ten children, and died
at Cooperstown, New York, 18 December 1894. He was
apprenticed in 1838 to H. & E. Phinney in Cooperstown
and there learned typesetting, stereotyping, printing,
and binding. He married Mary Ann Pennington of Cooperstown in April 1846, and in 1847 went to Buffalo, where
he worked as a stereotyper for Jewett, Thomas & Company,
publishers of the Commercial Advertiser. Erastus's
younger brothers, Irwin and James, came to Buffalo, and
in 1850 the three formed Beadle & Brother's [sic]
Buffalo Stereotype Foundry, which apparently became a
prosperous business. James, born in 1828, did not become a member of the publishing firm but evidently
stayed with the stereotype foundry until he moved to
Auburn, New York, in 1852, where he was mysteriously
murdered in 1856. Late in 1851 Erastus entered partnership with Benjamin C. Vanduzee, thus founding the Beadle
firm.

(Courtesy Edward T. LeBlanc, *Dime Novel Round-Up*)

Beadle & Co.

Robert Adams was born in Londonderry, Ireland, 15 January 1837 and died in New York City 2 February 1866. His family came to America in 1847, and when he was seventeen he became a stereotyper for Erastus Beadle. In 1856, when he was only nineteen, he became Erastus's partner in Beadle & Adams. After he died at the age of twenty-nine, his interest in the Beadle firm passed to his two younger brothers, William and David, both of whom had for some time been connected with it.

William Adams was born in Londonderry, Ireland, 17 October 1838 and died in New York City 19 December 1896, by that time the sole owner and last surviving member of the Beadle firm. He was working for Beadle as early as 1860 and in 1864 was the firm's superintendent. After his brother Robert's death, he became responsible for the business management of the firm. Beginning in 1876 he made twenty annual tours of Europe, which he described in letters printed in Beadle magazines.

David Adams was born in Londonderry, Ireland, 21 August 1846 and died in Brooklyn 1 October 1886. He was married by the Reverend Henry Ward Beecher to Leonora Kline in 1877. She died in 1881, and he married Mrs. Fredericka B. Cornwell in 1882. He ran the literary department of the firm but was not himself an author.

The most important employee was Orville J. Victor, editor of the Beadle publications for thirty-six years. He was born in Sandusky, Ohio, 23 October 1827 and died in Hohokus, New Jersey, 14 March 1910. He became the Beadle editor in 1861, a year after the publication of the first Beadle Dime Novel, and he resigned shortly before the firm was sold in 1898. He had graduated from the Seminary and Theological Institute of Norwalk, Ohio, and while reading for the law he began writing the poems and short stories that led to editorial positions on several journals. He became a Beadle author before he joined the firm, having written, among other things, the first of the Beadle's Dime Biographical Library, the "Life of Joseph Garibaldi." He married Metta Victoria Fuller in 1856, who as Metta V. Victor became one of Beadle's most important authors. Orville Victor himself continued to write not only for Beadle but for other

firms, and his numerous works include various scholarly
publications. He had strict moral standards for the
Beadle publications, and he maintained a quality not
always equaled by Beadle competitors. An anonymous
writer in The New York Public Library Bulletin in 1922
referred to Victor as "one of the most remarkable figures in the history of American literature." Certainly
he was a powerful influence in the Beadle firm.

The company began in 1851 with the preparation of
The Youth's Casket, a magazine for children (January
1852-December 1857). Benjamin Vanduzee, an artist and
wood engraver, furnished the illustrations and Erastus
Beadle did the stereotyping. The first editor was
Harley Thorne, the first printer Phinney & Co. The
Beadle firm did not do its own printing until many years
later; the exact date is unknown. Nor did the Beadles
and Adams's do much of their own editing, preferring to
hire experienced people. Vanduzee left in 1853, and by
May of 1855 the stereotyping plant had been sold. Soon
there was a new periodical, The Home, A Fireside Monthly
Companion and Guide for the Wife, the Mother, the Sister
and the Daughter, which began with the January 1856 issue and ran until June 1860. In 1857 Erastus went to
Omaha, Nebraska, where he speculated disastrously in
real estate, and returned in time for the move of the
firm from Buffalo to New York in 1858. Erastus Beadle
and Robert Adams continued to publish The Home, and
Irving Beadle began publishing dime songbooks and handbooks. He had been publishing broadside "penny" ballads, probably beginning in Buffalo before 1858, and
these he bound into 72-page, 6- by 3 3/4-inch booklets
selling for 10 cents. The first of these, Beadle's Dime
Songbook, was filed for copyright by Irving P. Beadle
19 April 1859, and it is the first of all the Beadle
dime booklets. The second publication was Mrs. Metta V.
Victor's Dime Cook-Book; or, Housewife's Pocket Companion.
Embodying what is Most Economic, Most Practical, Most
Excellent, 100 pages, 5 7/8 by 3 3/4 inches, buff wrappers, published sometime before July 1859. The third
publication was Mrs. Metta V. Victor's Dime Recipe Book.
A Directory For the Parlor, Nursery, Sick Room, Toilet,
Kitchen, Larder, etc., 100 pages, the same size as the

preceding, deposited for copyright 14 July 1859. These were followed by others, all of them published repeatedly in various editions for the next fifteen or twenty years, and all of them evidently good sellers. The booklets would be printed until the plates were so worn that they became illegible in places; they were then reset and re-stereotyped.

Credit for the first Beadle dime novel has been given variously to Erastus and to Irwin. Johannsen argues that Irwin published Mrs. Ann S. Stephens's Malaeska, and certainly the imprint does say Irwin P. Beadle & Co., but the address, 141 William Street, New York, is the same used by Erastus Beadle and Robert Adams. Regardless of who was responsible, its publication 9 June 1860 was the most important event in the firm's history.

Unknown today, Ann S. Stephens was during the nineteenth century one of the most famous of American authors, and her name alone would have helped create large sales when it appeared on the first Beadle Dime Novel, Malaeska: the Indian Wife of the White Hunter. This 128-page booklet, advertised as "A dollar book for a dime," became one of the best sellers of the century. Unlike most of the early Beadle novels, this was a reprint, having first appeared in 1839 as a serial in The Ladies Companion. Irwin Beadle paid Mrs. Stephens $250.00 for her moralistic tale about the tribulations of a mixed marriage in early colonial New York. This novel, like many of the early Beadle publications, received good reviews in respectable magazines.

Beadle was so famous for its dime novels that people have long tended to think the names Beadle and dime novel inseparable. The firm was probably the first to make this form widely popular, but others had preceded them, and the great success in 1860 of the first Beadle novel created strong competition that continued throughout the life of the firm. Malaeska was followed within three weeks by the second novel, The Privateer's Cruise, and the Bride of Pomfret Hall. A Sea Tale of '76, a story about privateering during the American Revolution, by "Harry Cavendish," the pen name of Charles Jacobs Peterson. The third novel, two weeks later, was another

41

by Mrs. Ann S. Stephens, <u>Myra, the Child of Adoption.
A Romance of Real Life</u>, the story of the disinherited
daughter of a wealthy man, based on an actual occurrence.
Unlike the first dime novel, this one was not a reprint.
Mrs. Stephens's name eventually appeared on thirty-
three Beadle publications.

On 29 September 1860 a famous advertisement
appeared in <u>The New York Tribune</u>, consisting of only
four words, "Who is Seth Jones?" So extensive was the
advertising campaign that these words "covered the
countryside." A few days later Beadle Dime Novel No. 8
appeared: <u>Seth Jones; or, The Captives of the Frontier</u>,
by Edward S. Ellis. A story of life in the early settlements of western New York in which a girl captured
by Mohawks is rescued by two scouts, this novel and
Mrs. Stephens's became the firm's two biggest sellers.

<u>Seth Jones</u>, like the earlier novels, bore the im-
print Irwin P. Beadle & Co., but beginning with No. 12,
Beadle & Co. appeared, changing to Beadle & Adams with
No. 259. Titles in this series included <u>The Slave
Sculptor; or, the Prophetess of the Secret Chambers.
A Tale of Mexico at the Period of the Conquest</u>, by
William Jared Hall; <u>The Land Claim. A Tale of the Upper
Missouri</u>, by Mrs. Francis F. Barritt, a story of pioneer
settlers in Nebraska Territory; <u>On the Deep; or, the
Missionary's Daughter</u>, a story of the Pacific Ocean by
"Roger Starbuck" in which a ship sailing from the Sand-
wich Islands to New York is destroyed by Malay pirates;
<u>The Red-Skin's Pledge; or, the Double Plot</u>, by James L.
Bowen, about horse thieves, Creek Indians, and bad men
in Alabama after the War of 1812.

The majority of the 3,158 different novels (usually reprinted from two to ten times) were adventure
stories and romances based upon American history, all
of them intensely nationalistic, the early ones giving
fairly accurate pictures of American pioneer life, although frequently mixed with legend. Some were tales
of the sea, the city, and foreign countries. Later
came various detective mysteries and a few rags-to-
riches moralities. The early publications were booklets
approximately 6 3/4 by 4 1/2 inches, about 100 pages,
35,000 to 40,000 words, in orange-colored wrappers that

gave way later to white paper covers with stenciled
color illustrations. Beginning in the 1870s the publications used larger paper, usually about 11 3/4 by
8 1/2 inches (quarto) or about 8 1/4 by 5 3/4 inches
(octavo), with no covers but with a black line illustration on the front page, multiple columns of print,
the quartos with 16 or 32 pages and the octavos with
32, usually from 70,000 to 80,000 words.

The firm published at different times about
twenty-five series of novels, the first being Beadle's
Dime Novels, 321 issues that ran from 1860 to 1874,
nearly all original stories about Indian and frontier
life. After 1874 the series continued to 1885 with the
name New Dime Novels, usually reprints of the earlier
Dime Novels, the two parts of the series containing a
total of 630 novels published during twenty-five years
and four months, the longest run of any of the Beadle
novels.

Another important series began in 1877 as Frank
Starr's New York Dime Library, became Beadle's Dime Library in 1878, and finally the Dime Library in 1879. It
continued under M. J. Ivers & Co. after 1898, the series
finally ceasing in December 1905, a run of 1,103 issues
during twenty-eight years. It was the first major series
to use the quarto form. The stories in the Dime Library
were usually first printings rather than reprints and
were the same kind as those in the earlier Beadle novels,
stories of the West, of trappers and hunters, scouts and
Indians, gold miners, road agents, bad men generally and,
in the later issues, detectives and criminals. There
were only a few sea stories with pirates, the popularity
of this subject having declined.

The Dime Novels and the Dime Library were intended
primarily for adults, but another important series, the
Half-Dime Library, was for boys. It began in 1877 and
lasted until 1905, having been continued by M. J. Ivers
& Co., a total of 1,168 issues running for twenty-eight
years. The early boys' stories were of Indians, pioneers, backwoodsmen, and the sea. Included were a few
standard reprintings such as Aladdin, Robinson Crusoe,
Gulliver's Travels, and Sinbad the Sailor. Later, detective plots predominated. Some stories repeated

43

leading characters such as Deadwood Dick (over a hundred novels), Broadway Bill, and Joe Phenix.

Of the eight periodicals published by Beadle, the most important was the Saturday Star Journal, also called the Saturday Journal, a weekly story paper begun in 1870, continued as Beadle's Weekly in 1882, changed to the Banner Weekly in 1885, and ending in 1897 for a run of twenty-seven years. Each number usually contained eight five-column pages and was illustrated by two or three woodcuts. The size of most issues was 21 1/4 by 14 1/4 inches. The total contents included 685 serial stories as well as innumerable short stories, sketches, informative articles, biographies of scouts, desperadoes, and mountain men. Authors included "Uncle Remus," Margaret E. Sangster, "Oliver Optic," Frank H. Converse, Ed. Mott, and many others. Most of the stories also appeared as individual publications in various Beadle series, and the later numbers of the magazine reprinted stories from the earlier ones.

The Beadle authors often used at least one pseudonym and sometimes as many as ten. Beadle's own authors, who could be depended upon to turn out a novel every few weeks, included Edward Sylvester Ellis, Prentiss Ingraham, Mrs. Metta V. Victor, Edward L. Wheeler (creator of "Deadwood Dick"), and others. Authors who sometimes wrote for Beadle were not considered a part of the company's "stable": Augustus Comstock ("Roger Starbuck"), Mrs. Mary A. Denison, Frederick Van Rensselaer Dey, Col. A. J. H. Duganne, E. Z. C. Judson, Charles Bertrand Lewis ("M. Quad"), "Leon" Lewis, Mrs. Ann S. Stephens, and others. American authors whose works in other publications were reprinted by Beadle included Newton Mallory Curtis, Dr. John Hovey Robinson, Dr. William Mason Turner, and others. Foreign authors, mostly English but a few German, Swedish, and French also appeared on the Beadle list.

The company worked hard to outwit its rivals by starting new series, changing names of authors, titles, and even firms, forming subsidiary companies, and creating a tangle difficult to follow. As the first novels appeared in 1860 they were quickly reprinted in England, evidently without permission, and the following year

Beadle & Co.

Erastus Beadle went to London to open the firm's own office, which immediately reprinted Seth Jones, the first issue of Beadle's American Sixpenny Library. This series was continued by George Routledge and Sons, the firm that bought the English subsidiary in 1866. The handbooks were also popular in England; these included the Six Penny Cooking Book and the Ready Remedies for Common Complaints.

With the beginning of the Civil War, Beadle publications soon became famous in homes and army camps throughout the country. It has been said that the novels were shipped in huge bales in order to meet the demand, and the Beadles are supposed to have given away many thousands of copies to soldiers. According to some reminiscences the Union government bought copies for distribution to army camps. Certainly the Beadle booklets were popular on the battlefronts. The stories were appropriate for the times, recounting reckless adventures and glorifying nationalism, protection of helpless women, and always the defeat of wrong and the triumph of right. In December 1861 one of the most famous of the Dime Novels (No. 33) was published: Mrs. Metta V. Victor's Maum Guinea and Her Plantation Children; or, Holiday-Week on a Louisiana Estate. A Slave Romance. According to Charles M. Harvey, writing in The Atlantic Monthly in 1907, this story of slave life was favorably compared by Abraham Lincoln to Uncle Tom's Cabin. Reviews of it appeared in the major publications, and it had such large sales in England that some people have believed it may have helped prevent that country from aiding the South.

No one knows why Irwin Beadle left the firm in 1863, but it was evidently an unhappy breakup, for Erastus Beadle and Robert Adams brought legal suit against Irwin Beadle and George Munro in an effort to prevent the new company from using the Beadle name or in any way indicating that their publications might be connected to the original business.

Soon after Irwin left, the Beadle firm entered into a direct relationship with the American News Company, which was formed in 1864 and took entire charge of selling the Dime Novels. Distribution of their

45

products had always been important to the Beadle firm, and much of their fame can be attributed to their skillfulness in the techniques of selling. The American News Company and the name of its president, Sinclair Tousey, were used in the imprint on some of the first publications in the American Tales series (1863-1874) and elsewhere. Most of the issues of this series were original stories of frontier life. The Beadle name first appeared on No. 45, but the entire series was probably published by them. There may have been further involvement between the two firms, since the attorney for the American News Company, Edward H. Spooner, became a partner in Beadle & Co. from approximately 1866 to 1868.

There is evidence that the Beadle firm tried to break away from its dime booklet image. During 1865 the firm published Beadle's Monthly, A Magazine of Today, which compared favorably with the contemporaneous Harper's Monthly. Other less ambitious efforts also failed to meet the firm's profit requirements. From 1866 to 1869 Beadle published Fifty Cent Books, an unnumbered series of five octavos, 9 by 6 inches, containing 80 to 300 pages: three romances, one murder mystery, and one nonfiction picture book of the West, Our New States and Territories. Another attempt was made in 1875 to present 25-cent novels in a series called Cheap Editions of Popular Authors. Most of the tales are love stories and all are reprinted from the Beadle periodical The Saturday Journal. Only twenty-five issues were published, the last in 1877. Another try was the 1875 series Beadle and Adams' Twenty Cent Novels, containing stories too long (140 to 200 pages) for the dime series; again all were reprints from The Saturday Journal or the double numbers of the Dime Novels. Only thirty-two titles were issued. During the 1870s several other series of novels were begun, priced at 15 cents, but they also were dropped.

One of the famous Beadle publications was the first appearance in book form of Mark Twain's Jim Smiley's Frog (Dime Book of Fun, No. 3, dated 1866), an abbreviated version of "The Jumping Frog of Calaveras County." Another famous publishing venture was the 1868 purchase from Captain Mayne Reid, a well-known Irish

46

writer, of a story for $700.00, for a long time the
record amount paid for the manuscript of a dime novel.
The usual compensation for authors who wrote for Dime
Novels series or for Half-Dime Libraries was $75.00 to
$150.00. Those who wrote for Dime Libraries typically
received $150.00 to $300.00. Those who wrote serials
for the periodicals usually received more. The $700.00-
story was The White Squaw, a story of the Seminole War
in Florida.

Beadle tried to expand its market with a family-
type series, The Fireside Library (1877-1882), which was
advertised as "a 'Welcome Guest' at Fireside and Social
Circles, in Homes and Libraries, in the Office and the
Shop." Most of the issues were love stories, many of
them reprints of English novels. At the same time the
firm began its new Dime Library series (1877-1905), the
first story of which was Philip S. Warne's A Hard Crowd;
or Gentleman Sam's Sister (the series at that time being
called Frank Starr's New York Library), a tale of Omaha
when it was a tough town and not yet part of the United
States. For this series, Albert W. Aiken, one of the
Beadle regulars, wrote The Spotter-Detective; or, the
Girls of New York, a story of Sing Sing and New York
City. Others were Prentiss Ingraham's Wild Bill, the
Pistol Dead Shot; or, Dagger Don's Double, a story of
Wild Bill Hickok in Kansas, and Joseph E. Badger's
Dandy Darling, Detective; or, the Boomers of Big Buffalo,
a tale of Oklahoma when it was thrown open for settlement.

The new series written chiefly for boys, the Half-
Dime Library (1877-1905), began with Edward L. Wheeler's
Deadwood Dick, the Prince of the Road; or, The Black
Rider of the Black Hills, in which Deadwood Dick pro-
poses to Calamity Jane and is turned down. Others were
T. C. Harbaugh's Old Frosty, the Guide; or, Niokana, the
White Queen of the Blackfeet. A Tale of the Far North-
west, a story of frontier days along the upper Missouri
River in Montana; Charles Morris's Dark Paul, the Tiger
King; or, Caught in his Own Trap, a city story of a
house with secret passages and trapdoors, a lady, and
a tiger; Edward L. Wheeler's Fritz, the Bound-Boy Detective; or, Dot Leetle Game mit Rebecca, a Horatio Alger
type of story about an amateur detective in Philadelphia;

47

and William R. Eyster's The Sport in Velvet; or, Big Burk's Bluff, about a mining camp in the West.

To correspond with this boys' series, Beadle brought out one for "young ladies," the Waverly Library (1879-1886), love and society romances which were, according to the advertisements, "Wholesome, Vigorous, and Fresh. . . Perfectly pure in tone . . . Everything to please and nothing to avoid . . . No . . . weak sentimentalism." English reprints predominated. Another boys' series, begun in 1881, was Beadle's Boy's Library, which lasted until 1890 and contained largely reprints from other Beadle series but with titles changed to make them more suitable for boys. The word "love," for example, was always omitted from the new titles.

The biographical booklets, like the novels, concentrated on adventurous men--Daniel Boone, Christopher Carson, David Crockett and, of course, General Grant, George Washington, and Abraham Lincoln. The biographies began in 1860, and the last was published in 1877. The handbooks, published from 1859 through 1880, included cheap guides to dressmaking, cooking, home nursing, housekeeping, etiquette, letter writing, dancing, fortune-telling, swimming, chess, croquet, skating, horse riding and other subjects. The songbooks had such titles as: Widow Machree Song Book, Stand by the Flag, The Old Arm Chair, and Kiss Me while I'm Dreaming. Included in the various series were not only the popular songs of the day but also original contributions. The Dime Dialogues and Dime Speakers (1859-1898) were successful series.

Beadle's Dime Baseball Player was the first continuous series issued on baseball. Usually annuals, 1860-1881, all were edited by Henry Chadwick; and when he went to Spaulding to edit his Base-Ball Guide, the Beadle series was discontinued. Beadle also issued various booklets related to the Civil War, which ranged from Beadle's Dime Drill Book for Squad and Company to The Soldiers' Directory to Pensions and Bounties. The Civil War national tax laws were printed in a number of booklets published as the laws were amended and revised.

The reputation of the dime novel deteriorated in the 1880s, and the firm resorted increasingly to

reprinting, as did other publishing houses; but up to
the last the Beadle firm was still buying some new
manuscripts. By 1877 the type of story was gradually
changing; instead of Indian and pioneer tales, the
readers wanted stories about newsboys, bootblacks, bad
men, detectives, and the Wild West. For the Beadle
firm, the struggle for a new market ended with the
death of William Adams in 1896. At the end of February
1898, the executors of his estate sold the assets of the
firm to M. J. Ivers & Co.,[1] which continued to publish
the Dime Library, the Half-Dime Library, and the Beadle
Boy's Library with their own imprint until December
1905, when that firm ceased production. Ivers also
reprinted sixty-four issues of Edward L. Wheeler's
novels in a series called The Deadwood Dick Library.
Some years later Ivers's plates and stock were bought
by the Arthur Westbrook Company of Cleveland, which
reissued the Deadwood Dick and Frontier Libraries, as
well as the tales of Aiken and a few other authors,
ceasing in 1937. Many English publishers have also
reprinted Beadle publications.

The Beadle firm existed to make money, though
there is no evidence that it built the huge fortune
legend has attributed to it. The company gave readers
what they wanted, and in this respect Beadle publications were more reinforcers of public tastes than crea-
tors of them. Thus they provide us with a mirror
reflecting much of nineteenth-century life. We can
still learn American history from Beadle publications;
although clouded with romantic nationalistic dreams,
parts of the early stories are close to reality. But
finding a Beadle booklet to read is not easy. They were
cheap, read once and thrown away or passed from hand to
hand until they disintegrated, and most of them disappeared. The few that remain are sold for high prices.

By the time Erastus Beadle died in 1894, his
products were remembered only as cheap paper stories
for boys, although the early publications were meant
for adults. At the beginning the novels were considered
favorably, but as tastes changed they were looked down
upon, and Beadle's reputation deteriorated. One of the
debts we owe Beadle publications is the fact that they

49

Beadle & Co.

helped the masses of people learn to read. In addition, Beadle novels and biographies contained the aspects of American history, attitudes, and legends that people wanted to know; they thus encouraged the national pride upon which much of the advancement of the country depended. In these respects, Beadle publications aided powerful forces in our society.

Lawrence Parke Murphy

References and Note

Albert Johannsen, The House of Beadle and Adams and Its Dime and Nickel Novels: The Story of a Vanished Literature (Norman: University of Oklahoma Press, 1950-1962. 3 vols.).

Madeleine B. Stern, "Ann S. Stephens: Author of the First Beadle Dime Novel, 1860," Bulletin of the New York Public Library, 64 (1960): 303-22.

[1] The Beadle files were accidentally destroyed after M. J. Ivers & Co. purchased the assets of the firm; supposedly they were used as fuel to heat the Ivers warehouse.

7 Irwin P. Beadle

Irwin P. Beadle (1859–1862; 1862–1864; 1865–1867) was from 1859 to 1862 one of the permutations of the firm best known as Beadle & Co., important for its innovations in publishing series of 10-cent novels, songbooks, and handbooks. Sometime after June 1862, Irwin Beadle's shares in Beadle & Co. were bought by Erastus Beadle and Robert Adams. Late in 1862 the second firm was established in partnership with a former Beadle employee, George Munro, and credit was established by 15 January 1863. Not only did it use an early form of the Beadle company name, it set up business at 137 William Street in the building that had housed the older firm from May 1859 to May 1860. Erastus filed suit claiming unfair competition in the use of the name, but lost. In August 1863 a third partner, Samuel Greenwood, joined the firm. Irwin severed ties with this firm in 1864, however, and the house became known as George Munro. This second firm had existed for slightly more than one year, from December 1862 to February 1864.

The third firm was established in mid-1865, for on 13 September 1865 the first number of Irwin P. Beadle's Comic and Sentimental Song Book for the People was advertised. This establishment was quartered at 51 and 53 Ann Street, moving to 102 Nassau Street sometime before July 1866. The house also published a fiction series that ran to forty-eight numbers called Irwin P. Beadle's American Novels (later name changes: Irwin's American Novels, American Novels), and Irwin's Six Penny Tales. In July 1866 the firm's name was changed to Irwin & Company and its address registered at 102 Nassau Street.

Major Authors: Edward S. Ellis, Edwin Evans Ewing, P. Hamilton Myers, "Leon" Lewis.

Irwin Pedro Beadle was born in Pierstown, New York, in 1826 and died in 1882. He moved to Buffalo in late 1849 or early 1850 to work as a bookbinder, a trade he

51

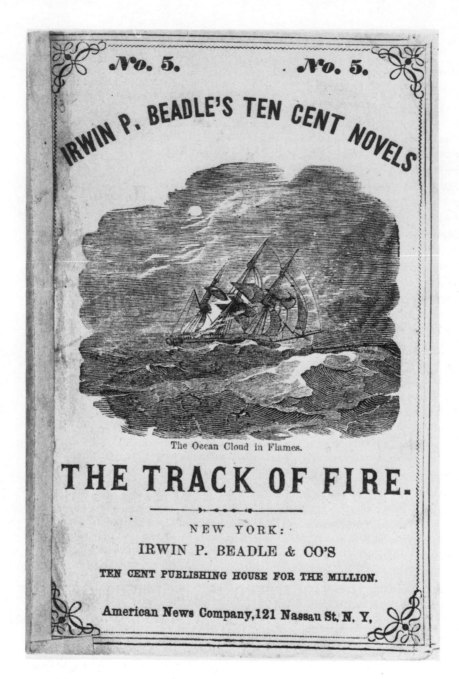

The Ocean Cloud in Flames.

THE TRACK OF FIRE.

NEW YORK:

IRWIN P. BEADLE & CO'S

TEN CENT PUBLISHING HOUSE FOR THE MILLION.

American News Company, 121 Nassau St, N. Y,

(Courtesy Edward T. LeBlanc, *Dime Novel Round-Up*)

had learned in Cooperstown and to which he returned when he retired from publishing. His brother Erastus Flavel, a stereotyper, had moved to Buffalo in 1847. In November 1850 they established Beadle & Brother's Buffalo Stereotype Foundry at No. 6 (later renumbered 5) West Seneca Street. Irwin apparently left the stereotype company in December 1853 or January 1854. Nothing is known of his activities from that time until he opened a bookstore at 227 Main Street in May or June 1856. Except as an address, this bookstore/newspaper depot seems not to have been connected with the Beadle & Adams publishing firm. Two years later, in late 1858, Irwin and Erastus Beadle and Robert Adams moved to New York. From 333 Broadway, Irwin published 10-cent handbooks and songbooks, while Beadle & Adams functioned as a separate establishment. Irwin's publications for this period show both New York and Buffalo imprints. The Buffalo city directory for 1859 lists him as publisher of broadside ballads--advertised in a later songbook at 1 cent each or 100 for 50 cents, no mail orders for less than 6 cents--and songbooks. The latter sold for 12 1/2 cents each. The New York directory for the same year shows him as publisher of The Dime Song-Book. In May 1859 he moved, with Beadle & Adams, from Broadway to 137 William Street.

Irwin had married Elizabeth M. Dunbar in Buffalo on 27 September 1850; after their divorce in 1858 or 1859, she ran the bookstore for many years. Shortly after moving to New York, he married Margaret Rice. They had four sons: William Irwin, Walter E., Franklin, and George. Irwin retired from publishing sometime between late 1867 and 1870. One directory shows him as a publisher at 21 Ann Street during the years 1868-1870. After 1870 he is shown as a bookbinder, and since no city directories list a company address for him, he may have worked at his various homes in Brooklyn. He died 9 June 1882.

Irwin Beadle's major contribution to nineteenth-century popular publishing, the concept of issuing inexpensive books in series, usually in sixteenmo format, grew out of his early publishing of penny songsheets. Because of that initial success, each time he began a

53

new firm its first publication was always a songbook.
<u>Irwin P. Beadle's New No. 1 Comic & Sentimental Song
Book for the People</u> was advertised on 13 September 1865,
the first publication of his third firm. This collection, reprinting many songs from books he had published
in 1859, contained 64 pages measuring 6 3/8 by 4 1/8
inches and sold for 10 cents. Number 2 was announced
for October 1865 but may never have been published.
Only two numbers have been seen.

One month later, 7 October 1865, Irwin P. Beadle's
American Novels, No. 1 was published in yellow-orange
wrappers. A portrait of James Fenimore Cooper replaced
the dime that marked Beadle & Co. wrappers, and a drawing illustrated the story. Pastel wrappers of different colors appeared on each of the four numbers published
during the remainder of the year.

Little information about the partnership structure
of the third Irwin P. Beadle venture survives. What is
known is closely tied to the complicated publishing history of this fiction series. Copyrights for the first
five numbers were registered in the name of "Irwin P.
Beadle" and for numbers 6-26 (possibly also 27) in the
name of "Irwin P. Beadle & Co.," although the "& Co."
never appeared in advertising or on wrappers. He may
have sold out temporarily or taken a partner about the
time of No. 6 (February 1866) because Chaney's American
Novels series advertised a number purporting to be the
sequel to Irwin's No. 5. It is not the same as Irwin's
No. 6, also advertised as a sequel to No. 5. The double
claim may simply indicate the keen competition among
dime novel publishers; however, at about that time the
copyright registration changed to "Irwin P. Beadle & Co."
Originally the books were issued monthly; beginning with
No. 11 (April/May 1866) they were issued semimonthly.
By No. 15 (July 1866)--although perhaps as early as No.
6--the series name was changed to Irwin's American Novels,
even though copyright notices still showed "Irwin P.
Beadle & Co."

It is likely that just prior to the July 1866 issue
(No. 15), the firm was refinanced, if not reorganized,
becoming Irwin & Company. Irwin Beadle's ownership of
this firm at its 102 Nassau Street location has been

established by contemporary business directories that
also show him at that address at least until July 1867.
Under the circumstances wrappers showing the new series
name, Irwin's American Novels, and the new imprint and
address would have been issued. An original issue of
No. 21 (December 1866) shows both the new series name
and imprint. The first copyright registration of Irwin
& Co. appears in No. 27 (21 March 1867), indicating that
the company may have been filing for copyright several
months in advance of publication or that it may have
been printing numbers several months before release.
Advertisements for 1866 and 1867 display the name of
Irwin & Co. In August 1867, with No. 33 or 34, the
series name was changed once more, to American Novels.
Both wrapper imprint and copyright notice show the publisher as the American Novel Publishing Company, 81
Nassau Street. Irwin Beadle's role in the remainder of
the series is problematic. The notice in No. 35 (first
issued December 1867) announcing his separation from the
series cannot be dated with certainty. The series ended
in December 1868 with No. 48.

The portrait of Cooper on the American Novel wrappers indicated the historical novel focus and hinted at
a forthcoming event: for No. 4, O-i-chee: A Tale of
the Mohawk appears to be the first book publication of
a story attributed to Cooper. Supposedly written in
1822, it had been published only once previously, in an
1843 issue of The Home Weekly.

Irwin Beadle's relations with his authors had always been good, but the loyalty of Edward Sylvester
Ellis (1840-1916) is noteworthy. Although he had written many books for Beadle & Co. after his novel Seth
Jones was published as the eighth dime novel, Ellis
followed when Irwin began his third venture; thereafter
the occasional book published by the original firm carried a pseudonym. For the new American Novels series,
however, Ellis published primarily under his own name.
No doubt this was a boon to the new firm because Ellis's
reputation as an author of juveniles ranked him in popularity and sales with Horatio Alger, Jr. and William T.
Adams. For this series, over a period of approximately
three years, he wrote eleven novels using his own name

(five of them in 1868 alone), four as Seelin Robins, two as Emerson Rodman, two as Boynton Belknap, and one as Lt. J. H. Randolph. One, as H. R. Millbank, was reprinted from the 1866 issue of the New York Weekly. In total he wrote twenty-one of the thirty-four books published during Irwin's tenure. In later life Ellis, a New Jersey teacher and superintendent, wrote mathematics and history books.

Other contributors to the series were Edwin Evans Ewing (1824-1901), a newspaperman; P. Hamilton Myers (1812-1878), a Brooklyn lawyer and novelist whose historical novels in this series were mostly reprinted from earlier publications, usually the Philadelphia Dollar Newspaper; and Illion Constellano, supposedly a Mexican military man but actually a Connecticut Yankee named Julius Warren "Leon" Lewis.

Irwin's Six Penny Tales began in 1866 or 1867. Only two numbers were advertised; No. 2 was 64 pages, measuring 4 7/8 by 3 3/16 inches, with buff wrappers.

Irwin Beadle never participated in the periodical ventures that Erastus inaugurated. Irwin's major contribution to nineteenth-century popular publishing, often erroneously attributed to his brother, was the idea of publishing 10-cent books in series. The combination of a fixed price and series organization made for easy marketing and standardized printing format. Irwin seems to have devised the formula first in songbooks, but to have perfected it in fiction.

Anna Lou Ashby

References

Albert Johannsen, The House of Beadle and Adams and Its Dime and Nickel Novels: The Story of a Vanished Literature (Norman: University of Oklahoma Press, 1950-1962, 3 vols.).

Irwin P. Beadle

"The Beadle Collection," Bulletin of the New York Public
Library, 26 (1922): 555-628.

8 Belford, Clarke & Company

Belford, Clarke & Company (1872-1899), publishers in
the United States (Chicago and New York branches, with
occasional San Francisco and St. Louis imprints) and
Toronto, Canada, published both cheap and expensive
subscription series sets, literary annuals, reprints
of American, English and European authors, plus a substantial amount of copyrighted fiction and poetry.
The various branches published many hundreds of titles
in various editions, and pioneered the use of department store bookstalls. First established with the name
Belford Brothers in Toronto in 1872, Clarke was added
in 1875. Later in the decade two Belford brothers
moved to Chicago on the corner of Congress and Wabash;
a third brother, Robert, opened a branch in New York
about 1879 at 384 and 386 Broadway. Prior to that move,
Robert was manager of Rose-Belford in Toronto. In 1888,
two years after a fire destroyed the Chicago store,
Clarke withdrew and the brothers split the New York and
Chicago branches into separate entities. In the 1890s
the remaining reprint stock was sold to the Werner Com-
pany, with one brother, Alexander, taking command of
Werner's publishing division. The Panic of 1898 drove
Werner into receivership by 1899, and that is the last
date for which any Belford imprint is seen.
   Major Authors: Original copyright editions by
Gertrude Atherton, Edgar Fawcett, Julian Hawthorne, Bill
Nye, G. W. Peck, Edgar Saltus, Ella Wheeler Wilcox, west-
ern writers such as J. W. Buel, political figures
Jefferson Davis and John C. Fremont, translations of
German and French authors, reprints of American and
English standard sets, Encyclopedia Britannica, Belford's
Monthly Magazine, and in Canada, The Fortnightly Review
(reprint) and London Society (reprint). Especially
noteworthy and controversial were their many piracies
of work by Mark Twain.

59

Belford, Clarke & Company

Alexander Belford, the youngest of the Belford brothers, was born 6 May 1854 in Valentia Island, County Kerry, Ireland. Shortly afterward the family (the father was a retired officer in the Irish constabulary) came to the United States and later to Canada. Both parents died in Toronto before Alexander ("Aleck" as he was known) reached the age of ten. He obtained little schooling and by age twelve was working for The Evening Telegraph of Toronto, owned by J. Ross Robertson and James B. Cook. While working at the Telegraph Aleck started the Canadian News Company, which a few years later became a branch of the American News Company.

In a handwritten memoir, Robert J. Belford reports that the Belford imprint was first used in 1872, and the firm known as Belford Brothers ran for several years under the guidance of three brothers, Alexander, Robert, and Charles, the last then a leading Conservative editor in Canada.

About 1875 James Clarke, a successful publisher, joined the Belfords. Shortly thereafter Charles died and the firm broke up. James Clarke and Aleck moved to Chicago and changed the name to Belford, Clarke. Robert remained in Toronto where he reprinted The Fortnightly Review, London Society, and Belford's Magazine (begun 1873). By 1877 a subsidiary of the Toronto firm Hunter, Rose and Company was formed, known as Rose-Belford Publishing Company, with George Maclean Rose as president and Robert J. Belford as manager. This firm continued the practice, begun by Belford Brothers of Toronto, of flooding the American market (as well as the Canadian) with cheap pirated reprints of Mark Twain and other popular American writers. Twain was a prime target as his works were being published in relatively expensive subscription editions in the United States. By advertising cheap reprints of these books in American newspapers, the Belfords--and later Rose-Belford--did a rush mail-order business. "A gross outrage," complained the New York Sun (as cited by Gundy): ". . . these Canada [sic] devils go to work to take our American books and reprint them for one tenth of our prices and sell them . . . to our own customers." In its 1882 edition of Clemens's The Prince and the Pauper, Rose-Belford felt compelled

60

to issue an explanation of its pirating practice. The
preface, dated 15 February 1882, said in part: "The
Importers of this cheap edition of Mark Twain's latest
production do not disguise their motive in placing it
on the Canadian market. Their object in its issue . . .
is to show, by its importation into, and sale in Canada,
as a foreign reprint of a work which has secured British
copyright, how anomalous is the present law. . . ." The
publisher explains that while Clemens was refused a Canadian copyright for his Montreal edition due to a too-
limited stay there, he was able to obtain a British
copyright. "That the laws of his own Government grant
no reciprocal privilege to British authors who seek
protection . . . presumably does not trouble Mr.
Clemens. . . . To extend an American author protection
in Canada as the result of British copyright legislation,
while the Dominion is the slaughter-market for American
piracies of English copyrights, seems the act of unwis-
dom." The publisher concludes that while this reprint
might hurt the Canadian industry that produced the
Montreal edition, the purpose was to nullify the effects
of the Imperial copyright in Canada.

Robert J. Belford reports further in his memoir
that the American firm of Belford, Clarke worked assid-
uously for a change in the copyright law: "Few . . .
tried more sincerely and persistently for an international copyright law. . . . Colonel Donn Piatt, who
represented the firm in Washington, did everything possible with a caustic pen and a persuasive tongue to put
an end to piracy."

Within a few years of starting in Chicago, "the
business ran up over a million a year." A branch was
opened in New York under Robert J. Belford. Aleck was
the creative and innovative member of the firm, whose
practices were soon controversial. With the debate over
piracies continuing, Aleck pioneered the use of bookstalls "in most of the big department stores until not
a city of note was without a Belford, Clarke & Company
retail department." Belford, Clarke had the Enclopedia
Britannica "Americanized," and newspapers and others
sold it on the installment plan.

Belford, Clarke & Company

The business, with much sniping at its methods, prospered during the early 1880s. Early in his publishing career, Aleck had become closely associated with Lyman J. Gage, then vice president of the First National Bank of Chicago, and money for expansion was always available. But the total destruction by fire in 1886 of the Chicago premises of Belford, Clarke was the beginning of the end. Much of the insurance was never collected, and in 1888 the New York and Chicago firms split, Clarke withdrawing from the company to go to New York to handle the Century Dictionary. Most of the remaining reprint stock was amalgamated by Aleck into the $3.5 million Werner Company. Aleck became the second largest stockholder and the general manager of the publishing division (the business failed in the Panic of 1898). Meanwhile, the split of 1888 saw the Belfords at perhaps their most creative time. Of sixty-seven copyright editions of American fiction listed by Lyle H. Wright in American Fiction 1876-1900, published by the Belfords, twenty-two were published in 1888, a substantial number in 1889, with only a scattering in other years between 1880 and 1899. An undetermined amount of copyright verse was published in these years as well.

The Canadian publishing houses with which the Belford brothers were associated were best known for their piracies. Their American firms were best known for cheap reprint editions of standard authors. As Mott says in Golden Multitudes,

> A cyclone struck the publishing industry and threatened for a time to wreck it completely. . . . They sold their millions at 10 and 20 cents a volume in double-column form, before the producers of cloth-bound books more suitable for library shelves edged into the game. These cloth-bound books sold for 25 or 30 cents; and when they became popular, their publishers were able to do a big business in the merchandising of sets of such favorite authors as Dickens. Thus Belford. Clarke & Company, of Chicago, sold in the neighborhood of 40,000 sets of Dickens in the eighties at $4 to $5.

Belford, Clarke & Company

When Belford, Clarke reported the suspension of business due to "the immense cheapening of standard works," one competitor editorialized in the pages of Publishers' Weekly (2 November 1879): "Who caused this 'cheapening' of such works? What other leading house has ever catalogued sets of standard works at $10., $12., $16., etc., and sold them at $2.40, $3.60, $4.80, etc., and even less? Belford, Clarke & Co., were the first and most reckless . . . after stocking up the jobbers and retail trade, [who] has put cheap John travelling bookstores into . . . the country to retail these books at less than jobbing prices?"

Belford, Clarke & Co. was for a time large and successful; its merchandising methods were often questionable but in large measure typical of the times. Its well-developed concept of selling books in department stores has been much copied and remains an important contribution to American merchandising. An examination of its fictional copyright output shows the house to have been a cut above a good deal of its mass merchandising competition. A number of its authors have made a lasting contribution to American letters, and in its own way it helped develop American literary tastes.

Daniel G. Siegel

References

Robert J. Belford, "Alexander Belford," manuscript memoir in the Growoll Scrapbooks in the R. R. Bowker Library, New York.

Publishers' Weekly, 14 May 1887, 28 September 1889, 2 November 1889.

Frank Luther Mott, Golden Multitudes, The Story of Best Sellers in the United States (New York: Macmillan Co., 1947).

Belford, Clarke & Company

H. Pearson Gundy, <u>Book Publishing and Publishers in
Canada Before 1900</u> (Toronto: Bibliographical
Society of Canada, 1965).

Lyle H. Wright, <u>American Fiction 1876-1900</u> (San Marino:
Huntington Library, 1966).   The following are numbers assigned by Wright to original editions of
fiction published by Belford, Clarke [et al.]:
163, 204, 486, 761, 1201, 1364, 1373, 1380, 1813,
1815, 1822, 1826, 1926, 1933, 2093, 2098, 2154,
2254, 2346, 2583, 2599, 2682, 2792, 2957, 2970,
3080, 3198, 3243, 3290, 3464, 3641, 3853, 4002-04,
4010, 4139-42, 4144-47, 4229-30, 4250-52, 4360,
4389, 4454, 4746, 4749, 4751-54, 4882, 5124,
5158-59, 5336, 5723, 5748, 5776, 6008.

9　A. L. Burt Company

A. L. Burt Company (1883-1937) was a leading publisher, primarily in reprint, of well-produced, low-priced popular fiction, titles by standard modern authors, older classics, series for children and youth, and home references. By 1910-1920 it had 3,000 or more titles in print and was considered second only to Grosset & Dunlap among America's largest publishers of reprint editions.

Starting in a small office at 105 John Street, New York, the business moved, as it grew, to 162 William Street, to 65 Beekman Street, and to 52 Duane Street in 1902, when the firm was incorporated. In 1914 it took 35,000 square feet of floor space at 114-120 East 23rd Street and later opened a Chicago office at 506 South Wabash Avenue. The firm remained at 23rd Street until its purchase in 1937 by Eugene Reynal.

Major Series: Copyright Fiction at Popular Prices, Burt's Home Library, Burt's Pocket Editions of Standard Classics.

Major Authors (mainly in reprint): Horatio Alger, Jr., Edgar Rice Burroughs, A. Conan Doyle, Zane Gray, G. A. Henty, Joseph C. Lincoln, E. Phillips Oppenheim, Edgar Wallace, Harold Bell Wright.

Albert L. Burt was born in 1842 at Belchertown, Massachusetts, and died 18 December 1913. He was educated in the Belchertown schools, started work in a grocery store, and became a traveling salesman. At the age of forty-one, while traveling for Case, Lockwood & Brainerd, a leather goods house in Hartford, Connecticut, he decided to enter what a later generation would call mass market publishing.

Burt's first book was a small volume, The National Standard Dictionary (probably a reprint), which he published in 1883. This was followed by home reference books for similar marketing. Demand for cheap paperback fiction was high, and Burt, with a line called the

65

(Courtesy Edward T. LeBlanc, *Dime Novel Round-Up*)

Manhattan Library, was one of a number of entrants into that field in the late 1880s. But Burt recognized also the popular hunger for good literature, and took a decisive step in 1890 by launching, with twenty-five titles, Burt's Home Library. This line of "the world's best literature" eventually embraced some 500 titles and became familiar to every bookseller.

During the period 1890-1900, however, much of Burt's strength lay in books for young readers by major writers in that field, among them Henty, Alger, Edward S. Ellis, James Otis, Edward Castlemon. These books, sometimes in paper covers, sometimes in cloth, at 25 and 50 cents, sold "millions" over a period of years. (John Tebell in Rags to Riches notes that Alger's Joe's Luck was title No. 1 of Burt's Home Library in 1887, and that Burt published nine additional Alger books through 1907.)

Meanwhile, the paperback market was becoming somewhat glutted, and some publishers in that field were failing. About 1895, as Tebbel recalls in his history of American publishing, the introduction of a cheap bookbinding cloth made it possible to sell hardcover books at very low prices. Grosset & Dunlap went into business in 1899 by purchasing unsold 25-cent paperback copies of new copyright fiction, binding them in cloth, and selling them at 39 and 50 cents. New titles were added mainly by buying reprint rights from original publishers.

In 1902 Burt took a second decisive step; it entered this field of reprint fiction with its first "popular copyright" title, Ellen Glasgow's The Voice of the People, obtained by arrangement with Doubleday, Page.

Aggressively acquiring more reprint rights, Burt soon emerged as Grosset & Dunlap's major competitor in the reprint field, occasionally taking on some original titles as well. The leading original trade publishers, as Lehmann-Haupt has observed, experimented with their own reprint lines now and then, but soon fell back on the more convenient procedure of selling reprint rights to either Grosset & Dunlap or Burt.

Some of Burt's earliest best-sellers were the high-spirited western novels of Zane Gray. In 1906

67

A. L. Burt Company

Burt was the original publisher of Gray's second novel, The Spirit of the Border, selling eventually more than 750,000 copies. About 1910, Burt was among the eighteen publishers reprinting one of the all-time sellers, Charles M. Sheldon's inspirational story, In His Steps. In 1911 Burt, in the person of the founder's son, Harry P. Burt, arranged with Book Supply Company of Chicago to publish 50-cent editions of books by another intensely popular inspirational writer, Harold Bell Wright: The Shepherd of the Hills, The Calling of Don Matthews, and The Winning of Barbara Worth. Mott reports that by 1914, total sales of Shepherd were a million each and, of Barbara, a million and a half. Burt's long line of Joseph C. Lincoln best-sellers in reprint began at the same time. With its list augmented month by month, Burt built up a coast-to-coast staff of trade salesmen who became widely known and trusted by the booksellers, according to the travelers' biographies carried every February in Publishers' Weekly.

After his death in 1913 Albert L. Burt was succeeded by his eldest son, Harry Prentice Burt, as president and treasurer. Another son, Edward F. Burt, became assistant treasurer and a third son, Frederick A. Burt, secretary.

Harry P. Burt (1873-1941) joined the business in 1891, and by the time he was thirty was taking a leading part in its expansion. He became known in the book industry for his acumen in title selection for a mass market, and in establishing sound and friendly trade relationships. He arranged for the Harold Bell Wright reprints and later for the Tarzan books of Burroughs, with sales, the firm claimed, of over half a million copies per title. Tarzan on the screen helped sales of Tarzan in print; The Return of Tarzan was one of two early movie tie-ins advertised by Burt in Publishers' Weekly in 1919; the other was The Unpardonable Sin by Rupert Hughes.

By the 1920s the Burt firm was in full flower. Its complete catalog in the Publishers' Trade List Annual of 1921 showed the accumulation of titles. The "popular copyright" authors included, along with those already mentioned, E. Phillips Oppenheim, Samuel Hopkins Adams,

68

A. L. Burt Company

Mary Roberts Rinehart, Max Brand, George Barr McCutcheon,
Baroness Orczy, V. B. Ibanez, Charles Norris, Kathleen
Norris, Rex Beach, P. G. Wodehouse, and many more.
Books in the Home Library, about 400 titles, were good-
looking, handy-sized volumes in "uniform binding, gilt
tops," carrying a $1.25 retail price. Burt's Pocket
Editions of Standard Classics offered tried-and-true
writers--Dickens, Darwin, Thackeray, Scott, Barrie, and
so on--"in flexible bindings, . . . gilt tops, durable
light-weight paper." The Cornell Series offered standard older works at 85 cents, and there were half a dozen
lines of various sizes and formats. Some lines featured
multicolored binding designs.

Books for children and youth had been Burt specialties almost from the start. By 1921 the firm featured
numerous series for boys and girls, including the widely
sold Fairy Library and several for very young children,
notably the Uncle Wiggly Series and other bedtime stories "for reading aloud to the little folks each night."

Expansion continued in the 1920s. Oppenheim's
mystery stories were already among Burt's popular reprints when the firm added The Great Impersonation,
first published in 1920 by Little, Brown. Burt was an
early reprinter of Wodehouse; later it acquired from
Doran the 1924 success Jeeves, sold 160,000 reprint
copies, and eventually listed twenty Wodehouse books.

Low-cost reprint lines held up well during the
Great Depression. In 1931 Burt listed its largest selling staff, sixteen men plus McLeod's in Canada. In the
early 1930s it started the Crescent Library of $1.00
nonfiction, adding two or three titles a month. In 1932
it bought the Sully Company line of game, etiquette, and
home reference books, and in 1936 the Putnam Reference
Handbook titles.

Burt's catalogue in the 1935 Publishers' Trade
List Annual listed nearly 1,700 Popular Fiction titles
at 75 cents. Among 400 or more writers, Edgar Wallace
was the leader with sixty-three books; among still
others were Robert Benchley, Gertrude Atherton, James
Warner Bellah, John Buchan, W. R. Burnett, Robert W.
Chambers, Ethel M. Dell, J. S. Fletcher, A. Fielding,
Jeffery Farnol, Edison Marshall, Carolyn Wells, Will

Rogers, and those cited from the 1921 list. One feature was Dr. Marie C. Stopes's <u>Married Love</u>, "over 500,000 sold." In all, about 3,000 titles were listed.

It was a strong showing, but at the same time there was competition from reprinters of a more contemporary kind, including Modern Library, Garden City and, especially, Blue Ribbon Books, which had been formed by a consortium in 1930 and purchased by Eugene Reynal in 1933. In 1937 Harry P. Burt decided to retire and sold the firm to Reynal. The latter merged it with Blue Ribbon, under Reynal & Hitchcock, which in turn sold all its reprints in 1939 to Doubleday.

The firm of A. L. Burt had come to the end of its era. But during its fifty-four years it had developed reprint marketing on a national scale, and had contributed greatly to the pleasure of millions of readers and to the elevation of popular culture.

Chandler B. Grannis

References

"Obituary Note, Albert L. Burt," <u>Publishers' Weekly</u>, 85 (3 January 1914): 21.

<u>Publishers' Trade List Annual</u> (New York: R. R. Bowker Company, 1921, 1935).

"Obituary Notes: Harry P. Burt," <u>Publishers' Weekly</u>, 139 (29 March 1941): 1374.

Frank Luther Mott, <u>Golden Multitudes: The Story of Best Sellers in the United States</u> (New York: Macmillan Co., 1947).

James D. Hart, <u>The Popular Book: A History of American Literary Taste</u> (New York: Oxford University Press, 1950).

A. L. Burt Company

Hellmut Lehmann-Haupt, The Book in America (New York: R. R. Bowker Company, 1951).

John Tebbel, From Rags to Riches: Horatio Alger, Jr. and The American Dream (New York: Macmillan Co., 1964).

John Tebbel, A History of Book Publishing in the United States Vols. II and III (New York: R. R. Bowker Company, 1975-1977).

10 Carey & Lea

Carey & Lea (1822-1838), probably the largest general publishers in the nation during the period, expanded considerably the markets for both their primary American authors and the English authors they chose to reprint. Successors to M. Carey & Sons, they were situated on the southeast corner of Fourth and Chestnut streets in Philadelphia, where they operated not only as Carey & Lea, but also as H. C. Carey & I. Lea (1822-1827); (with Edward L. Carey as junior partner) Carey, Lea & Carey (1827-1829); and Carey, Lea & Blanchard (1833-1838). Of the 930 titles they produced, 290 were novels. They also issued several journals, an encyclopedia, and three literary annuals.

Major Authors: Jane Austen, Robert Montgomery Bird, James Fenimore Cooper, Charles Dickens, Theodore Hook, Washington Irving, John Pendleton Kennedy, Thomas Moore, Sir Walter Scott.

Henry Charles Carey, son of Mathew Carey, was born in Philadelphia on 15 December 1793 and died in 1879. Bred to the trade, he conducted business on his own account at the nation's first literary fair in New York in 1802. He managed his father's branch store in Baltimore in 1806 and was charged with much of the firm's financial affairs beginning two years later. In 1817 he became a partner and five years later, together with his brother-in-law Isaac Lea, he bought out Mathew's equity in the firm.[1] He was the senior and dominant partner throughout.

Isaac Lea was born into a Quaker family in Wilmington, Delaware, in 1792 and died in 1886. He moved to Philadelphia in 1807. In 1821 he married Mathew Carey's daughter and entered his father-in-law's business.

Mathew Carey's younger son, Edward L. Carey, entered the firm's employ in 1822.

73

William A. Blanchard entered Mathew Carey's service in 1812 and became a junior partner in 1833.

The significance of the firm directed by these men lies primarily in four areas: its reprinting of English novelists; its publishing of American authors; its special and subscription ventures; and its general publishing in science, history, medicine, law, the social sciences, and other fields.

When Henry C. Carey took over direction of his father's firm in 1817, the reprinting of English novelists in this country was entirely a matter of piracy practiced on a relatively petty scale. The reprint trade was nominally and loosely guided by the "courtesies of the trade," which allowed that any publisher who announced a title should have exclusive rights to it until his edition was sold off. As long as editions were small, calm had prevailed. In 1814, however, Sir Walter Scott's Waverley had appeared in Edinburgh, and its unprecedented marketability bred fierce competition among American reprinters and rendered the traditional "courtesies" largely ineffective for self-policing purposes. By the time H. C. Carey & I. Lea went into business in their own name in 1822 the reprint industry was in chaos, with small fortunes being made and lost on as little as one day's priority into the market of a particular edition of a Waverley novel.

Henry Carey set out from the beginning to gain control over the reprint trade. Two factors had given his firm dominance in the nation's fastest growing book markets in the South and West. The first was his father's sustained effort to sponsor aspiring young booksellers, often displaced Irish immigrants like himself, in the southern and western towns, where once established they became outlets in Carey's growing retail network. The second factor was Philadelphia's geographical proximity to the South and its situation at the head of the wagon road over the mountains to Pittsburgh and thence down the Ohio to the western country. Advantageous delivery schedules and freight costs thus gave Philadelphia a trading monopoly over western markets.

74

Able thus to dispose of larger printings of their books, Carey & Lea could invest more in their production, a fact that enabled them from the beginning to pay popular authors. In the absence of international copyright, they did this among English authors by purchasing not rights but priority. In 1822 C & L negotiated the purchase of advance proofsheets of future Waverley novels with Scott's agent, Archibald Constable of Edinburgh, for prices averaging £75 each. The priority they gained in America by being able to compose and print from pre-publication English copy enabled the Philadelphians to control Scott's novels on this continent and rendered them in effect his "authorized" American publishers, a status they enjoyed until Scott's death in 1832.

Carey & Lea looked hard for another British author popular enough to take Scott's vacated place on their reprint lists. They published all six of Jane Austen's novels in 1832 and 1833 and were moderately surprised at the sale; Mathew Carey had published one of her books before her death in 1817 and had found it unsaleable at that time, but with that exception she had not previously been published here. They produced Mary Shelley's Frankenstein, Last Man, and Perkin Warbeck in 1833 and 1834, and they published six novels by Bulwer-Lytton. They produced three novels by Disraeli, six by Theodore Hook, and many by others, but none was able to capture the readership enjoyed by Scott.

Somewhat diffidently C & L issued late in 1836 a small anonymous work entitled The Posthumous Papers of the Pickwick Club, Part I, in 1,500 copies. To their great and pleasant surprise it sold out immediately, requiring four more editions in the next twelve months. Never before had the work of an unknown author sold so well. C & L continued to publish Charles Dickens's works as rapidly as they could be obtained, and they profited substantially from them. C & L never concluded a contract with Dickens as they had with Scott, but they corresponded with him on friendly terms throughout the period of Henry Carey's partnership in the firm. On one occasion they even sent Dickens a draft for £25 as a gift, which the author returned, saying that he would prefer instead to be sent copies of C & L editions of his works.

In order to understand Carey & Lea's significance as publishers of American authors, it is important to recall that when the firm was established in 1822 the United States had seen no such thing as a publisher in the modern sense of that word. There were printer-booksellers, but publishers--that is, firms that were prepared to share financial risk, purchase printing, cultivate markets, and work with an author to develop his reputation to their mutual profit--were as yet unknown. C & L in 1822 set out to be America's first such publisher.

Their profitable experience with the reprinting of Scott led C & L to conclude that, if they could recover the cost of early copy from England by marketing larger editions, they could also afford to purchase rights in popular American authors. They tried this first in 1822 with John Neal, offering him $300.00 worth of books for the rights to his novel Logan. Neal accepted but the book failed, so the publishers were not able to test their new intention.

In 1822 and 1823 C & L tried to coax James Fenimore Cooper, then rapidly gaining recognition as a novelist, to join them. Cooper, however, had been in effect acting as his own publisher, buying small printings at his own risk and selling direct to booksellers at short discounts, and he was wary of entrusting these activities to another party. C & L entreated with Cooper, claiming that with their marketing acumen they could sell thousands more copies of his books than he could sell. By 1825 Cooper was ready to deal, and the firm concluded a contract with him for the first 5,000 copies of his next novel plus rights to the work for four years in return for $5,000 plus cost of manufacturing. That next novel was The Last of the Mohicans, which sold so well that both author and publisher profited greatly from it. Cooper stayed with the firm for some twelve years thereafter and was paid more than $40,000 for the rights to his books during that period, unprecedented earnings by an American author.

Carey & Lea

Carey & Lea made similar representations to
Washington Irving in 1822, but at that time with similar
negative results. They did publish Irving's Tales of a
Traveller in 1824, but Irving did not bring all of his
properties to the firm until 1828. Thereafter, with a
single exception, C & L handled all of Irving's publishing until after Henry Carey's retirement. This period
included Irving's best work and saw the publication of
The Alhambra, Astoria, Conquest of Granada, and the
Crayon Miscellany.

Carey & Lea published novels by other American
authors as well. The firm published John Pendleton
Kennedy's Swallow Barn in 1832 and his Horseshoe Robinson
three years later. Also in the mid-1830s they published
Robert Montgomery Bird's Hawks of Hawk Hollow, Calavar,
The Infidel, and Nick of the Woods, and they produced
Ralph Ingersoll Lockwood's Insurgents and Rosine Laval.
Still other American authors, including Edgar Allan Poe
and Nathaniel Hawthorne, offered to write for C & L,
although no contracts were consummated. Clearly the
Philadelphians were viewed by American authors in a
favorable light.

Carey & Lea contributed to the popular culture and
reading of the times in more ways than the issuing of
English and American fiction. They also involved themselves in several special and subscription publishing
ventures that proved to be important in the rise of the
American book industry, of significance to American readership, and of profit to themselves and to authors. One
such venture was their production in 1825 of America's
first literary annual, the Atlantic Souvenir for 1826.
It was their desire to produce as fine an annual gift
book, in terms of authorship and artwork, as was possible at the time, and they sought the services of leading
American authors and engravers in the effort. During
the seven years that the Atlantic Souvenir appeared over
the C & L imprint, it contained works by such writers as
Catherine M. Sedgwick, William Cullen Bryant, James
Kirke Paulding, Lydia Sigourney, Washington Irving, and
Fitz-Greene Halleck. Artwork was supplied by Charles
Robert Leslie, Peter Maverick, James B. Longacre,
Asher B. Durand, and others. Editions of the annual

77

rose to exceed 10,000 copies before C & L sold the title
to S. G. Goodrich in 1832 to be combined with his Token.
The Atlantic Souvenir had by that time pioneered a fashion of literary annuals that was to continue in popularity in this country for forty years thereafter.

Carey & Lea also conceived and published a literary
review. Feeling that its publications were not receiving adequate attention in the North American Review,
which had been established in Boston in 1815, C & L set
out in 1827 to balance the scene with their own American
Quarterly Review. Subscriptions to the American soon
stabilized at about 2,500, and C & L kept the title until 1831 when they sold it. During this period the review not only published writings of such literary authors
as Paulding, Cooper, and Henry D. Gilpin, but also included pieces by Albert Gallatin, Peter Duponceau, George
Bancroft, George Ticknor, and other men of affairs, many
of whom were from the North.

In 1828 Dr. Francis Lieber proposed to Carey & Lea
that he would translate for them, if they were interested,
the Brockhaus Konversations-Lexikon that was then enjoying great popularity in Germany. Although C & L was not
interested in a simple translation, it became persuaded
that an original American encyclopedia would be market-
able and contracted with the young immigrant scholar to
produce one. Retaining such authors as Edward Everett,
Caleb Cushing, Joseph Story, and George Ticknor to write
for one dollar per page, Lieber delivered thirteen volumes between 1829 and 1833, which C & L published as the
Encyclopaedia Americana. The work was exceedingly popular and remained a staple item in the American book markets through the time of the Civil War.

By the late 1830s, however, much was changing that
would affect American publishing generally and Carey &
Lea in particular. The technology of printing was changing, paving the way for cheap publishing in the years
just ahead. The Erie Canal had been opened, giving New
York the ability to compete equitably with Philadelphia
for the rapidly growing western markets. The seat of
American publishing was coming increasingly to be located in New York.

11 G. W. Carleton

G. W. Carleton (G. W. Carleton and Company) (1857-1886),
publishing house known for its humorous publications
as well as for its best-selling novels, published
about 300 titles in various editions. The business began as Rudd and Carleton (1857-1861) on Broadway near
Duane Street, New York. With the death in 1861 of
Edward P. Rudd and the retirement of his father,
George R. Rudd, it became G. W. Carleton (1861-1871)
at Broadway and Lispenard Street (413 Broadway). In
1869 the firm leased the Worth House for its Fifth Avenue Bookstore, the upper section of which was run by
Carleton as a hotel. In 1871, with the copartnership
of George Dillingham, the house was restyled G. W.
Carleton and Company. The following year it moved to a
larger establishment under the Fifth Avenue Hotel (192
Fifth Avenue), where it remained until 1883. In that
year it abandoned its retail trade, limited itself to
its own publications, and moved to West 23rd Street
above Dutton and Company. On 8 May 1886 the copartnership was dissolved; G. W. Carleton retired and was succeeded by G. W. Dillingham. After Dillingham's death
the firm was incorporated (1896) as the G. W. Dillingham
Company.

Major Authors: Charles Farrar Browne ["Artemus
Ward"], Charles G. Halpine ["Private Miles O'Reilly"],
Azel Stevens Roe, Henry Wheeler Shaw ["Josh Billings"],
Augusta Evans Wilson.

George Washington Carleton was born in New York in
1832 and died in 1901. Educated at St. Thomas Hall,
Flushing, he clerked for a commission house, Burnham,
Plumb and Company. During his leisure time he designed
illustrations for the humorous journals The Lantern and
The Picayune. Some of his work attracted the attention
of the publisher George Merriam, who asked him to design
an illustration for an advertisement of Webster's Dictionary. Carleton supplied a sketch of two cherubs

81

weighted down with Webster's Unabridged, which was used for nearly fifty years. In 1857, with the retirement of Edward Livermore of Livermore and Rudd, Carleton joined that firm, which was restyled Rudd and Carleton.

Rudd and Carleton's principal publication was Nothing to Wear: An Episode of City Life by William Allen Butler (1857), a poem on fashionable city life that immortalized Miss Flora M'Flimsey of Madison Square. Illustrated by Augustus Hoppin and published as an eighteenmo priced at 50 cents, it had a sale of some 20,000 copies in spite of the Panic of 1857 and in spite of the fact that it had already appeared in Harper's Weekly. A claim of plagiarism served only to heighten interest in the book. Rudd and Carleton proceeded to offer Mortimer Thomson ["Q. K. Philander DoesLicks"] one dollar a line for a burlesque on the poem. The result was Nothing to Say (1857), which was published in the same format and cased in a binding similar to that of Butler's poem.

Rudd and Carleton also published The Course of True Love Never Did Run Smooth (1858), a versified love story by Thomas Bailey Aldrich, of which 2,200 copies were sold. That publication was the first to use the Arabic symbol for books which, viewed upside down, seemed to spell the initials "G. W. C." This became Carleton's trademark. Two other Rudd and Carleton successes were Edmund Clarence Stedman's The Prince's Ball (1860), which sold in the thousands and for which the author received a 10 percent royalty; and The "Wigwam Edition." The Life, Speeches, and Public Services of Abram Lincoln (1860), which was the first campaign biography of Lincoln and is today the keystone of any Lincoln collection.

In 1861, with the death of Edward P. Rudd and the retirement of George R. Rudd, G. W. Carleton became a publisher under his own name. He was assisted for a short time by the poet Thomas Bailey Aldrich; by his brother Charles Carleton; by Henry S. Allen, formerly of Appleton, during the 1860s; and by George W. Dillingham, who had been associated with the Boston firms of Crosby, Nichols and A. K. Loring. Dillingham started as Carleton's head clerk and became his co-partner in 1871.

From the start, the firm of G. W. Carleton catered to mass entertainment by the publication of books of humor. Among the firm's most famous authors in this field was Charles Farrar Browne, who used the pseudonym "Artemus Ward." Browne presented Carleton with a blotted, almost illegible manuscript stuck with mucilage, plastered with newspaper clippings, and bundled into a green baize bag. This was transformed, after judicious editing, into Artemus Ward His Book (1862), of which over 40,000 copies were sold in six months. As his share of the profits the author received $6,000, or 15 cents per copy. Other Artemus Ward publications followed in which the author assumed the role of an itinerant showman exposing the absurdities of American life by such devices as graphic caricature, execrable spelling, and gross exaggeration. Carleton published in succession Artemus Ward; His Travels (1865), Artemus Ward in London, and Other Papers (1867), Artemus Ward's Panorama (1869). The Complete Works of Artemus Ward appeared in 1887 over the imprint of G. W. Dillingham, Carleton's successor, and as late as 1898, after over 100,000 copies had been printed, was still selling.

Another celebrated humorist published by Carleton was Henry Wheeler Shaw, who used the pseudonym "Josh Billings." Billings impersonated the comic itinerant lecturer whose brief essays were peppered with exaggerated misspellings and characterized by ludicrous sententiousness. Among the Billings titles published by Carleton's firm were Josh Billings, Hiz Sayings (1866), Josh Billings on Ice, and Other Things (1868), and Josh Billings' Farmer's Allminax (1870-1879). When "Billings" offered to sell his Farmer's Allminax outright for $250.00 and to supply one for each of ten succeeding years at the same price, Carleton advised him to accept instead a royalty of 3 cents a copy. As a result the humorist earned $30,000 instead of $2,500 during that period. The Farmer's Allminax, a burlesque of the traditional Farmer's Almanac, was published as a 25-cent paperback and sold more than a half million copies after a slow start. It was succeeded by an annual comic

Allminax until 1879, as well as by an omnibus collection, Josh Billings' Old Probability, Perhaps Rain--
Perhaps Not (1879), priced at $1.50. In 1880 the firm
published Josh Billings: His Works, Complete.

A third humorist on the Carleton list was
Charles G. Halpine, who used the pseudonym "Private Miles
O'Reilly" of the 47th Regiment of New York Volunteers,
an Irish private in the Union army whose gentle satire
of military and political life was relished during and
after the Civil War. Carleton published The Life and
Adventures, Songs, Services, and Speeches of Private
Miles O'Reilly (1864) and Baked Meats of the Funeral.
A Collection of Essays, Poems, Speeches, Histories, and
Banquets. By Private Miles O'Reilly (1866).

The Carleton firm reached a mass audience not only
with its humorous publications but with its popular novels. One of the most successful was St. Elmo by Augusta
Evans Wilson (1867), in which the heroine, a model of
virtue and erudition, reforms a man of the world and
marries him. Carleton suggested that Charles H. Webb
write a burlesque of the novel which Webb published as
St. Twel'mo; or, The Cuneiform Cyclopedist of Chattanooga
(1867). The burlesque sold well and increased the sale
of St. Elmo. According to Frank Luther Mott in Golden
Multitudes, "children were named 'St. Elmo'; towns,
streets, hotels were christened with the magic name,"
and the novel had "a sale of a million copies." When
Carleton purchased the stereotype plates of other
Augusta Evans Wilson titles, he informed her that he
had been obliged to pay so much for the plates of Macaria
(which he published in 1868) that he could allow her only
a moderate percentage on future sales. After the successful publication of St. Elmo (1867) and Vashti; or,
"Until Death Do Us Part" (1869), Carleton increased the
author's royalty.

Novels by Mary J. Holmes, who produced one a year,
were published by Carleton as clothbound books at $1.50
following their serialization in Street & Smith's New
York Weekly. They were surefire successes, the author
receiving a royalty of 15 percent. Among her novels on
the Carleton list were Cousin Maude, and Rosamund (1864),
The Cameron Pride; or, Purified by Suffering (1867),

Ethelyn's Mistake; or, The Home in the West (1869),
Darkness and Daylight (1870).

In 1869 the Carleton firm purchased the copyrights
of Mary Virginia Hawes Terhune ["Marion Harland"] from
Sheldon and Company. The following Harland novels appeared under the Carleton imprint: Phemie's Temptation
(1869), At Last (1870), Helen Gardner's Wedding-Day; or,
Colonel Floyd's Wards (1870), The Empty Heart; or, Husks
(1871), Jessamine (1873), My Little Love (1876), Alone
(1876).

Other popular novelists published by Carleton's
firm were Miriam Coles Harris, represented by Rutledge
(1862), the sentimental narrative of a girl's rise in
the world, Frank Warrington (1863), A Perfect Adonis
(1875), Missy (1880), Happy-Go-Lucky (1881); Julie P.
Smith, represented by Widow Goldsmith's Daughter (1869),
His Young Wife (1877), Kiss, and Be Friends (1878), Lucy
(1880), Blossom-Bud and Her Genteel Friends (1883); and
A. S. Roe [Azel Stevens Roe], represented by Like and
Unlike (1862), The Star and the Cloud; or, A Daughter's
Love (1864), James Montjoy: or, I've Been Thinking
(1864), The Cloud on the Heart (1869), How Could He Help
It? or, The Heart Triumphant (1879).

Among Carleton's popular society novels that pro-
vided mass readers with spicy hammock literature were
Epes Sargent's Peculiar; A Tale of the Great Transition
(1864), May Agnes Fleming's A Wonderful Woman (1873), A
Terrible Secret (1874), and A Mad Marriage (1875).
Equally popular were Cora Agnew's Peerless Cathleen; or,
The Stolen Casket; An English Society Story (1877) and
Faithful Margaret (1877) by "Annie Ashmore" [pseudonym
of Mrs. J. M. Simpson].

With Mayne Reid's stories, purchased by Carleton
in 1868, the firm reached a masculine mass market, publishing The Scalp Hunters; or, Adventures among the
Trappers (1877) and The Rifle Rangers; or, Adventures
in Southern Mexico (1879) as well as Reid's magazine
Onward (1869-1870), which brought to American readers
the romance of the Rocky Mountains and the Texan hunters.

The Carleton firm, in cooperation with Street &
Smith, also published three books by Horatio Alger, Jr.:
The Western Boy, or, The Road to Success (1878), The

Train Boy (1883), and Dan, The Detective (1883). According to Ralph D. Gardner in Horatio Alger, or The American Hero Era: "Since a number of Carleton's books were reprints of stories originally printed in New York Weekly, it is safe to assume there was a close business connection, and possibly a partial ownership of the Carleton organization by Street & Smith."

The firm of G. W. Carleton attracted a mass audience not only with humor and fiction but with digests of information, treasuries of knowledge, and social handbooks. Among these were The Habits of Good Society, originally published in 1860 by Rudd and Carleton, republished by Carleton in 1863 and frequently reprinted; The Art of Conversation, with Directions for Self Education by Charles Godfrey Leland (1864); 595 Pulpit Pungencies (1866); Carleton's Hand-Book of Popular Quotations (1877); Carleton's Household Encyclopædia and Handbook of General Information (1879); Carleton's Condensed Classical Dictionary (1882); Carleton's New Hand-Book of Popular Quotations (1883). Such publications catered to the almost universal desire for self-improvement.

The Carleton list also included several books translated from the French that reached a mass market. Indeed, in its handling of French translations the firm seems to have established a nineteenth-century speed record. La Femme by Jules Michelet was translated in three days by Dr. John W. Palmer for the sum of $1,000. The 450-page volume was printed and bound, with 20,000 copies sold, in less than thirty days. Woman (La Femme) from the French of M. J. Michelet was published by Rudd and Carleton in 1860 and republished by G. W. Carleton in 1864. As for lavish advertising, the Carleton firm spent $10,000 to advertise Victor Hugo's Les Miserables Translated from the Original French, by Chas. E. Wilbour, which it published in 1862.

The few failures and mistakes in the firm's history serve only to highlight its achievements. Carleton was sued by Fannie Bean, author of a novel, Dr. Mortimer's Patient, on the charge that its publication had been delayed and that the book had never been advertised or placed on sale except in the publisher's offices, although she had paid $900.00, which was to have been returned after the first 2,000 copies had been sold. The plaintiff won the case. The firm made a more grievous error, revealed in Mark Twain's Notebook. Referring to his "Jumping Frog" story, the humorist noted: "Wrote this story for Artemus [Ward]--his idiot publisher Carleton, gave it to Clapp's Saturday Press."

Carleton himself was the author and illustrator of several books of travel, including Our Artist in Cuba (1865), Our Artist in Peru (1866), and an omnibus volume, Our Artist in Cuba, Peru, Spain and Algiers (1877) which brought the firm a profit of $10,000. Following his retirement, G. W. Carleton spent his time (1886-1901) traveling and reporting his travels.

During three decades the firm of G. W. Carleton supplied a variety of books for mass entertainment. In publishing and widely distributing popular novels and self-improvement handbooks, the company was successful without being innovative. In publishing books of humor, it was not only successful but innovative and influential. Reaching a mass audience with such publications, it helped an expanding nation to laugh at its own foibles.

Madeleine B. Stern

References

"G. W. Carleton & Co.," New-York Evening Post (28 April 1875).

"G. W. Carleton, Retiring from Business, Tells Some of His Experiences [1886]," Adolf Growoll Collection. American Book Trade History (R. R. Bowker Library) IV, 10-12.

"Obituary. George W. Carleton," Publishers' Weekly (19 October 1901).

G. W. Carleton

Madeleine B. Stern, _Imprints on History: Book Publishers and American Frontiers_ (Bloomington: Indiana University Press, 1956; reprinted, New York: AMS Press, 1975).

12   T. R. Dawley

T. R. Dawley (1860s) published series of cheap libraries
in the wake of the success of Beadle & Co. The firm was
located at 13 and 15 Park Row, New York.

Major Series: Camp & Fireside Library, New War
Novels, Ten-Penny Novels.

T. R. Dawley reached the height of its productivity
in 1865. According to J. Edward Leithead, writing on
"The Anatomy of Dime Novels" in Dime Novel Round-Up
(15 December 1967), "the Dawley output seemed to dwell
on guerrilla raids, killings, wrecking of trains, etc.,
rather than the conflict between the regular armies in
blue and in gray." Nonetheless there was much of Civil
War interest in the Dawley series.

The Camp & Fireside Library, published in 1865,
consisted of eight numbers, each cased in a colored
cover, with illustrations, priced at 15 cents. The
series included Incidents of Camp Life; Mercedes, the
Outlaw's Child; Norma Danton, or the Children of the
Light-House; Justina, the Avenger; The Mad Bard; or,
The Mystery of Melrose Castle; Sue Munday, the Guerrilla
Spy; Rippard, the Outlaw; Bottle Nose Ben, the Indian
Hater. Of those titles, two were based upon Civil War
events and personalities: No. 1, Incidents of Camp Life,
and No. 6, Sue Munday, the latter narrating, as Edward T.
LeBlanc declares in Dime Novel Round-Up (July 1952),
"gruesome accounts of [Jerome] Clark's atrocities."

The firm also launched in 1865 a series entitled
Dawley's New War Novels consisting of eleven numbers in
colored pictorial covers, illustrated, priced at 25
cents each, and concerned with the Civil War. Titles
included Mosby, the Guerrilla; Pauline, the Female Spy
(based upon the adventures of Pauline Cushman); Semmes,
the Pirate; Killdare, the Black Scout; Osgood, the Demon
Refugee; Cheatham; or, The Swamp Dragon; Perdita, the
Demon Refugee's Daughter; Larry, the Army Dog Robber;

89

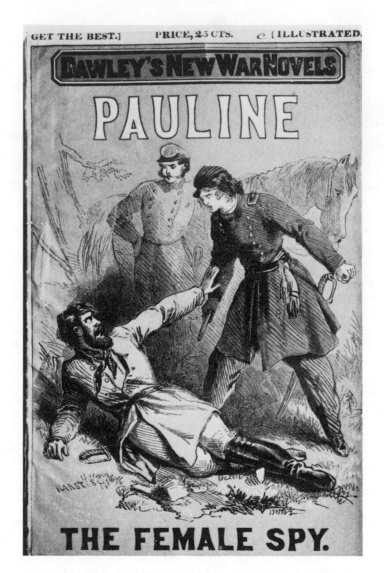

(Courtesy Edward T. LeBlanc, *Dime Novel Round-Up*)

Booth, the Assassin; Hawks, the Conscript; Clarissa, the Conscript's Bride. Several of these tales were by "Dion Haco, Esq."

Dawley's Ten-Penny Novels, also produced in 1865, were in direct competition with Beadle's dime books. Cased in colored covers, illustrated, and priced at 10 cents each, the series consisted of general adventure narratives and included at least thirteen items, among them Kennedy, the Incendiary Spy and Quantrell, the Terror of the West.

One of the numerous early imitators of Beadle, T. R. Dawley flourished for a short period during the 1860s, providing stories of violence, adventure, and the Civil War in cheap paperbacks for a mass audience.

Jacob L. Chernofsky

Reference

Dime Novel Round-Up 20 (July 1952): 49-52; 36 (15 October 1967): 103; 36 (15 December 1967): 115; 42 (15 June 1973): 59; 43 (15 September 1974): 105; 43 (15 November 1974): 129, 134.

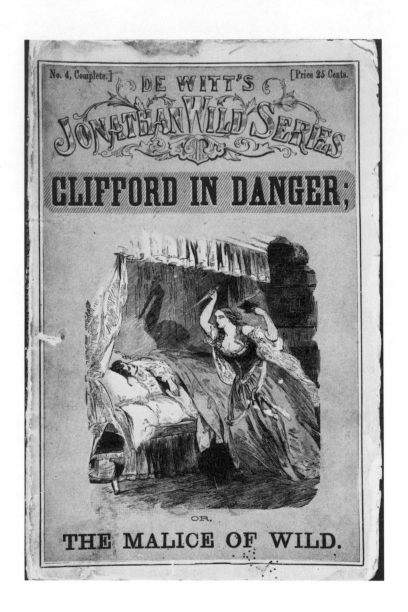

No. 4, Complete.] [Price 25 Cents.

DE WITT'S
JONATHAN WILD SERIES
CLIFFORD IN DANGER;

OR,

THE MALICE OF WILD.

(Courtesy Edward T. LeBlanc, *Dime Novel Round-Up*)

13   Robert M. DeWitt

Robert M. DeWitt (1848-1877), publisher, produced popular romantic fiction and dime novels based upon life in
New York City, the American West, pirates, highwaymen,
headhunters, and other villainous types. Songsters,
jokebooks, plays, elocution books, self-help manuals,
and reports of sensational contemporary murders and
divorces were also published. The firm produced over
1,200 titles in twenty-eight different series with
frequent reprinting, as well as maintaining a substantial
list of less popular materials, including architecture
and medicine. From 1849 to 1852 as DeWitt and Davenport,
the firm was located at 156 Nassau Street and from 1853
to 1856 at 160 and 162 Nassau Street. In 1856 Davenport
left the firm and after a period of reorganization the
firm Robert M. DeWitt Publisher was formed, located at
the old address until 1859. From 1860 to 1869 the firm
was located at 13 Frankfort Street and from 1870 to
1877 at 33 Rose Street.

Major Authors: Osgood Bradbury, Joseph Holt
Ingraham, E. Z. C. Judson, Cornelius Mathews, Mayne
Reid, Solon Robinson, Charles W. Webber, Henry L.
Williams.

Major Series: DeWitt's Claude Duval Series,
DeWitt's Ten Cent Romances, DeWitt's Ethiopian and
Comic Drama, DeWitt's Twenty-Five Cent Novels, DeWitt's
Acting Plays.

Robert M. DeWitt was born in New York City 25
April 1827 and died in Stratford, Connecticut, 16 April
1877. He attended public schools in New York, entering
the trade at age sixteen as an errand boy for Israel
Post, a bookseller and newsdealer in the Bowery. Soon
thereafter he became a clerk in the publishing office
of William H. Graham, where he stayed until the establishment of his own firm. His strong sense of nationalism led him to become active in the American or

"Know-Nothing" Party. He was a strong supporter of the
Union cause and the war. From 1861 until his death his
home was in Stratford, Connecticut, where he spent only
Sundays and holidays, residing at a hotel in the city
during the week. His only son, Clinton T. DeWitt, took
over the firm in 1877 but survived him by only three
years, dying at age twenty-five.

James Davenport was born July 1812 in Stamford,
Connecticut, and died 4 February 1887 in Saint Paul,
Minnesota. He was educated in New York City but poor
health prevented him from attending college. He married
Katherine Eliza Bennett in 1843. The combination of his
wife's poor health and poor business conditions caused
him to sell his interest in the firm DeWitt and Davenport
to his partner in 1856. He moved to Saint Paul, where
he was a bookseller and publisher until his death.

In August 1848, the firm of DeWitt and Davenport
was formed, succeeding William H. Graham for whom
Robert M. DeWitt had worked. James Davenport had been
a bookseller in the firm of Davenport and Wood prior to
this. The firm's first books were published in 1849,
among them Charles W. Webber's The Gold Mines of the
Gila. From the very beginning many of the firm's books
were illustrated by such artists as William Coome,
Jacob A. Dallas, F. O. C. Darly, and John McLennan. To
supply the public's demand for adventure stories, such
authors as Joseph Holt Ingraham were reprinted and the
work of Mayne Reid was introduced to the American reading public. Lurid recitations of gambling, dance halls,
illicit sex, brothels, and alcoholism accompanied by
pious moralizing formed the background for many books
similar to E. Z. C. Judson's The G'Hals of New York
(1850) and Solon Robinson's Hot Corn: Life Scenes in
New York Illustrated (1854). The proceedings of sensational murder trials, divorce cases, and public execu-
tions were published regularly. The firm had a varied
list of publications: popular romantic fiction, songsters, adventure stories based on frontier life, the
American Revolution, highwaymen, pirates and hunters,
anti-Catholic pamphlets and novels, reprints and translations. Its publications were meant to entertain and
were well received by the public, if not always the

reviewers. George G. Foster's New York by Gas-Light
(1850) had sold over 40,000 copies by 1854. His New
York Naked (1855) was considered very close to being
"yellow-covered" literature, with its chapter on fallen
women and its wretched title. Solon Robinson's Hot
Corn: Life Scenes in New York Illustrated created a
sensation in 1854 and sold over 50,000 copies. Mayne
Reid's novels sold over 12,000 copies per title.

The company advertised regularly in the Tribune,
in 1853 alone at a cost of over $1,500. Rapid expansion,
however, caused the firm to become overextended in 1856/
1857, and it was forced to suspend publishing. The partnership was dissolved when James Davenport left the firm
in 1856 to become a bookseller and publisher in Saint
Paul, Minnesota. After a brief period of reorganization,
DeWitt resumed publishing in 1857 under his own name,
assuming all the indebtedness of the partnership and
eventually repaying everyone. In 1867 he became one of
the founders of the New York News Company and served as
its first secretary. In 1870 he moved to his own building at 33 Rose Street, where he had his publishing office,
printing plant, and bindery.

The publications under the imprint of Robert M.
DeWitt changed little except that most began to appear
in numbered series. Previously published works were
reprinted and made part of a series. DeWitt published
hundreds of plays, jokebooks, self-help manuals, and
adventure stories, all in series. Many of these bore
crudely illustrated paper covers, but for his adventure
novels in such series as DeWitt's Ten Cent Romances and
DeWitt's Twenty-Five Cent Novels he used brilliant pictorial covers, mostly a garish yellow. These were issued
monthly, each novel 100 pages in length. His Ten Cent
Romances ran to 118 numbers; his Twenty-Five Cent Novels
to 55; his Ethiopian and Comic Drama series to 143; his
Acting Plays to 300; his Popular Song and Joke Books to
238. From 1857 to 1877 he published over 1,200 titles
in twenty-eight different series.

Like many nineteenth-century American publishers,
DeWitt pirated the work of English and American authors.
Mayne Reid's works were first published in America by
DeWitt over Reid's strenuous objections, not only because

he got no royalties but because of misprints and nonsensical notes. DeWitt also attributed to Reid several novels he did not write. In 1873 he pirated Francis Brett Harte's <u>Mliss: An Idyll of Red Mountain</u>; in 1874 Harte sued DeWitt for suppression of the book and won. DeWitt interpreted this to mean that if he left out Harte's name he could continue to publish it. In 1875 DeWitt was taken to court again and ordered to cease publishing Harte's work.

Robert M. DeWitt was a successful mid-nineteenth-century publisher. He recognized the potential of catering to the entertainment needs of America and successfully met them for twenty-nine years. During his entire career he published sensational literature, for the most part by authors now long forgotten. His plays, songsters, and jokebooks had strong ethnic and racial overtones, but were no different from those of other publishers. All these publications, which seem quaint and remote today, were extremely popular in their time and certainly are indicative of popular literary taste in mid-nineteenth-century America.

Nathaniel H. Puffer

References

"Robert M. DeWitt," <u>The American Bookseller</u>, 2
     (1 June 1877): 327-28.

Rev. Edward D. Neill, <u>History of Ramsey County and the
     City of St. Paul</u>. (Minneapolis: North Star Pub-
     lishing Company, 1881).

Edward T. LeBlanc, "A Checklist of Robert M. DeWitt
     Publications," <u>Dime Novel Round-Up</u>, 45 (August
     1976): 97.

Joan Steele, <u>Captain Mayne Reid</u> (Boston: Twayne Pub-
     lishers, 1978).

14   DeWolfe, Fiske, & Company

DeWolfe, Fiske & Company (1880–circa 1905) published cheap clothbound twelvemos, sets of standard English classic prose and poetry, works in history, travel, and biography, some literature of regional interest, and a strong line of juveniles. Producing some 400 titles in various editions, the firm began publishing at 365 Washington Street, Boston, around 1880, and two years later expanded to an adjoining store, 361 Washington. In 1891 it established a branch house in New York at 18 Astor Place, with W. B. Perkins in charge. In 1905 DeWolfe, Fiske & Company was dissolved by mutual consent of the partners and became a corporation under the name DeWolfe & Fiske Company. It moved to Park Street, Boston; its publishing activities ceased and it became a whole-sale and retail business. In 1907 it purchased a four-story building at 14-20 Franklin Street. Perez Morton DeWolfe, Charles F. Fiske, and Ephraim Adams were offi-cers at the time.

Major Authors: N. H. Chamberlain, Sally Pratt McLean, W. H. H. Murray, Johanna Spyri, Susan Warner.

Of the men associated with DeWolfe, Fiske & Company, Perez Morton DeWolfe (1850-1931) was its major figure. He was born in Nova Scotia to an old family for whom the town Wolfville, Nova Scotia, was named. After attending Acadia University, he immigrated to the United States in the late 1860s. Before entering business on their own account, DeWolfe and Charles F. Fiske, one as bookkeeper and the other as shipping clerk, worked for Albert W. Lovering, whose Boston book business failed in 1876 and again in 1879.

Having learned the trade from Lovering (but not his unsound merchandising methods), DeWolfe and Fiske started their business around 1880. It reached the height of its productivity in the decade of competitive price wars among American publishers of cheap reprints.

97

Aggressive in its efforts to become a leading Boston
publisher and jobber, the firm claimed in advertisements:
"We are the only house east of New York carrying a complete line of Books for the General Jobbing Business."
And it always emphasized its low prices: "Also many
bargains in specialties and remainders."

The company began buying plates and books owned
by competitors: in 1882 the Waverley novels from
John W. Lovell; in 1887 the entire stock of the book
jobbing business of C. H. Whiting of Boston; in 1889
plates and stock from Henry A. Young and Company; in
1891 the Anna B. Warner books from the estate of Robert
Carter & Brothers. From Cupples & Hurd it obtained the
works of W. H. H. Murray (1840-1904), who was famous at
the time for having promoted the Adirondack wilderness
to the world. At one time a clergyman, Murray preached
the virtues of fresh air, fishing, and a simple life-
style in Adventures in the Wilderness; or, Camp Life in
the Adirondacks, Lake Champlain and Its Shores, and other
travelogue/nature books that were among the firm's most
successful sellers.

The company sold works of particular interest to
its region: Boston Illustrated; Boston Harbor; Boston:
What to See and How to See It; Harvard: The First American University, and Cape Cod Folks. Additional books
under its imprint were medical guides: Insane: Hand-
book for Attendants; Gynaecological Case Book; The Mystery of Pain, as well as other advice books: How to
Write the History of a Family; Etiquette, and Hints to
Young Men on the True Relations of the Sexes.

In 1890 DeWolfe, Fiske & Company sold some of its
plates to John Lovell's United States Book Company. Although the firm retained its hardcover properties, it
increased promotion of its illustrated juvenile and
novelty lines. "The finest line of Juveniles ever
offered to the American public," it advertised in 1892,
with colored plates "fully equal to the finest German
works" at less than half the price of imported books,
"pronounced by all a wonder." By 1894 some of its novelty items for little folks had become panoramic "toy
books," "wall hangers," or "die cut" items--peacocks or
a Santa Claus that could stand on a table.

DeWolfe, Fiske, & Company

Over its imprint appeared a wide-ranging series of
English classics. Its standard sets included the works
of Thackeray, Dickens, Lytton, Eliot, and Carlyle, in a
line of 110 illustrated clothbound volumes, selling in
1891 for $1.25 each. Charles Reade's works were offered
for $1.50, inasmuch as this was "the only good, uniform
set of Reade in the market," the advertisement proclaimed.
Odd volumes for any dealer who wished to break the sets
would be supplied.

By the turn of the century, DeWolfe, Fiske & Com-
pany's publishing enterprises were declining, although
the firm continued to advertise in Publishers' Weekly
for a few years. In 1901 advertisements featured a new
"Board-Book" line and copyright novels. By 1904 the
firm still offered for sale works formerly published by
Cupples & Hurd; the next year, Cupples & Leon, 101 Fifth
Avenue, New York, became sole selling agents for DeWolfe,
Fiske & Company. That year, the partners of DeWolfe,
Fiske & Company dissolved their partnership and organized
the business as a corporation under the name of DeWolfe &
Fiske Company. From this time forward, the firm's pub-
lishing activities dwindled until they soon ceased altogether, but DeWolfe & Fiske Company continued its retail
and wholesale book business for many years.[1]

The works published by DeWolfe, Fiske & Company
were mainly reprints and juveniles. The firm's importance lies in its dissemination of many popular works at
favorable prices in New England, and for a time in New
York.

Marie Olesen Urbanski

References and Note

Publishers' Trade List Annual (New York: R. R. Bowker
    Company, 1875-1910).

DeWolfe, Fiske, & Company

Raymond H. Shove, <u>Cheap Book Production in the United States, 1870 to 1891</u> (Urbana: University of Illinois Library, 1937).

Charles E. Goodspeed, <u>Yankee Bookseller</u> (Boston: Houghton Mifflin, 1937).

Madeleine B. Stern, <u>Imprints on History: Book Publishers and American Frontiers</u> (Bloomington: Indiana University Press, 1956; reprinted, New York: AMS Press, 1975).

[1]Perez Morton DeWolfe, II, Marblehead, Massachusetts, grandson of the founder, has some publishing archives.

15   Dick & Fitzgerald

Dick & Fitzgerald (1858-1916), book publishers, specialized in publications for mass entertainment in the home.
The firm, located at 18 Ann Street, New York, published
over 1,000 titles in various editions.   The copartnership
of Dick & Fitzgerald was begun 30 June 1858 and was dissolved after Fitzgerald's death in 1881.   The business
was, however, continued under the style of Dick &
Fitzgerald by William B. Dick, who retired in 1898.   At
that time his son, Harris B. Dick, took over the concern
and continued it under the original name until his death
in 1916.   The firm of Dick & Fitzgerald was reorganized
in 1917 as the Fitzgerald Publishing Corporation, Successor to Dick & Fitzgerald, at 18 Vesey Street and later
at East 38th Street, New York.   The Fitzgerald Publishing Corporation was dissolved in 1940.
    Major Authors: Mary Elizabeth Braddon, Harris B.
Dick, William B. Dick, Sarah Anne Frost Shields,
Mrs. Henry (Ellen) Wood.
    William Brisbane Dick was born in Philadelphia in
1826 and died in 1901.   Son of John and Arabella Dick,
he was related to Wesley Burgess of the New York publishing and bookselling firm, Burgess, Stringer & Company.
William B. Dick located in New York and worked for that
firm, which underwent various changes in style.   After
Stringer's retirement to form the firm of Stringer and
Townsend, the business was styled Burgess and Garrett,
with Ransom Garrett as copartner.   After the withdrawal
of Burgess, it was restyled Garrett & Company, publishers
of popular fiction and games at 18 Ann Street, New York.
Finally, the firm became Garrett, Dick & Fitzgerald.
With Garrett's retirement, Dick & Fitzgerald formed a
copartnership on 30 June 1858.
    Lawrence R. Fitzgerald was born in Philadelphia in
1826 and died in 1881.   Trained in the mercantile business, he became a salesman for Burgess and Zieber,

101

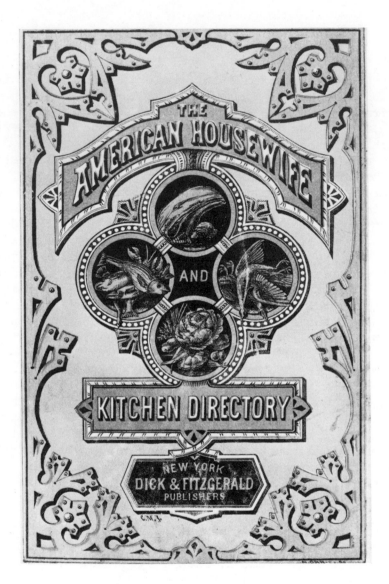

THE
AMERICAN HOUSEWIFE

AND

KITCHEN DIRECTORY

NEW YORK
DICK & FITZGERALD
PUBLISHERS

(Courtesy Nathaniel H. Puffer Collection)

publishers. He accompanied his friend William B. Dick
to New York and with him served an apprenticeship in the
firm of Burgess, Stringer & Company. He, too, remained
with that firm in the course of its various changes in
style [Burgess and Garrett; Garrett & Company; Garrett,
Dick & Fitzgerald] until in 1858 Dick & Fitzgerald became
a copartnership.

From its inception the firm specialized. Instead
of publishing the miscellaneous books that had characterized Burgess's lists, it followed the line established
by Ransom Garrett by producing books that would fill
nineteenth-century American demands for entertainment
and self-improvement. Indeed, some of the firm's publications had originally been Garrett publications.

Even before the articles of copartnership were
formally signed, Dick & Fitzgerald began publication of
a monthly journal, The Home Circle Devoted to Literature,
News, Fun, Poetry &c. (1858-circa 1863). Priced at 3
cents a copy, it contained poems, tales of adventure and
animal life, informative articles, stories, useful receipts, family pastimes, riddles, charades, rebuses, and
parlor pastimes--everything for "the home circle." The
Home Circle was in effect a microcosm and a foretaste of
the publications that were to become identified with the
house of Dick & Fitzgerald.

At least half the Dick & Fitzgerald imprints may
be described as parlor entertainments. Some of them were
compiled by William B. Dick himself, who at times used
the pseudonyms "Leger D. Mayne" and "Trumps." Designed
for domestic social amusement, those publications offered
family games, tableaux, musical pastimes, explanations of
round or forfeit games, puzzles, illusions, waxworks,
games of action or of memory--a variety of entertainments
for a family seeking its pleasures within the home.
Among the most popular general books for parlor entertainment were The Sociable; or, One Thousand and One
Home Amusements (1858) by George Arnold, Fireside Games;
for Winter Evening Amusement (1859) by Wiljalba Frikell,
Uncle Josh's Trunk-Full of Fun (1869) by William B. Dick
using the pseudonym "Joshua Jedidiah Jinks," and the

103

(Courtesy Nathaniel H. Puffer Collection)

compendium What Shall We Do To-Night? or Social Amusements for Evening Parties (1873), also by William B. Dick writing under the pseudonym "Leger D. Mayne."

Within the specialty of publications for home entertainment were numerous subspecialties, all of which found a place on the Dick & Fitzgerald list. In an elocuting age, recitation, dialogue, and jokebooks were extremely popular, and many of them appeared over the Dick & Fitzgerald imprint. The series entitled Dick's Recitations and Readings, published during the 1870s, supplied parlor entertainers in city and country homes across the nation with appropriate material. Several collections of that nature were compiled by William B. Dick himself: Dick's Dutch, French and Yankee Dialect Recitations (1879), Dick's Irish Dialect Recitations (1879), Dick's Book of Toasts (1883), Dick's Dialogues and Monologues (1885), Dick's Comic Dialogues (1886), Dick's Comic and Dialect Recitations (1888), Dick's Diverting Dialogues (1888), Dick's Stump Speeches and Minstrel Jokes (1889), Dick's Festival Reciter (1892).

The firm did not limit itself to Dick's own arrangements of recitations and readings. The compilations of numerous other authors were also produced, among them Floyd Baker Wilson's Book of Recitations and Dialogues (1868), Jerome Barton's Comic Recitations and Humorous Dialogues (1868), Sarah Anne Frost Shields's Humorous and Exhibition Dialogues (1870), Joseph Barber's American Book of Ready-Made Speeches (1871), H. Elliott McBride's All Kinds of Dialogues (1874), Alvah C. Beecher's Recitations and Readings (1874), Alfred Burbank's A Collection of Humorous, Dramatic and Dialect Selections (1878). Jokebooks were particularly popular, and Dick & Fitzgerald published several of them, including Chips from Uncle Sam's Jack-Knife (186?), Ned Turner's Clown Joke Book (1870), and Jack Johnson's Jokes for the Jolly (1873).

Card games vied with recitation, dialogue, and jokebooks for home entertainment, and the firm of Dick & Fitzgerald became expositors of their many varieties: patience, cribbage and whist, bezique, euchre, commercial pitch, and whisky poker. Using the pseudonym "Trumps," William B. Dick produced The American Hoyle;

or Gentleman's Hand-Book of Games (1864) following two
years of consultations with the best cardplayers in the
country. The firm also published The American Card-
Player (1866) by William B. Dick, Dick's Games of Patience (1883), and Dick's Hand-Book of Cribbage (1885),
as well as Gamblers' Tricks with Cards, Exposed and Ex-
plained (1859) by the reformed gambler Jonathan Harring-
ton Green, The Complete Poker-Player (1880) by John
Blackbridge, Poker Principles and Chance Laws (1883) by
Professor Richard A. Proctor, The Theory of the Modern
Scientific Game of Whist (1889) by William Pole, and
American Leads at Whist (1891) by Henry Jones.

From card games to card tricks, and from card
tricks to sleight of hand and magic in general was a
natural progression. Dick & Fitzgerald, having published Parlor Tricks with Cards in 1863 by Wiljalba
Frikell, went on to publish The Fireside Magician (1870)
by Thomas Picton and books on related subjects that
lent themselves to parlor entertainment, such as Dick's
Mysteries of the Hand; or, Palmistry Made Easy (1884)
and Ventriloquism Self-Taught (1894) by Professor
Robert Ganthony.

Reading palms was only one method of telling fortunes. Dick & Fitzgerald produced a long line of
fortune-tellers and dreambooks, from Madame Le Marchand's
Fortune-Teller and Dreamer's Dictionary (1863) to Madame
Le Normand's Unerring Fortune-Teller (1866) and Mother
Shipton's Fortune Teller; or, Future Fate Foretold by the
Planets (1878?). The firm's dreambooks introduced the
lucky number device to the American public, and its
fortune-tellers suggested to parlor entertainers a variety of methods for telling fortunes, from egg whites to
apple parings, from moles and fingernails to dreams.

The nineteenth-century American parlor formed the
backdrop not only for such fireside entertainments as
recitations, card games, and displays of magic, but for
dancing and singing. The last two subjects ranked high
on the Dick & Fitzgerald list. The firm produced numerous volumes to explain the steps of polonaise, lancers
and caledonians, redowa and schottische to terpsicho-
reans in city and country. Among them were Thomas
Hillgrove's Complete Practical Guide to the Art of

Dancing (1863), Dick's Quadrille Call-Book, and Ball-Room Prompter (1878), and Professor Emile De Walden's Ball-Room Companion; or, Dancing Made Easy (189?). Dick & Fitzgerald helped to make dancing easy by publishing directions for calling figures or for executing the steps of jig, german, or galop. As a companion piece to its terpsichorean publications, it also produced Frank B. Converse's Banjo Instructor, Without a Master (1865).

Singing was perhaps even more popular as a parlor pastime than dancing. Whether family and guests gathered around a banjo player or around an upright piano, they needed the songsters that rolled from the Dick & Fitzgerald presses and presented, for 10 cents a copy, love songs and sentimental songs, Ethiopian and comic songs, patriotic and convivial songs, songs with such titles as "Life on the Bloomingdale Road," "The Angel Dressed in White," "She Smiled When I Had Done It," and "I Always Take It Cool." Among the most notable Dick & Fitzgerald songbooks were those published during the 1860s: The Convivial Songster (1862), The Shamrock; or, Songs of Old Ireland (1862), The Tent and Forecastle Songster (1862), The Camp-Fire Songster (1862), Bob Hart's Plantation Songster (1862), William Birch's Ethiopian Melodist (1862), The Arkansas Traveller's Songster (1863), Tony Pastor's "444" Combination Songster (1864), Christy's Bones and Banjo Melodist (1865), Tony Pastor's Waterfall Songster (1866), Tony Pastor's 201 Bowery Songster (1867), Berry's Laugh-and-Grow-Fat Songster (1867), John F. Poole's Champagne Charley Songster (1867), William Lingard's On the Beach at Long Branch Song Book (1868), and even E. C. Buell's Ku-Klux-Klan Songster (1868). Music, required for the 10-cent songsters, was provided by W. A. Pond or William Hall of New York.

As Andrew Fletcher of Saltoun suggested in 1703, the songs of a nation may be of far greater significance than the laws of a nation. If this is so, then the songsters on the Dick & Fitzgerald list do indeed reflect accurately the moods and interests, the preoccupations and pleasures of the nineteenth-century Americans for whom they were published. Equally indicative of the

American yesterday are the plays written and published
for home performance; the Dick & Fitzgerald books for
parlor theatricals graphically evoke the latter part of
the nineteenth century. The firm provided to a public
eager for home amusement scripts of plays and farces,
dramas and vaudeville sketches at 15 or 25 cents each,
along with manuals on costume, lighting, and the use of
greasepaint.

Unlike the firm of Samuel French, which produced
plays for both private and public performance, Dick &
Fitzgerald limited its dramatic publications to private
theatricals designed especially for performance at home.
Within that limitation, the firm's stock of plays ran a
wide gamut, including Irish, rural, western, temperance,
and military plays, as well as Ethiopian acts and monologues, mock trials and initiations, tableaux, shadow
pantomimes, and acting charades. The Dick & Fitzgerald
list offered dramatic collections, such as George
Arnold's Parlor Theatricals (1859), Sarah Anne Frost
Shields's Amateur Theatricals and Fairy-Tale Dramas
(1868) and her Book of Tableaux and Shadow Pantomimes
(1869), Frances Hudson's Private Theatricals for Home
Performance (1870), Dick's Ethiopian Scenes (1873?),
Sarah Anne Frost Shields's Parlor Acting Charades, Intended Solely for Performance in the Drawing Room (1876),
and Dick's Parlor Exhibitions (1882).

Among the most popular individual plays distributed
from the firm's headquarters at 18 Ann Street were those
published toward the end of the century: the three-act
western drama Crawford's Claim; or, Nugget Nell, the Pet
of Poker Flatt (1890) by J. E. Cowley, the one-act farce
Darkey Wood Dealer (1890) by Charles Townsend, Josiah's
Courtship (1896) by Horace C. Dale, and the ever-popular
temperance drama Ten Nights in a Barroom by T. S. Arthur
(1898). In addition Dick & Fitzgerald published a substantial theatrical reference book, T. Allston Brown's
History of the American Stage (1870), and also provided
Weldon's Fancy Costumes (1887), Dick's Theatrical Make-
Up Book (1900), and a five-dollar makeup box containing
crimped hair, nose putty, and moustache cosmetique.

The majority of Dick & Fitzgerald publications
were directed to American parlor life during the latter

108

half of the nineteenth century. The remainder of its
list was devoted to how-to books for self-education and
to novels for mass entertainment. Among the former, the
firm concentrated upon books for the kitchen, books
about sports, and general encyclopedias of information.

The Dick & Fitzgerald books for the kitchen were
represented by several successful compilations: Mrs.
Matilda M. C. Pullan's Lady's Manual of Family Work
(1859), The American Housewife and Kitchen Directory
Containing the Most Valuable and Original Recipes, in
All Various Branches of Cookery (1866), which the firm
pirated, Mrs. T. J. Crowen's American Lady's Cookery
Book (1866), How to Cook and How to Carve (1869), How
to Cook Potatoes, Apples, Eggs, and Fish 400 Different
Ways (1869) by Georgiana Hill, A. S. Wright's Book of
Three Thousand American Receipts (1869), and, as late
as 1890, Dick's Home Made Candies.

Besides catering to intellectual entertainment
with its parlor pastimes and theatricals, and to gus-
tatorial pleasure with its manuals for the kitchen, the
firm of Dick & Fitzgerald published a range of books
that would develop physical fitness among Americans and
increase their enjoyment of outdoor life. The literature of calisthenics and sport figures notably on the
firm's list. Among the former were Dick's Art of Gym-
nastics Containing Practical and Progressive Exercises
(1885) compiled by William B. Dick, Dick's Dumb-Bell and
Indian-Club Exercises (1887), and George Cruden's Calisthenic Training and Musical Drill (1889). The firm's
books on sports were represented by The American Boy's
Book of Sports and Games (1864), Athletic Sports for
Boys (1866), The Athlete's Guide (1872) by William
Edgar Harding, George P. Delisser's Horseman's Guide
(1875), Stanley Harding's Amateur Trapper and Trap-
Maker's Guide (1875), William Wood's The Laws of Athletics (1880), Wakeman Holberton's The Art of Angling
(1887), Dick's Art of Bowling (1890), Henry Arthur C.
Dunn's Fencing Instructor (1893). The Dick & Fitzgerald
books on sport were especially strong in the pugilistic
art, including Edmund E. Price's The Science of Self-
Defense (1867), W. J. Elliott's Art of Attack and Defence (1887), Dick's Art of Wrestling (1887), Professor

109

James Muldoon's <u>Wrestling</u> (1893), and C. Mitchell's <u>Art of Boxing</u> (1893).

   In addition to its manuals on the culinary and calisthenic arts, Dick & Fitzgerald published an extremely varied group of how-to books that satisfied nineteenth-century America's desire for self-improvement, self-instruction, and self-development. A Reason Why Series and a Shilling Library of reference books were published, along with guides to ready reckoning, punctuation and printing, the care of household pets and the family aquarium. The firm's general encyclopedias and how-to books ranged from William B. Dick's <u>Encyclopedia of Practical Receipts and Processes</u> (1872) to an <u>American Boys' Manual of Practical Mechanics Containing Instruction in Carpentry, Boat Building, Glass Blowing, Turning, etc.</u> (1891).

   Priced at 10, 25, or 30 cents, the Dick & Fitzgerald manuals were concerned with many aspects of life, including etiquette in its various manifestations. As early as 1858 <u>The Arts of Beauty; or, Secrets of a Lady's Toilet</u> by Lola Montez made its appearance, followed by <u>The Perfect Gentleman; or, Etiquette and Eloquence</u> (1860). In due course, Dick & Fitzgerald produced <u>The Ladies' Guide to Beauty</u> (186?) by Sir James Clark, private physician to Queen Victoria, Arthur Martine's <u>Hand-Book of Etiquette, and Guide to True Politeness</u> (1866), <u>The Art of Dressing Well</u> (1870) by Sarah Anne Frost Shields, and even <u>The Art and Etiquette of Making Love</u> (1875).

   A degree of self-education was made possible by the firm's manuals on the three Rs and related subjects: William D. Brisbane's <u>Golden Ready Reckoner</u> (1863), Franz Thimm's <u>French Self-Taught</u> (1878), M. C. Hart's <u>The Amateur Printer; or, Typesetting at Home</u> (1883), and guides for potential correspondents, from Ingoldsby North's <u>Book of Love Letters</u> (1867) to William B. Dick's <u>Society Letter Writer</u> (1884) and <u>Commercial Letter Writer</u> (1886). Indeed, there was little the reader could not teach himself, provided he or she was armed with appropriate Dick & Fitzgerald guidebooks. They ran a wide gamut, from George Bishop's <u>Every Woman Her Own Lawyer</u> (1858) to James Carter Beard's <u>Painting on China</u>

(1882), from Henry D. Butler's The Family Aquarium (1858)
to a Book of Household Pets, and How to Manage Them
(1866), from Jerry Thomas's How to Mix Drinks, or the
Bon-Vivant's Companion (1862) to Joseph Fleischman's
The Art of Blending and Compounding Liquors and Wines
(1885), from Georgiana C. Clark's Dinner Napkins and
How to Fold Them (1884) to Jared Flagg, Jr.'s How to
Take Money Out of Wall Street (1887).

Dick & Fitzgerald did not confine its list to parlor pastimes and how-to books. Like most nineteenth-
century American houses that directed their publications
to mass entertainment, the firm published both series
and individual cheaply priced novels, some of which had
already appeared on the Garrett list. During the 1860s
and into the 1870s Dick & Fitzgerald published at least
four series of novels consisting of paperbacks priced
at 25 cents. Its Series of Military Novels was represented by William H. Ainsworth's Don Bernardo's Daughter;
or, Love, War, and Adventure (186?), which had previously
been published by Garrett, Dick & Fitzgerald. The Dick &
Fitzgerald series Tales of Celebrated Highwaymen consisted of at least seven stories, including The Life and
Adventures of Claude Duval, The Dashing Highwayman (187?)
and Life and Adventures of Dick Clinton, The Masked Highwayman (187?). The firm's Series of Sea Tales comprised
thirteen or more novels by Joseph Holt Ingraham, Sylvanus
Cobb, Frederick Marryat, and others. At least one novel
in that series, The White Cruiser; or, The Fate of the
Unheard of (ca. 1860) by Edward Zane Carroll Judson, had
been a Garrett publication.

The most extensive Dick & Fitzgerald novel series
was its Series of Prize Novels, which included at least
thirty titles, among them English and French reprints.
For the most part, these were published without dates
during the 1860s and 1870s, and included such colorful
titles as The Matricide's Daughter; or, Life in the
Metropolis by Newton M. Curtis, Paul Feval's The White
Wolf; or, The Secret Brotherhood, Osgood Bradbury's The
Belle of the Bowery, and May Agnes Fleming's The Mid-
night Queen.

Among the most popular of the Dick & Fitzgerald
novels were Mrs. Henry Wood's East Lynne, which the firm

published in 1861 as a 75-cent paperback, and Mary
Elizabeth Braddon's Lady Audley's Secret, which it published in 1863 as a 50-cent paperback. Both books were
English imports. The former had been published as a
three-decker by Richard Bentley in 1861 and, according
to Frank Luther Mott in Golden Multitudes, "became a
favorite with the publishers of cheap editions," sold
at least a million copies, and was widely presented in
dramatic form. As for Lady Audley's Secret, "it was
long one of the leaders in this [melodramatic] class of
fiction." Other popular novels on the Dick & Fitzgerald
list included Friedrich W. C. Gerstäcker's The Hunter's
Trail; or, The Indian's Ruse (1863) and Pierce Egan's
Imogene; or, The Marble Heart (1864).

One of the firm's most interesting publications
was entitled The Adventures of Mr. Obadiah Oldbuck
Wherein Are Set Forth His Unconquerable Passion for His
Lady-Love, His Unutterable Despair on Losing Her, His
Five Attempts at Suicide and His Surprising Exploits in
Search of the Beloved Object. Also, His Final Success
(undated). Actually, as was pointed out by Marianne C.
Gourary in the Bulletin de la Société d'Études
Töpffériennes (February 1979), this was by the celebrated
Swiss writer and illustrator Rodolphe Töpffer and, as a
charming book of caricatures, played an important role
in the beginnings of the comics. The Dick & Fitzgerald
undated edition was pirated.

In the days before international copyright, pirating was prevalent among American publishing houses, and
Dick & Fitzgerald was no exception. When the firm did
not pirate its publications, it often obtained manuscripts by arrangement or consultation with experts in
a given field. Occasionally plates were purchased from
such companies as Street & Smith. Another source of
supply was the prolific William B. Dick himself who,
according to Nathaniel H. Puffer in This Book-Collecting
Adventure Presented by The Delaware Bibliophiles, "was
responsible for well over thirty titles" and whose "son,
Harris B. Dick, carried on that tradition by contributing nearly a dozen new titles."

Dick & Fitzgerald operated primarily as a mail-
order house, shipping cheap books across the country

from its post office box. Its publications were listed
in catalogs often attractively illustrated and sent
forth gratis. Among them were several undated catalogs:
Dick & Fitzgerald's Descriptive Book Catalogue and Dick's
Descriptive Catalogue of Dramas, Comedies, Farces, as
well as Dick & Fitzgerald's Catalogue for 1881, which
listed 200 titles.

Upon William B. Dick's retirement in 1898, his son
Harris Brisbane Dick took over the Dick & Fitzgerald
house. Born in 1855, the younger Dick had been trained
in the firm and, using the pseudonym "Trumps, Jr.,"
carried on tradition by compiling or editing the later
series of reciters and card games that had originally
been launched by his father. With employees Rudolph
Behrens and William Train, the firm continued to prosper,
catering to mass entertainment in the home. In 1916
Harris B. Dick died suddenly. According to the terms of
his will, his executor was to "convert into money . . .
the good-will and assets (but not the firm name) of the
book publishing business now carried on . . . under the
firm name of 'Dick & Fitzgerald.'" The firm of Dick &
Fitzgerald was reorganized in 1917 as the Fitzgerald
Publishing Corporation, Successor to Dick & Fitzgerald,
and as such it continued in business until 1940.

For more than half a century Dick & Fitzgerald
supplied the demands of a nation that sought its entertainment within the confines of the home. In publishing
novels and novel series, encyclopedias and how-to manuals, the firm catered to mass entertainment and instruction much in the manner of other publishing houses of
the time. In producing extensive lines of books that
enabled nineteenth-century Americans to entertain themselves at home, Dick & Fitzgerald were more innovative.
Today the recitation and jokebooks, the books of card
games, the dreambooks and fortune-tellers, the dance
books and songsters, the plays for parlor performance
that bear the Dick & Fitzgerald imprint recall nostal-
gically domestic America of the latter half of the

nineteenth century. Those Dick & Fitzgerald publications raise yesterday's curtain upon a nation at home.

Madeleine B. Stern

References

Madeleine B. Stern, Imprints on History: Book Pub-
    lishers and American Frontiers (Bloomington:
    Indiana University Press, 1956; reprinted,
    New York: AMS Press, 1975).

Stephen Powell, Short-Title List of Dick & Fitzgerald
    Publications (undated typescript, courtesy
    Stephen Powell, Torrington, Connecticut).

Dime Novel Round-Up, 44 (15 July 1975): title page,
    46 (June 1977): title page, 46 (December 1977):
    title page and 126, 47 (June 1978): title page
    and 75.

Nathaniel H. Puffer, "Dick & Fitzgerald, Publishers,"
    This Book-Collecting Adventure Presented by The
    Delaware Bibliophiles (Newark, Delaware: The
    Delaware Bibliophiles, 1978): 21-25.

Marianne C. Gourary, "A la poursuite des éditions
    anglaises et américaines de Töpffer," Bulletin
    de la Société d'Études Töpfferiennes 5
    (February 1979): 1-6.

16   Donnelley, Loyd & Co.

Donnelley, Loyd & Co. (1875-   ), Chicago publishers,
pioneered in the publication of cheap libraries of un-
copyrighted authors after the Civil War.   The firm's
Lakeside Library was an offshoot of the extensive
Donnelley printing and publishing enterprise that had
existed in Chicago since 1864.   When the series was begun in 1875, it was published by Donnelley, Loyd & Co.
at the corner of Clark and Adams streets.   In 1879 the
Lakeside Library was sold to George Munro; at the time
of sale, Norman T. Gassette was a partner in the house,
which operated under the style of Donnelley, Gassette &
Loyd.   In 1885 the firm was located at 144 Monroe Street.
By 1887 it had become R. R. Donnelley & Sons (the name
in which it was later incorporated), quartered at 140-
146 Monroe.   Between 1897 and 1929 it was housed in the
Lakeside Press Building at 731 Plymouth Court.   R. R.
Donnelley & Sons is a thriving twentieth-century
concern.

     Major Series: Lakeside Library.

     Richard Robert Donnelley was born 15 November 1836
in Hamilton, Ontario, and died 8 April 1899.   After ap-
prenticing as a printer while a boy, he went to New
Orleans in 1857 where he worked for several years for
the True Delta and became a partner of John Hand.   Because of rising Civil War sentiment, he returned to
Canada, where he worked in the printshop of Joseph
Lawson.   In 1863 he married Naomi Shenston and moved to
Chicago to run the printshop of Church & Goodman at 51
and 53 LaSalle Street.   He became a member of the firm
in October 1864.   In 1870 Church, Goodman, and Donnelley
merged with the Lakeside Publishing and Printing Company
with Donnelley as manager.   Construction on their new
building at Clark & Adams streets was almost complete
when it was destroyed by the great Chicago fire of 8-10
October 1871.   The destruction included all of Donnelley's

machinery and his home. He raised money and equipment
in New York and reestablished the firm in leased quarters
on the third floor of the building at 103-105 South Canal
Street while constructing a new building at the old site.
That new structure was occupied in June 1873. With A. J.
Cox, a Chicago bookbinder, as its head, he added a binding department in 1873 or 1874. From this base Donnelley
joined forces with Alexander T. Loyd in late 1874 or
early 1875 to establish Donnelley, Loyd & Co. By the
time he died the firm had become the corporation R. R.
Donnelley & Sons, including his three sons, Reuben
Hamilton, Thomas Elliott, and Benjamin.

The idea of forming an inexpensive fiction series
to keep the press busy appears to have come from Alexander
Loyd, although it has been attributed to Donnelley as
well. The first volume of the Lakeside Library was published about 20 January 1875. Unlike dime novels the
books were clothbound, although they sold for much less
than regular casebound books of the time--10 cents to
50 cents, depending on length, generally 32 to 80 pages.
The books were printed in quartos measuring about 12 1/2
by 8 inches, two or three columns to the page, and frequently containing wood engravings. The authors included
foreign writers whose works were not subject to United
States copyright: Charles Reade, Anthony Trollope,
Charles Dickens, Jules Verne. Also represented were
American writers Irving, Cooper, and those whose works
were in the public domain. One of the most popular
books in 1876 was a reprint of John Habberton's Helen's
Babies (50 cents), which had its turn at being pirated
in Europe. This library, which consisted of 270 volumes
by 1879, was among the early attempts to publish general
literature in cheap format.

The series was an instant success, developing
such competition that by 1877 some fourteen libraries
were produced by various publishers. The library moved
rapidly from twice monthly to weekly numbers. It was
not advertised in bookselling periodicals but was distributed by the Western News Company. In 1879 the
firm's partner Gassette, unsuccessful in negotiations
to buy the Seaside Library from rival George Munro,

agreed to sell the Lakeside Library to him. It was consequently subsumed into Munro's Seaside Library.

The mass entertainment venture that was the Lakeside Library constituted a short-lived episode in the
firm's history. Another project was the publication of
the Chicago City Directory. In the final decade of the
nineteenth century Donnelley's was responsible for the
printing of such respected publishers as Stone & Kimball,
after its move to Chicago, and most of the Way & Williams
books of the 1890s.

Donnelley's innovative move to provide "cheap" fiction of good quality, printed on strong paper and casebound, served a public need in the 1870s for an
affordable alternative to the dime novels while countering the influx of cheap foreign books being dumped in
the American market. The library format appealed to the
public, thus providing a market that would absorb the
product of advancing technology in the printing industry.

Anna Lou Ashby

References

J. Stearns Cushing, "Death of R. R. Donnelley," Inland
Printer 23 (1899): 238-40.

Raymond H. Shove, Cheap Book Production in the United
States, 1870 to 1891 (Urbana: University of
Illinois Library, 1937).

Frank L. Schick, The Paperbound Book in America: The
History of Paperbacks and Their European Background (New York: R. R. Bowker Company, 1958).

17   Donohue & Henneberry

Donohue & Henneberry (1871-1900), Chicago bookbinders and publishers, produced popular series for mass consumption from its address at 407-425 Dearborn Street during the 1890s.

Major Authors: Bertha M. Clay, Thomas W. Handford, Norman D. Wood.

Michael A. Donohue was born 25 September 1841 in Gort, County Galway, Ireland, and died in Chicago in 1915. At eight he crossed the ocean alone to join his father in Philadelphia. In 1856 they settled in Chicago, where Michael became a bookbinder in the firm of Cox and Donohue.

William P. Henneberry was born in 1848, and after studying in the Chicago High School worked as a bookbinder.

In 1871, the first week after the Chicago Fire, Donohue & Henneberry began operating as bookbinders, later adding a line of stationery and printed forms-- the "Red Line Series,"--the only form of printing done by the firm during the 1880s. In 1890 the company began publishing with its Dearborn Series of popular copyrighted novels, including Two Women in Black by James Mooney, A Respectable Family by Roy Thompson, Lucia Lascar (A Romance of Passion) by Luman Allen. At the same time, Donohue & Henneberry produced a line of non-fiction, notably biographies and self-help manuals, several by Thomas W. Handford.

The following year the firm published the Optimus Series of twelvemos priced at 50 cents each, featuring, according to its elegant catalog, "the best American and foreign authors . . . printed on fine toned and calendared paper. Profusely illustrated in line and half-tone studies with enameled paper covers of special and attractive designs." Consisting of some thirty titles, the Optimus Series featured George F. Ormsby's

The Madonna of Pass Christian, Dangerous Delights by
André Theuriet, translated by E. P. Robins, and Marco
Brocier's Jovel Fortunat, A Roumanian Romance, translated by Hettie E. Miller from the German. The hero of
Jovel Fortunat was advertised as "a grand ideal of a
noble and exalted young manhood. The manly way in which
he resists the wiles and temptations of the beautiful
but too passionate women and remains true to . . . the
pure and true in womanhood, constitute some of the grand-
est conceptions of character in all the range of fiction."
Works by Alphonse Daudet, Pierre Loti, Théophile Gautier,
as well as Washington Irving and William Gilmore Simms
also appeared in the Optimus Series.

By 1894 Donohue & Henneberry was producing, be-
sides the Dearborn and Optimus Series, the Ideal Library,
standard sets, juveniles, birthday, and gift books. It
reprinted some 183 titles, including works by Dickens,
Wilkie Collins, Marie Corelli, H. Rider Haggard, George
Eliot, Charlotte Brontë, Jules Verne, as well as Bertha M.
Clay's Lord Lynne's Choice, Thorns and Orange Blossoms,
Claribel's Love Story, Her Only Sin.

Such juvenile series as The Little Footprint at 50
cents a copy and Pleasant Picture Series at 15 cents a
copy were also published by the firm. One of the house's
most interesting ventures was its publication of a work
sympathetic to the plight of the black man, The White
Side of a Black Subject by Norman D. Wood, which appeared
in its appropriately entitled Advance Series.

Between 1890 and 1893, when the United States Book
Company was operated as a giant trust by John W. Lovell,
its act of incorporation included, among many firms,
that of Donohue & Henneberry. The firm continued operation after the end of the United States Book Company,
lasting until 1900 when it split, Donohue forming Donohue
Brothers, which specialized in adventure books for young
people, and Henneberry forming the Henneberry Company.

Through the efforts of Donohue & Henneberry, as
through the publications of most publishers for mass

entertainment, hosts of readers were assured good reading at reasonable prices during the 1890s.

William Clarkin

References

Publishers' Trade List Annual (New York: R. R. Bowker Company, 1895).

"Obituary of Michael A. Donohue," Publishers' Weekly, 87 (14 October 1915): 1183.

Albert N. Marquis, The Book of Chicagoans: A Biographical Dictionary of Leading Living Men and Women of the City of Chicago and Environs (Chicago: A. N. Marquis Company, 1917).

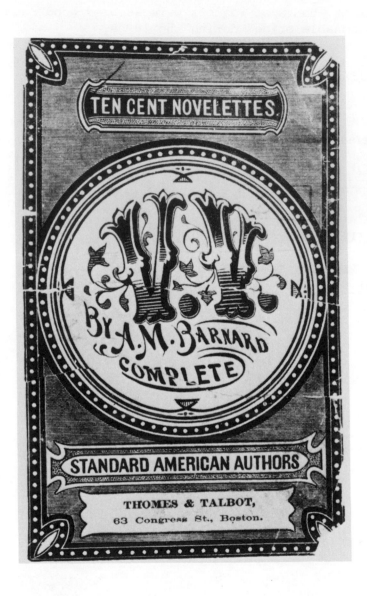

A.M. Barnard was the pseudonym of Louisa May Alcott.
(From *Plots and Counterplots,* Madeleine B. Stern, ed.)

18   Elliott, Thomes & Talbot

Elliott, Thomes & Talbot (1861–1885), publishers of periodicals and cheap series, published dime novels based
upon foreign and American history, especially the winning
of the American West, and became competitors of Beadle &
Company. They published some 500 titles in various editions. As Elliott & Thomes (1861–1863), the enterprise
began publishing at 100 Washington Street, Boston. With
the admission of Newton Talbot the firm was restyled
Elliott, Thomes & Talbot in 1863 and relocated at 118
Washington. Subsequently the company moved to 63 Congress Street. In 1870 Thomes & Talbot separated from
Elliott. In 1872 Thomes & Talbot moved to 36 Bromfield
Street and later to 23 Hawley Street, where the firm
remained until its dissolution in 1885.
     Major Authors: Louisa May Alcott, Maturin M.
Ballou, William H. Bushnell, Sylvanus Cobb, Jr.,
E. Z. C. Judson, Ben Perley Poore.
     James R. Elliott was born in Mason, New Hampshire,
circa 1820 and died circa 1890. In 1852 he became a
member of the Boston firm of Moulton, Elliott, and
Lincoln, publishers of the True Flag, a weekly devoted
to adventure stories. His work was primarily editorial
in nature. In 1861 he joined Thomes, founding the firm
of Elliott & Thomes.
     William Henry Thomes, the best known of the partners, was born in Portland, Maine, in 1824 and died in
1895. Early orphaned, he was reared in Boston by a
guardian. At age eighteen he shipped aboard the Admittance to engage in the California hide trade. Back in
Boston, he served as printer on the Boston Daily Times
and married the daughter of Captain Peter Peterson, his
former master on the Admittance. His second marriage
was to Frances Ullen. In 1849, having joined the
Boston and California Joint Stock Mining and Trading
Company, he sailed to San Francisco, helping to edit a

shipboard paper, the Barometer. He dug for gold at
Bidwell's Bar, and before returning home he sailed
aboard an opium smuggler plying between China and
California, worked in the gold mines of Victoria,
and kept a store at Ballarat. His personal adventures
may well have governed his choice of texts when he became a publisher. Between 1854 and 1860 he was a reporter for the Boston Daily Times and the Boston Herald.
In 1861 he began his publishing career in partnership
with James R. Elliott.

Newton Talbot was born at Stoughton, Massachusetts,
in 1815 and died in 1904. Educated in the Stoughton
public schools, he went to Boston at age twenty-one,
and after working as a shoe dealer and an inspector in
the custom house, sailed aboard the Crescent City for
Chagres, New Granada, in 1849--an experience similar to
Thomes's adventures. Returning to Boston in 1850, he
became a cashier in Frederick Gleason's Publishing Hall
in 1851, continuing as business manager when Maturin M.
Ballou took over the Gleason publications. He married
Calista Harvey in 1867 and had one child, Bessie Talbot
(1869-1883). In 1863 he joined Elliott & Thomes.

In 1863 the newly formed firm of Elliott, Thomes
& Talbot published a line of periodicals that included
the American Union, The Flag of Our Union (a miscellaneous weekly designed for the home circle but emphasiz-
ing violent narratives and flamboyant adventure)
previously published by Frederick Gleason and later by
Maturin M. Ballou, and Ballou's Dollar Monthly Magazine,
which had been founded by Ballou. They also published
the Novelette, originally published by Ballou as a
weekly devoted to four-part stories, and converted it
into a magazine that contained one long complete story
and a few short stories.

In the same year Elliott, Thomes & Talbot added
dime novels to its line of periodicals, entering the
field on 10 November 1863 with publication of its Ten
Cent Novelette No. 1, Sylvanus Cobb, Jr.'s The Golden
Eagle; or, The Privateer of 1776, which was published
in a special edition of 25,000 copies. Erastus F.
Beadle had begun the large-scale publication of dime
novels in 1860 with Ann Stephens's Malaeska: the

124

Indian Wife of The White Hunter. By 1863 several competing publishers emerged, of whom Elliott, Thomes & Talbot
was first. The firm published a new Ten Cent Novelette
the last Monday of every month. Bound in pink wrappers,
later in blue, these dime novels contained from 100 to
128 pages. The yearly series of twelve was priced at
$1.00 and included reprints as well as original stories.
In addition to its series of Ten Cent Novelettes,
Elliott, Thomes & Talbot published a line of Brilliant
Novelettes priced at 20 cents. Bound and richly illustrated, each contained a complete story, as well as
short stories and anecdotes.

The firm generally paid its writers $2.00 for a
short column of print or $3.00 for a column inside length
(a full-length column)--a sum that amounted to approximately $50.00 or $75.00 for a complete story. Among
its most successful cheap publications (many of which
were Gleason reprints) between 1863 and 1870 were The
Bravo's Secret, The Yankee Champion, and The Ducal Coronet by Sylvanus Cobb, Jr.; The Duke's Prize, The Turkish
Slave, and The Child of the Sea by "Lieutenant Murray"
[Maturin M. Ballou]; The Scout; or, Sharpshooters of the
Revolution and Mameluke; or, The Sign of the Mystic Tie
by Ben Perley Poore; The Volunteer and The Black Avenger
by "Ned Buntline" [Edward Zane Carroll Judson]; The Nov-
ice and Kinah's Curse by Jane G. Austin; and V. V.: or,
Plots and Counterplots by "A. M. Barnard" [Louisa May
Alcott].

The firm's relationship with Louisa May Alcott is
of particular interest. In 1865 "V. V.: or, Plots and
Counterplots," a heavily plotted story about a malevo-
lent and manipulating heroine, appeared as a four-part
serial in The Flag of Our Union. Subsequently (circa
1870) it was reprinted as No. 80 in the firm's series
of Ten Cent Novelettes. Eager for an abundance of such
stories, the editorial member of the firm, James R.
Elliott, wrote to Louisa May Alcott on 7 January 1865
requesting more narratives from her, and assuring her,
"You may send me anything in either the sketch or Novelette line that you do not wish to 'father', or that you
wish A. M. Barnard, or 'any other man' to be responsible
for, & if they suit me I will purchase them." In May

and June 1865 her "A Marble Woman: or, The Mysterious
Model" was published in The Flag of Our Union, followed
in October and November 1866 by "Behind a Mask: or, A
Woman's Power," and in January 1867 by "The Abbot's
Ghost: or, Maurice Treherne's Temptation." In 1867
Elliott, Thomes & Talbot published Alcott's The Skeleton
in the Closet as a trailer to The Foundling by Perley
Parker in No. 49 of their Ten Cent Novelettes. In the
same year the firm published Alcott's The Mysterious Key,
and What It Opened as No. 50 in the Ten Cent Novelette
series. The ingredients of these Alcott thrillers included opium addiction, disguises, violent deaths, and
Gothic devices. Alcott, shortly to be known almost
universally as the author of Little Women (1868-1869),
supplied Elliott, Thomes & Talbot with some of its most
sensational narratives and may certainly be ranked as
the most famous of its authors.

Many of the Elliott, Thomes & Talbot dime novels
resorted to the American past for their backgrounds and
plots. Stories based upon colonial America included
Zelda. A Tale of the Massachusetts Colony by Jane
Howard (No. 31 of the Ten Cent Novelettes, 1866) and
The White Rover: or The Lovely Maid of Louisiana
by Dr. J. H. Robinson (No. 2 of the Ten Cent Novelettes,
1863), the story of hunter and red man in the days when
Louisiana was a French colony. Several Elliott, Thomes
& Talbot dime novels were based upon the American Revolution, among them the first of the Ten Cent Novelettes,
Sylvanus Cobb, Jr.'s The Golden Eagle; or, The Privateer
of 1776 (1863); Ben Perley Poore's The Scout; or, Sharpshooters of the Revolution (Brilliant Novelette, 1863);
and Sylvanus Cobb, Jr.'s The Patriot Cruiser. A Revolutionary Story (No. 52 of the Ten Cent Novelettes, 1868).
Similarly, the Mexican War provided the historical background for The Volunteer: or, The Maid of Monterey (No.
16 of the Ten Cent Novelettes, 1865) by "Ned Buntline"
[E. Z. C. Judson], in which facts about the Texas Rangers
and the Battle of Buena Vista were mingled with the story
of a false accusation and a court-martial.

The winning of the American West inspired a stream
of dime novels, notably William H. Bushnell's Hack, The
Trailer. A Story of The Shoshonee Indians (No. 68 of

126

the Ten Cent Novelettes, 1869), a romance of "the time
when the first daring spirits had turned their backs
upon civilization; when they banded together to resist
the attacks of the Indians." The hero, Hack, was "all
bone and muscle," his face "swarthy from exposure to
sun and wind," his tall frame clothed in "well-worn and
stained buckskin," his cap "formed of the shaggy skin of
a wolf." His name was "familiar to all who have travelled through Dacotah Territory." A "man amongst men,"
he guided his "unfaltering steed" through a "trackless
wood," and he may well be regarded as a prototype for a
host of western heroes.

Such cheaply priced Elliott, Thomes & Talbot publications, with their ingredients of painted Indians
and squaws, thundering cannon and hatchets, emigrant
wagons and frontier forts, made the Wild West come alive
for readers en masse. The Mexican War and the California Gold Rush were scarcely two decades in the past when
these novels recalled to the original forty-niners their
own experiences and embodied for a younger generation
the lure of American adventure. The only book outside
the domain of cheap literature published by the firm was
John B. Hill's Proceedings at the Centennial Celebration
of the One Hundredth Anniversary of the Incorporation of
the Town of Mason, N.H., August 26, 1868 (1870), published because of James R. Elliott's connections with
the town.

In 1870 Thomes and Talbot severed their connections
with Elliott, who became publisher of the Western World,
a family journal. The Boston fire of 1872 destroyed many
of the Thomes & Talbot publications. By the end of the
decade, the reputation of the dime novel as a respectable
literary genre had begun its decline. In 1883, the Honorable Abel Goddard, a member of the New York Assembly,
introduced into that body a bill declaring: "Any person
who shall sell, loan, or give to any minor under sixteen . . . any dime novel . . . without first obtaining
the written consent of the parent or guardian of such
minor, shall be deemed guilty of a misdemeanor, punish-
able by imprisonment or by a fine." Largely as a result
of this denigration of the dime novel, the firm of
Thomes & Talbot was dissolved in 1885.

127

A prolific author himself, William Henry Thomes produced a number of books more or less based upon his personal experiences and similar in content to many of the dime novels he published. They included The Gold Hunters' Adventures; or, Life in Australia (1864), The Bushrangers (1865), The Gold Hunters in Europe; or, The Dead Alive (1868), The Whaleman's Adventures in the Sandwich Islands and California (1871), Life in the East Indies (1872), A Slaver's Adventures (1872), Running the Blockade (1875), The Belle of Australia (1883), On Land and Sea (1883-1884), and The Ocean Rovers (1896). In 1885 Thomes returned to California as president of the New England Society of California Pioneers. Newton Talbot became treasurer of Tufts College.

The publishing list of Thomes & Talbot was turned over to George W. Studley, who was located at the Thomes & Talbot address of 23 Hawley Street, Boston. In his Owl Library, Studley reprinted the earlier Thomes & Talbot series.

Elliott, Thomes & Talbot was one of several moderately successful nineteenth-century American firms catering to mass entertainment by publishing dime novels that competed with the larger output of the Beadle house. Imitative rather than innovative, it was nonetheless steadily productive for a generation. During the 1860s and 1870s the demand for colorful, often sensational, escapist literature reached a height. During those decades the firm of Elliott, Thomes & Talbot responded to that demand with its lines of Ten Cent and Brilliant Novelettes, which provided an avid public with the historic romance that had been shaped from the nation's romantic history. The dime novels published by Elliott, Thomes & Talbot were all but thumbed out of existence. Today they have become highly desirable as rare collectibles. Moreover, the tides of taste have again undergone a change. The sensational narratives devoured during the 1860s and 1870s and denigrated during the 1880s when the firm dissolved are now regarded by some critics as graphic documentary source material for the evocation of the American past.

Madeleine B. Stern

References

Hosea Starr Ballou, "Hon. Newton Talbot, A.M.," New-England Historical and Genealogical Register, 58 (October 1904): 329-34.

George R. Stewart, Take Your Bible in One Hand. The Life of William Henry Thomes (San Francisco: Colt Press, 1939).

Leona Rostenberg, "Some Anonymous and Pseudonymous Thrillers of Louisa M. Alcott," Papers of the Bibliographical Society of America, 37 (1943): 1-10.

Madeleine B. Stern, Imprints on History: Book Publishers and American Frontiers (Bloomington: Indiana University Press, 1956; reprinted, New York: AMS Press, 1975).

129

19 Samuel French

Samuel French (1846–   ) was the foremost American publisher of plays produced as cheap, paper-covered pamphlets in numbered series. As Samuel French the firm operated until 1871, the year before its founder moved to London. Beginning some time in 1871 and continuing into 1891 the firm was known as Samuel French & Son; from 1891 to 1899 T. H. French or T. Henry French was used; and since 1899 the form has been Samuel French, Inc. The firm has published from the following addresses in New York: 293 Broadway from 1846–1850; 151 Nassau, 1850–1854; 121 Nassau, 1854–1857; 122 Nassau, 1857–1878; 38 East 14th, 1878–1887; 28 West 23rd and 19 West 22nd, 1887–1896; 24 and 26 West 22nd, 1896–1910; 28 West 38th, 1910–1924; and 25 West 45th from 1924 to the present.

Major Publications: French's Standard Drama, 425 numbers; French's Minor Drama, 403 numbers.

Samuel French was born in Randolph, Massachusetts, 25 October 1821, to Samuel French (1785–1838) and his wife Sarah Sawyer (1792–1871). He died at his home in Kensington, England, 9 April 1898. On 9 March 1848 he married Mary Amelia Mitchel (1826–1887), and their only surviving child, Thomas Henry, was born in New York 7 December 1848. On 9 August 1893 he married Ada Emily (Foster) Astley-Sparke, a widow.

French entered the book trade in New York as a seller and distributor of paperbacks, particularly at first of novels reprinted from story papers. In the 1840s he was Gleason's New York agent; in the 1850s he reprinted about fifty novels from The Flag of Our Union and similar sources, many of them following Gleason's editions. They included some seventeen titles by Sylvanus Cobb, Jr., and a handful by such authors as M. M. Ballou, J. H. Robinson, and A. J. H. Duganne. About 1850 he became general agent of William Taylor &

131

Samuel French

Company of New York, publishers of the principal contemporary American collections of British and American plays: The Modern Standard Drama, 104 numbers in thirteen volumes, and The Minor Drama, 56 numbers in seven volumes. After that he published about 100 numbers of his own French's American Drama. He then bought Taylor's printing plates and those of Spencer's Boston Theatre and incorporated nearly all his purchases and much of French's American Drama in two new series. French's Standard Drama and French's Minor Drama continued to expand until the late 1890s.

Sometimes in partnership with his brother James and sometimes with another partner or on his own, he operated retail shoe stores, ran a book bindery for a time, and from 1859 to 1870 engaged in job printing with George W. Wheat, beginning on the premises vacated by Taylor. (Probably French & Wheat printed the plays that Samuel French published.) The only publication for which French & Wheat is known is the Illuminated Western World (1869-1870) edited by Orville J. Victor, who serialized in its pages his wife's celebrated story "The Dead Letter." It also contained the only nineteenth century printing of William Gilmore Simms's "Voltmeier or, The Mountain Men." Each of the fifty-two issues of 1869 was decorated with a masthead and two cuts "printed in oil colors, from one to seven, at a single impression." After sixteen further numbers, uncolored, the paper was sold to Wide World, Boston.

In 1870 Thomas Henry joined the firm, and was left in charge of the New York office in 1872 when his father moved to London. There Samuel French bought out Thomas Hailes Lacy (1809-1873), the foremost British publisher of plays. French had been Lacy's American representative. Like French, Lacy had been buying up the series and stock of rival play publishers. At a cost of £5,000 French had consolidated his transatlantic monopoly of the trade in printed plays.

French's important innovation at the London office, one that affected his son's career and later the business in New York, was the collection of royalties from both professional and amateur performances. By 1895 the London office held one thousand plays on which it

collected royalties, and by 1900 it represented two
hundred authors, proprietors, or executors. French
also purchased performance rights from authors or es-
tates, retaining in those cases the whole performance
fee instead of a percentage. French retained agents
throughout the British Isles to keep him informed of
all amateur and professional productions, and the firm
took the issue to the courts when necessary. French's
purchases of American performance rights from contemporary British and continental authors was to transform
his son from publisher to man of the theatre.

Beginning in the 1870s Thomas was able to offer
for sale the American performance rights of some very
important British and European plays and musicals. Soon
Thomas was producing plays (White Lies), taking first-
run companies on tour (Mother and Son, The Silver King),
and organizing and touring his own Lillian Russell Opera
Company. With Frank W. Sanger he organized four companies to tour simultaneously in Little Lord Fauntleroy,
a venture marred by disputes and climaxed by a $68,000
judgment against him. From about 1885 to about 1893 he
leased and managed the Grand Opera House (8th Avenue and
23rd Street); with Frank W. Sanger he ran the Broadway
Theatre (7th Avenue and 41st) from about 1888 to 1893,
managing it from 1893 to 1896; from 1890 to 1893 he managed the Garden Theatre, Madison Square Garden (Madison
Avenue and 27th); and he built and managed the American
Theatre, including its Roof Garden (260 West 42nd Street),
1893-1897, losing it by foreclosure. He became one of
the principal producers of the Gilded Age.

The Samuel French enterprise catered to the stage-
struck--readers and playgoers, professional and amateur
actors. Its influence in the theatre, as documented by
the numerous copies of French editions that survive with
the manuscript annotations of professional prompters,
producers, and actors, is not surprising, for no one in
America published a more extensive catalog, and no other
catalog was so widely distributed. As early as 1856
French advertised over 100,000 plays on hand. Even before he absorbed his competitors he stocked their plays,
so series published by Cumberland (incorporating
Duncombe), Oxberry, Webster, and Dicks--to say nothing

133

of Lacy--were available through French. French encouraged other publishers (Lee & Shepard, Baker) to retail his stock by allowing them to send out his catalogs over their own imprints.

Until the twentieth century French specialized in reprints; few first editions of plays important to the professional theatre came from his office. Dion Boucicault (1820-1890) and John Brougham (1810-1880) were the only playwrights whose output he attempted to collect in print. Nonetheless, the 1856 American copyright law with its then practically unenforceable performance rights clause brought him several plays which remain historically important and which he printed for the first time: Dion Boucicault's The Poor of New York and Oliver Bunce's Love in '76 (1857); George L. Aiken's Uncle Tom's Cabin and Benjamin A. Baker's A Glance at New York (1858?); Thomas Dunn English's The Mormons and Clifton W. Tayleure's Horseshoe Robinson (1858).

French's role in supplying texts to the professional theatre should not be minimized, but it is his part in encouraging amateur dramatics that makes him important in the history of popular publishing: his published catalogs of pamphlets and paraphernalia reflect a popular American pastime that penetrated all classes in both city and country in the second half of the nineteenth century. Amateur theatricals, already established in the home parlor, made their way to sanitary fairs, schools, and even church parlors while amateur dramatic clubs--the semiprofessionals--flourished. French supplied how-to-do-it books, makeup, wigs, lights, costume and set designs, and even sets, in addition to the plays themselves.

French's principal series, priced 12 1/2 cents until 1864, when they went up to 15 cents, were French's Standard Drama in 425 numbers and French's Minor Drama in 403 numbers. The former consisted of principal vehicles or featured plays, while the latter were afterpieces or short comic works. There were also Shadow Pantomimes, The Series of Charade Plays, Home Plays for Ladies, French's Amateur Operas, Booth's Series of Acting Plays, Henry Irving's Series of Acting Plays,

134

French's Parlor Comedies, and The Ethiopian Dramas
(eighty-six skits from the minstrel stage).

Tony Denier's manual is typical of its class:
The Amateur's Hand-Book and Guide to Home or Drawing
Room Theatricals . . . To which is added how to "get up"
theatricals in a country house. Together with rules,
by-laws, selected scenes, plays, and everything useful
for the formation of amateur societies [^C1866]. Related works offered by French include C. W. Smith's The
Art of Acting [186-], L. T. Rede's The Guide to the
Stage (1861), and Prof. J. E. Frobisher's Acting and
Oratory (1879) and A System of . . . Voice and Action
(1867). Makeup offered in French's priced catalogs included makeup boxes and books, prepared burnt cork,
blue, carmine, mascara or water cosmetique, patches,
mongolian, spirit gum, and greasepaints. Over fifty
different theatrical and fancy costume wigs were offered,
together with tableaux lights, colored fire in bulk, and
magnesium tableaux lights.

French purveyed French's Costumes. Dramatic, National and Historical, a collection of two hundred colored plates assembled originally by Lacy in the 1860s.
His Scenes for Amateurs, 16 1/2 by 12 1/2 inches, 15
cents plain or 30 cents colored, were meant to guide the
painting of the real thing, while his scenery, 8 by 15
feet or 20 by 11 1/2 feet, was the real thing: garden,
wood, drawing room, cottage interior, proscenium and
drop scene, and so on. No aspect of amateur dramatics
was omitted, not even the costumes. If you could not
make the ones you needed from French's Costumes you
could rent them from the agencies that advertised in
French's plays.

French published little that was not listed in his
catalogs. From March through December 1857 he carried
on a Frank Leslie magazine as The New York Journal of
Romance, General Literature, Science and Art; in 1855
he published Max Maretzek's Crotchets and Quavers: or,
Revelations of an Opera Manager in America; and in 1860
he published Joseph N. Ireland's Fifty Years of a Play-
Goer's Journal: or, Annals of the New York Stage, from
A.D. 1798 to A.D. 1848. With biographical notices of
all the principal performers. By H.N.D.

Samuel French

Thomas Henry French died 1 December 1902, his wife and only child having predeceased him. The London and New York offices were sold separately. Under Thomas R. Edwards, and with editorial help from Barrett H. Clark, the New York office began to publish the principal contemporary plays; they collect royalties to this day on the basis established by Samuel French at the London office.

French was not the only American play publisher in his day, but he was the only one with such an extensive historical catalog. He achieved his commanding position through the purchase of the stock and printing plates of his competition, growth made possible by the widespread use in those days of electrotype printing plates. Those same plates allowed him to replenish his stock cheaply and quickly: once the plates were cast, reprints were virtually automatic. His dealings in performance rights kept him and his son close to the professional theatre, a fact reflected in the plays they published. While certain other publishers dealt in a lower grade of fare (Sunday school plays, drills, children's plays) and must be studied in order to complete the picture of amateur dramatics in nineteenth-century America and of the publishers who promoted it, French remains unrivalled as the dominant play publishing house.[1]

Roger E. Stoddard

Reference and Note

Roger E. Stoddard, "Notes on American Play Publishing, 1765-1865," Proceedings of the American Antiquarian Society, 81 (1971): 161-90.

[1] A collection of about 15,000 plays, given by M. A. Van Nostrand, president of Samuel French, Inc., is located in the Amherst College Library.

20 Gleason's Publishing Hall

Gleason's Publishing Hall (1845-1890), Boston publisher
of periodicals and novelettes, specialized in seafaring
tales, stories about the American Revolution, didactic
sketches, and stories set in exotic locales. The firm,
variously styled "Gleason's Publishing Hall" and "The
United States Publishing Company," published a half-
dozen periodicals and fewer than one hundred single
titles. It began in Boston at 1 1/2 Tremont Row; moved
to Court Street, at the corner of Tremont, in 1847; to
the Museum Building, 24 and 26 Tremont, in 1850; and to
100 Tremont Street, at the corner of Bromfield, in 1852.
After Frederick Gleason's "retirement" in 1854, it returned to 100 Tremont, where its former associate,
Maturin Murray Ballou, had kept shop in the interim.
Later the Gleason offices were variously listed as on
Washington Street and at 40 or 22 Summer Street.
     Major Authors: Horatio Alger, Jr., Maturin
Murray Ballou, Sylvanus Cobb, Jr., A. J. Duganne,
J. H. Ingraham, Justin Jones, E. Z. C. Judson, Edgar
Allan Poe, Ben Perley Poore, Mrs. Lydia H. Sigourney,
Ann S. Stephens.
     Frederick Gleason was born circa 1816 and died
6 November 1896. His business ventures in Boston began
in the early 1840s, when he first appears in the city
directories as the proprietor of a printing and publishing firm specializing in prints and chromos. In an article in Granite State Magazine (February 1907), George
Waldo Browne quotes Gleason on the subject of his entry
into the publishing of popular fiction: "As early as
1840 I conceived of the idea of giving at low prices
such reading matter as it seemed to me the average reader
would demand, and would appeal to the great majority.
Accordingly I entered into preparation with this purpose
in view, and in 1842 I launched my first venture from
the old Scollay building in Boston. It was a

137

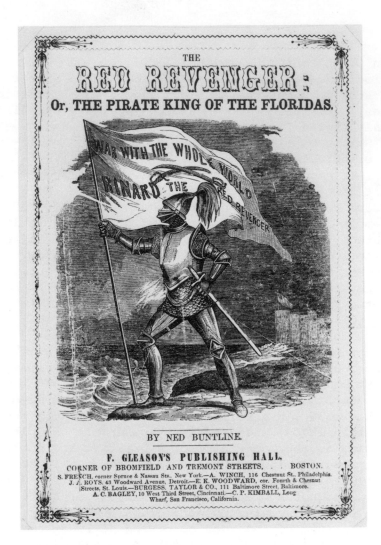

(Courtesy Edward T. LeBlanc, *Dime Novel Round-Up*)

paper-covered book that sold for 10¢, and contained a complete novelette with several minor articles for 'filling.' This was received with so much promise that I concluded to give even more reading for the money, and in the fall of the same year I began the publication of The Flag of Our Union, the first story and literary paper in the country." In fact, however, The Flag of Our Union was not founded until January 1846, and Gleason and his collaborator, Maturin Murray Ballou, cannot have begun work on their first novelettes much before 1844.

The ideas for the novelettes seem to have been jointly conceived by Ballou (then a twenty-five-year-old writer with some local editorial experience) and Gleason, but Ballou did the actual writing under his pseudonym "Lieutenant Murray." Gleason contributed his business acumen and his insight into the vast, untapped market for popular adventure stories. Ballou's first three efforts, Fanny Campbell; or the Female Pirate Captain, Red Rupert; or the American Buccaneer, and The Naval Officer; or the Pirate's Cave, published at a shilling per copy and distributed through a chain of booksellers in major American cities, were phenomenally successful. Fanny Campbell alone sold 80,000 copies within the first few months. Gleason's development of a national system of distribution, then an innovation, was as important as his and Ballou's knowledge of what the public would want.

Gleason hired a staff of writers, including J. H. Ingraham, Justin Jones [Harry Hazel], and Mrs. Ann Stephens, expanded the novelettes from 50 to 100 pages, increased the size from 8 1/2 by 5 inches to 9 1/2 by 6 inches, and began including a single illustration, a hand-colored woodcut. He also doubled the price, from one shilling (12 1/2 cents) to two. The stories themselves did not vary from Ballou's original design. They proceeded from "chilling deed" to "daring rescue," from "forlorn hope" to "joyous reunion," dealing out in the process violent retribution to all enemies of virtue and modesty. Despite the lurid details of vice and violence, the stories are most remarkable for the Calvinistic self-righteousness. Called "steam literature" because they were printed on the new rotary steam presses, these

139

"subliterary stories of adventure deliberately concocted for a mass audience," to use literary critic Henry Nash Smith's apt definition, were meant to flatter, not criticize, an American public that believed in its own superior common virtues: hard work, honesty, bravery, social democracy, and patriotism.

The first issue of The Flag of Our Union, a weekly family paper designed to cash in on the same mass audience that had made Gleason's novelettes so profitable, appeared 24 January 1846. Primarily devoted to sensational fiction, the Flag contained a serialized novelette, a half-dozen shorter stories and didactic sketches, a few sentimental poems, an editorial miscellany and a few columns of news clippings. Gleason's most important boast about the Flag was its red-blooded Americanism. His authors, he never tired of announcing, were Americans; he did not reprint material from British magazines. He preferred American heroes and heroines or, failing that, working-class protagonists in foreign countries who overcame aristocratic villains. (In disquieting fashion, however, the working-class hero, once his virtues have been accepted for their own sake, generally turns out to have had aristocratic blood all along.)

The Flag soon surpassed its few competitors among early story papers, increasing its circulation from a small initial printing to 40,000 copies by 1848. In its effort to find new contributors, it employed as a promotional device the "prize story." Gleason announced the first prize competition for new novelists in the 31 July 1847 issue-- a "GRAND SCHEME," in which $5,000 in prizes would be awarded to fifty successful competitors, $100.00 to each. Gleason added: "We do not offer prizes like some of our contemporaries, retaining the liberty of keeping all manuscripts and stories, awarding pay only to the premium one. We do not wish to publish anything in the Flag that we are not willing to pay for, and that liberally." Gleason's second prize competition, announced in February 1848, however, offered only a single $150.00 prize, specifying that the successful tale was to be publishable as a 100-page novelette. The winning story was announced as "Rosalette; or the Flower Girl of

Paris" by "Lieutenant Murray"--that is, by Ballou,
Gleason's own editor. Gleason finally created a legit-
imate stir in October of that year, making up for the
spuriousness of the February competition by offering a
first prize of $1,000, a second prize of $500.00, and
assurances of the Flag's impartiality. Gleason's call
for contributions sought to define his sort of fiction:
"We wish for such contributions as shall be strictly
moral in their tone, highly interesting in their plot,
replete throughout with incident, well filled with exciting yet truthful description, and, in short, highly readable and entertaining. Domestic stories, so-called, are
not exactly of the class we desire; but tales--of the sea
and land--of the stirring times of the revolution--or of
dates still farther back, are more in accordance with
our wishes."

Gleason's campaign to discover new authors was
certainly successful. In 1847 E. Z. C. Judson [Ned
Buntline] began his long and somewhat controversial
career with a string of successful serials in the Flag,
among them "The King of the Sea; a Tale of the Fearless
and Free," "The Black Avenger of the Spanish Main; or
the Fiend of Blood," "The Volunteer; or the Maid of
Monterey," and "The Red Revenger; or the Pirate King of
the Floridas." He is reputed, later in his career, to
have completed a 600-page book in sixty-two hours, and
on another occasion to have earned $12,500 in six weeks
of marathon writing.

In 1850 Sylvanus Cobb, Jr., of Norway, Maine, who
was to become the mainstay both of the Flag and of
Gleason's Pictorial Drawing Room Companion, contributed
his first popular serial at the age of twenty-five. Like
Ballou the son of a Universalist preacher, Cobb had tried
to sell a story to the Olive Branch, a sectarian paper,
and he had already written for religious and temperance
journals, although only for nominal fees. Gleason, with
very little on which to make a judgment, let Cobb try a
serial. He was not disappointed: not only was Cobb to
be even more productive than Judson, churning out dozens
of pieces each week under a half-dozen pseudonyms; but
he was perfectly willing to tailor his contributions to
Gleason's precise requirements, writing his fiction to

141

order around a specific setting, conflict, or even a specific engraving. Their most popular author, Cobb wrote
hundreds of stories and novelettes for Gleason and Ballou,
under such pseudonyms as "Austin C. Burdick" and "Dr. S.
Le Compton Smith," before he left Ballou for Robert
Bonner's New York Ledger in 1856.

Gleason's poets were widely known, although for the
most part he cannot be said to have discovered any of
them. Edgar Allan Poe, during the last few years of his
life, grudgingly accepted $5.00 per poem from Gleason,
who promptly trumpeted him as "our regular contributor."
At this rate, several other well-known poets joined Poe
in the pages of the Flag, among them Mrs. Frances
Sargent Osgood, Park Benjamin, Mrs. Lydia H. Sigourney,
and Mrs. Ann Stephens.

By 1851 Gleason's Publishing Hall was established
as the clear leader in its field, inspiring a whole flock
of moderately successful imitators and one deadly rival,
Robert Bonner's New York Ledger (which Bonner purchased
that same year). Browne later quoted Gleason's own esti-
mate of his success with the Flag: "Inside of ten years
[sic] I had a circulation of nearly 100,000 and an income of $25,000 from it."

Gleason and Ballou shared managerial duties--both
were fond of extended trips abroad--and two newcomers
became more and more important in the firm. The first,
Newton Talbot, began in 1850 as a cashier and stayed on
to become business manager after Gleason left. The second, a young Englishman, Henry Carter ("Frank Leslie"),
who had worked on the Illustrated London News, conceived
with Ballou the idea of founding America's first major
illustrated weekly, Gleason's Pictorial Drawing Room Companion. Both new staff members were to become important
in nineteenth-century popular publishing, Talbot as a
founder of the firm of Elliott, Thomes & Talbot, which
succeeded Gleason's firm as a leader in the story paper
and novelette field after 1863, and Carter, who adopted
the name Frank Leslie in 1853, as one of America's most
successful publishers of illustrated periodicals.

The Pictorial too was an almost immediate success.
According to Granite State Magazine (February 1907),
Gleason later commented: ". . . I originated the idea

142

of publishing an illustrated paper of from sixteen to
twenty-four pages weekly, the descriptive matter to be
accompanied by the best woodcuts and engravings to be
obtained. There was no publication of this kind in the
country at that time. . . . When I sold out in 1854 I
had an actual circulation of 110,000 copies weekly."
He had started with an edition of only 5,000 copies, but
soon was printing almost 50,000; and circulation continued to grow in 1852 in spite of the fact that the price
per year's subscription was raised from $3.00 to $4.00.
By the time he sold the paper to Ballou, just three
years after its founding, the Pictorial was earning
Gleason as much as the Flag, providing him with a personal income of $50,000.

By 1854, Gleason's last year with his original
publishing house, the story-paper field had shifted
somewhat, away from Ballou's original nautical and revolutionary stories and toward border tales or western
adventures. Sentimental fiction was also becoming more
important, as T. S. Arthur (who later wrote Ten Nights
in a Bar-Room, a best-selling temperance novel) and
Horatio Alger, Jr., joined Cobb as contributors of moral-
istic stories and sketches for Gleason's two weeklies.
Bonner's New York Ledger, adopting Gleason's promotional
methods, began to pose a serious threat to the Flag. And
Frank Leslie's departure to work for Barnum and Beach's
Illustrated News, a rival paper in New York, was an un-
healthy sign for the Pictorial. But both periodicals
were still steaming ahead, churning up admirable profits
for their proprietors. Gleason's sale of his firm came
quickly, unexpectedly, and in spite of his unquestion-
able success: Ballou suddenly announced that he wished
to buy Gleason out, threatening in the process to publish
rivals to the Flag and the Pictorial. Gleason quickly
capitulated, accepting an unspecified sum of money and
leaving immediately for an extensive European tour. In
a final issue under his proprietorship, Gleason declared
that he had "realized an ample competency" and now wished
to "retire from business altogether," at about the age of
thirty-five. Ballou, meanwhile, settled into the company's offices at 100 Tremont Street to preside over
both periodicals' later declining fortunes.

Gleason's retirement did not last long, nor did his savings. He reestablished himself at 100 Tremont Street, Boston, began selling chromos at 15 cents each, and published a succession of new story papers and illustrated weeklies with varying degrees of success. The first of these, Gleason's Line of Battle Ship, begun in November 1858, probably constituted Gleason's most ambitious attempt to regain his former predominance. Unfortunately, his literature no longer equaled his illustrations and competition in the field had become fierce. Ballou was struggling to keep the Pictorial afloat in the face of competition from Bonner's Ledger, Street's New York Weekly, Harper's Weekly, and Frank Leslie's Illustrated. In company with Ballou's Pictorial, Gleason's Line of Battle Ship went under in 1858, fourteen months after its founding.

Gleason continued with other periodicals over the next thirty years: Gleason's Literary Companion, founded in 1860, lasted ten years under his proprietorship, making a major splash only once, in 1863, when it came out with eight different colors on its front page. The magazine finally suspended in 1870. It was followed by Gleason's Monthly Companion (1872–1887) and Gleason's Home Circle (1871–1890). The latter, an eight-page illustrated folio that sold for $2.00 a year (5 cents a copy), was a modest weekly, imitative of the story papers but founded primarily to capitalize on Gleason's business in chromos, which it frequently advertised. The Monthly Companion, a crudely illustrated quarto on poor paper, borrowed broadly from the editorial format of magazines like Scribner's while retaining many features from the story papers, including their spurious news clippings and cant wisdom. When Gleason finally did retire, after 1890, it was not to "a life of leisure and ease," but to ill-fortune and adversity, spending his last years in complete obscurity at Boston's Home for Aged Men.

The Gleason firm was an important innovator and pioneer, developing the story paper as a network for the mass distribution of popular fiction. It made available to hosts of readers novelettes and serials, especially narratives of sensationalistic character. It led to the work of Beadle, Leslie, and the Harpers, and helped create the demand for popular fiction which it also supplied.

Peter Benson

References

George Waldo Browne, "Pioneers of Popular Literature," Granite State Magazine, 3 (February 1907): 51-55; and 3 (March 1907): 111-13.

Henry Nash Smith, Virgin Land (Cambridge: Harvard University Press, 1950).

Mary Noel, Villains Galore . . . The Heyday of the Popular Story Weekly (New York: Macmillan Co., 1954).

Madeleine B. Stern, Imprints on History: Book Publishers and American Frontiers (Bloomington: Indiana University Press, 1956; reprinted, New York: AMS Press, 1975).

Frank Luther Mott, A History of American Magazines, Vol. 2 (Cambridge: Harvard University Press, 1957).

The Counting-Room of the Harper Establishment.
(From *Imprints on History* by Madeleine B. Stern)

21 An Introductory Review of Harper Highlights

In the year 1817 four Harper brothers migrated from eastern Long Island (where they were engaged in farming) to New York City, establishing there a small printing office, J. & J. Harper. The brothers were James, twenty-one, John, twenty, Wesley, seventeen, and Fletcher, eleven.

The first Harper book was an English translation of Seneca's Morals, produced for bookseller Evert Duyckinck. The small printing establishment was located at the corner of Front and Dover Streets.

The Harpers soon went into publishing in their own right and by 1830 were producing a title a week; soon they started to issue series of books, one of which was called the Boy's and Girl's Library. The most famous title in this series was The Swiss Family Robinson. In 1830 J. & J. Harper published Harper's Family Library, consisting of 187 volumes, mostly by British authors. They also brought out a large number of popular books at low prices.

The year 1833 was a memorable one in Harper history, the year that the name of the firm was changed from J. & J. Harper to Harper & Brothers. That same year a newly invented steam press was installed, replacing a horse-powered press. (The horse that operated the press was honorably retired to the Harper farm on Long Island. It had worked the press by walking steadily in a circular path; alone in the pasture, the horse betook himself to a tree and walked steadily around it from 7 a.m. to 6 p.m., with an hour out for lunch--the same routine he had followed for years in New York.)

Two Years Before the Mast by Richard Henry Dana, Jr. and Daniel Deronda by George Eliot appeared under the Harper imprint in 1840. At that time Harper & Brothers was putting out clothbound novels that retailed at $1.00 or $2.00.

147

Harper Highlights

Two fires occurred at Harper in the middle of the nineteenth century. One, in 1842, was set by a burglar employed by a rival publisher who sent him to steal some Harper printing plates. The other in 1853--a far more serious one--destroyed the Harper offices and cost the brothers $1. million, since the building was only partially covered by insurance. Following this disaster, the Harper brothers built for the firm a new fireproof building fronting on Franklin Square, close to the Brooklyn Bridge. The large new building was the first iron business edifice in New York and, at the time, was considered an exciting structure. Visitors from abroad would go to Franklin Square in order to view this "modern" wonder, as they do today to visit the World Trade Center.

Not long after the fire in 1853, Harper & Brothers became the largest publisher in the world. The New York Times wrote, "For the last few years Harper & Brothers have published, on the average 25 volumes a minute for 10 hours a day." Harpers pioneered in the production of low-priced books. The competition was severe and in 1877 American publishers were cutting each others' throats by bringing out paperbacks at lower and lower prices; books in Harper's Franklin Square Library (1878) retailed at 10 cents apiece.

In the 1870s American publishers imported from England sheets of works by such famous authors as Charles Dickens, William Makepeace Thackeray, and George Eliot. For the privilege of obtaining advance sheets Harper & Brothers paid Dickens sums ranging from £250 to £1,250. (Before the United States joined the International Copyright Union, such imported books appeared at low prices because Harper and its competitors usually paid no royalties.)

In 1850 Fletcher Harper started Harper's Magazine and, seven years later, Harper's Weekly under the editorship of George William Curtis. Harper's Weekly was successful, featuring Thomas Nast's famous cartoons attacking New York's corrupt Tweed political ring. The Weekly covered the Civil War pictorially with great effectiveness; Winslow Homer was one of its principal illustrators. In 1863 Charles Parsons was taken on as manager of Harper's

148

art department and he promoted such artists as Edwin A. Abbey, C. S. Reinhart, A. B. Frost, Charles Dana Gibson, and Howard Pyle.

Succeeding Fletcher Harper as the firm's major editor was Joseph W. Harper, Jr., the first Harper to be a college graduate. He was responsible for General Lew Wallace's novel, Ben Hur, with sales seven years after its publication amounting to more than 230,000 copies. Henry James appeared on the Harper list, as well as William Dean Howells and Mark Twain.

During the 1890s deaths among the Harper partners and subsequent withdrawals of capital coincided with the decline of the Weekly, causing the dissolution of the seventy-nine-year-old Harper family partnership. This occurred in spite of the acquisition of a number of new authors, including A. Conan Doyle, Richard Harding Davis, and John Kendrick Bangs. With the help of J. Pierpont Morgan the firm was reorganized and Colonel George B. Harvey became president; his regime lasted from 1900 to 1915.

In the nineteenth century Harper & Brothers published every type of cloth and paperback book. Among its popular authors were Wilkie Collins and Herman Melville. Famous books published by the firm included King Solomon's Mines by H. Rider Haggard, John Halifax, Gentleman by Dinah Maria Mulock, The Virginian by Owen Wister, Toby Tyler by James Otis, Lorna Doone by R. D. Blackmore, Trilby by George du Maurier, The Boy Traveller Stories, a series by Thomas W. Knox, and books for boys by W. O. Stoddard.

Cass Canfield

References

Eugene Exman, The Brothers Harper, 1817-53 (New York: Harper & Row, 1965).

Harper Highlights

Charles A. Madison, <u>Book Publishing in America</u> (New York: McGraw-Hill Book Co., 1966).

Eugene Exman, <u>The House of Harper, 150 Years of Publishing</u> (New York: Harper & Row, 1967).

22 Harper & Bros.

Harper & Bros. (1817-   ), for years the largest publishing house in the United States, was also important
to the field of mass market reading. The firm was established as J. & J. Harper, Printers, by James and John
Harper at the corner of Dover and Front streets, New York,
in 1817. On 5 August of that year the firm's first book
was delivered to the bookseller who published it. During
the following eight years, as its own publishing business
slowly prospered, the firm moved to Fulton Street near
Broadway, to 230 Pearl Street, and in 1825 to 81-82
Cliff Street. The younger brothers, Wesley and Fletcher,
became partners in 1823 and 1825, and in October 1833 the
firm's name was changed to Harper & Bros., as it was to
remain until the merger with Row, Peterson & Company on
30 April 1962 that created Harper & Row Publishers, Inc.
     When fire destroyed everything except a few papers
and the plates that were stored in a different location
on 10 December 1853, the Harpers took temporary quarters
at 82 Beekman Street while constructing two fireproof
buildings in Franklin Square. These buildings, occupied
in the summer of 1855, served the firm for about seventy
years.
     Harper's was innovative in its use of new technol-
ogy--it was one of the first to use stereotyping, and
electrotyping was perfected by one of its artists for an
edition of the Bible--and in its marketing. In order to
respond to nineteenth-century economic depressions and
the competition of cheap publications, the firm reoffered
its backlist in inexpensive style and published the first
Library of Select Novels as early as May 1831 in a 50-
cent twelvemo format. To meet the competition of
Donnelley and Munro in 1877, this price was reduced to
25 cents. The Franklin Square Library was begun in 1878.
Under the editorial guidance of Fletcher Harper, the firm
always aimed at providing good reading at affordable

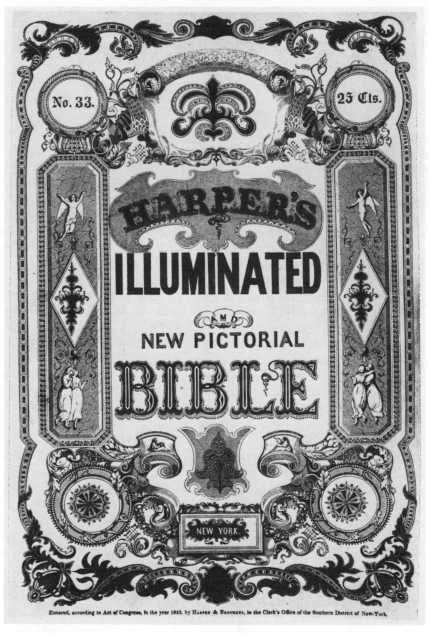

Harper's Illuminated and New Pictorial Bible, No. 33. Harper Bros., 1843-1846. 54 parts, folio, engraved paper wrappers and more than 1600 engravings.
(Arents Collection, The New York Public Library; Astor, Lenox and Tilden Foundations)

prices, and several periodicals were established for that purpose: Harper's New Monthly Magazine (1850-   ), Harper's Weekly (1857-1916), Harper's Bazar (1867-1913), and Harper's Young People (1879-1899).

Major Popular Authors: Rex Beach, Robert W. Chambers, Zane Gray, Booth Tarkington, Mark Twain.

James Harper was born in 1795 at Newtown, Long Island, the son of a farmer, and died on 27 March 1869. He served an apprenticeship as a printer 1816-1817. He supervised the firm's manufacturing activities until his death. His popularity and civic activity led to his being elected mayor of New York for one term in 1844.

John Harper, two years younger, was born on 11 January 1797 and died 22 April 1875. Like all four of the original Harper brothers, he served an apprenticeship as a printer, but as the firm grew his area of responsibility became record-keeping and finances.

Wesley Harper, who managed the composing room and supervised proofreading, was responsible for most of the correspondence. He was born in 1801 and died on 14 February 1870. His son, Joseph Wesley, Jr., called "Joe Brooklyn," was the major force in the second-generation management of the house.

Fletcher Harper served as editor from the time he joined the firm in 1825 until his retirement in 1875. His was the personality, as manager of publishing activities, that shaped both books and periodicals. He died on 29 May 1877 at the age of seventy.

One major factor in nineteenth-century publishing was the lack of an international copyright law. As a result, many American publishers were able to publish and sell books very cheaply; consequently, competition was keen. After the ships arrived carrying proof of the newest English fiction, the first publisher to get the books on the street made the sales. Harper & Bros. came out well in this competition because its plant was large and efficient enough to produce books rapidly. In 1826 Harpers was the largest printing house in the city, by 1830 the largest in the United States, and in 1853 the largest in the world.

About 1830 the house was publishing reprints of its stock for about $1.00, down from earlier prices of

$1.50 to $1.75. As early as 1843, however, Harper produced an inexpensive series of novels by English authors in brown wrappers for as little as 25 cents to meet competition from such sources as the story papers. The Library of Select Novels, first published in May 1831, antedated by four decades the "library" period of cheap book production. By 1885, 615 volumes had been published in that series, selling for approximately 20 cents.

Perhaps the most famous of the cheap series was the Franklin Square Library, begun in the summer of 1878. Most of the books for this series were taken from the firm's own backlist. By this time Harper's had established ties with many English writers and was paying for advance sheets and permission to publish American editions. As a consequence, royalties continued to be paid on the books that went into the Franklin Square Library. The books in this series were produced once or twice per week in early 1879 in answer to cheap books flowing in from England and Canada and emerging from American presses.

Some of the inexpensive books published in 1871 included four series that sold for 75 cents: the Harper's Boy's and Girl's Library, Harper's Classical Library, Harper's Family Library (the first low-priced nonfiction library, it was begun in 1830, priced at 50 cents and republished in wrappers in 1843 at 25 cents), and Harper's Fireside Library. Later the nonfiction Handy Series (1885) selling for 25 cents was added, as were the Library of American Novels and the English Men of Letters series. In 1839 Harper & Bros. published the School District Library, the first instance of school board adoption in the United States. This series was in addition to other textbooks that were an important factor in the company's business until the 1890s.

The Adams Bible (1844) is a good example of the philosophy and method of operation of this publishing house created by four God-fearing, upright men. Not only was it a sound text that would serve the public, its merchandising and production were in keeping with the innovative practices of the firm. The Bible was copiously illustrated with wood engravings by Joseph A. Adams, who had developed an electroplating process to support and preserve the blocks in the press. Special presses were designed and purchased to produce the Bible with these fine illustrations. It was published (with flourishes of advertising in advance) in 54 numbers, of some 28 pages on good paper, hand-sewn and wrapped in two-color covers in an edition of 50,000. Each number sold for 25 cents. A 25,000-copy edition, bound in hand-tooled gilt morocco was published in 1846. According to Exman in The House of Harper, this was the "first richly illustrated book" and the first effort at fine bookmaking in the United States. Certainly it demonstrates Harper & Bros.' commitment to quality and the best technology of the period, innovative and competitive merchandising, and constant concern that its products be affordable.

These commitments are evident not only in the firm's general list, but in the series and libraries it published both before and during the high tide of cheap book production in the United States, in an effort to capture a mass market.

Anna Lou Ashby

References

Publishers Weekly, 15 (22 March 1879): 345.

Raymond H. Shove, Cheap Book Production in the United States, 1870 to 1891 (Urbana: University of Illinois Library, 1937).

Hellmut Lehmann-Haupt, The Book in America (New York: R. R. Bowker Company, 1951).

Frank Luther Mott, A History of American Magazines, Vol. 2 (Cambridge: Belknap Press of Harvard University Press, 1957).

Frank L. Schick, The Paperbound Book in America: The History of Paperbacks and their European Background (New York: R. R. Bowker Company, 1958).

155

Harper & Bros.

Eugene Exman, The Brothers Harper, 1817-53 (New York: Harper & Row, 1965).

Eugene Exman, The House of Harper, 150 Years of Publishing (New York: Harper & Row, 1967).

John Tebbel, The American Magazine: A Compact History (New York: Hawthorne Books, 1969).

23 Henry Holt and Company

Henry Holt and Company (1873-1959), thereafter Holt, Rinehart & Winston (1959-   ), published a wide variety of trade books including novels by American, British and foreign authors, cheap reprints of classic authors and popular writers, and a classic series of college and science texts in the nineteenth century under the personal supervision of Henry Holt. A "quality" house, it published the Leisure Hour Series, which offered well-written novels and literary classics at $1.25. Many of the titles of this series were later incorporated in the Leisure Moment Series and sold at 30 cents in competition with the "cheap book" publishers. Also noteworthy was the American Science Series.

Frederick Leypoldt had established a publishing business in 1864 at 646 Broadway, New York. Henry Holt joined that firm, now known as Leypoldt and Holt, on 1 January 1866 when it moved to 451 Broome Street at the corner of Mercer. In 1870 the firm, now at 646 Broadway, moved to 25 Bond Street. Ralph O. Williams, a former college classmate of Holt's, joined the firm, which was renamed Leypoldt, Holt and Williams. In 1871 Leypoldt sold his equity to the remaining partners, the company thereafter being called Holt and Williams. When Williams withdrew in 1873 the firm became known as Henry Holt and Company. The growth of the company necessitated a move in 1879 to 12 East 23rd Street, in 1882 to 29 West 23rd, and in 1908 to 34 West 33rd.

Major Authors to 1901: Henry Adams, John Buchan, John Dewey, John Fiske, Paul Leicester Ford, Thomas Hardy, Anthony Hope, William James, Jerome K. Jerome, Fanny Kemble, Henry S. Maine, John Stuart Mill, Lewis H. Morgan, Simon Newcomb, William G. Sumner, John Addington Symonds, H. A. Taine, E. L. Voynich, H. G. Wells.

Major Series: Leisure Hour Series, Leisure Moment Series, American Science Series.

157

(Courtesy Edward T. LeBlanc, *Dime Novel Round-Up*)

Henry Holt and Company

Frederick Leypoldt was born in Stuttgart, Germany, in 1835 and died in 1884. He came to America in 1854. His first position was with F. W. Christern, and five years later he opened a bookshop in Philadelphia. During the Civil War he began publishing translations of foreign books, some of which he translated himself. He wrote under the thinly disguised pseudonym "L. Pylodet." In 1864 he established a publishing business at 646 Broadway, New York. Henry Holt brought his translation of Edmond About's The Man With the Broken Ear in November 1865 to Leypoldt for publication. The manuscript was not accepted but the result of the contact was Holt's joining Leypoldt to establish the firm of Leypoldt and Holt. Holt's investment was $6,000.

Leypoldt's interest turned toward the bibliographical and functional aspects of publishing. In 1868 he converted the firm's promotional circular into the monthly Literary Bulletin and Trade Circular, which included a record of the publication of American and foreign books. His ambition to make it a general periodical for the industry was achieved when in January 1872 he purchased George F. Childs' American Literary Gazette and Publishers' Circular and combined it with his own publication to form Publishers' Weekly. Leypoldt, who had previously sold his share of the partnership to Holt and moved to separate quarters, carried on the publication until his death in 1884, whereupon his widow continued in charge of the publication for another thirty years.

Ralph Olmstead Williams was born in Palmyra, New York, on 12 May 1838 and died in 1908. Upon graduation from Yale in 1861 he joined the Seventh Delaware Volunteers as a private and served until 1864. He was admitted to the New York bar the following year. After the end of his partnership in Leypoldt, Holt and Williams, and later in Holt and Williams (1871 to 1873) he devoted himself to literary work as a lexicographer, teacher, and librarian. He died 17 July 1908 in New Haven, Connecticut.

Shortly before Holt joined Leypoldt, Joseph Vogelius had come into the firm. He was to remain with Henry Holt and Company as its leading figure, other than

159

Holt himself, until his retirement in 1919, a period of fifty-five years. Henry's brother Charles joined the company upon graduation from the Yale Scientific School but did not play a major role. Edward N. Bristol joined the firm in 1882 and was put in charge of the important textbook division. The business was incorporated in 1903 with Henry Holt as president, his son Roland, who had entered the firm in 1890, as vice-president, Vogelius as treasurer, and Bristol as secretary. In 1904 Donald Harcourt joined the firm, and brought in Donald Brace. Both left in June 1919 to establish Harcourt, Brace and Company. The company was reorganized in November 1928 with E. N. Bristol as majority stockholder. Both Henry's sons resigned. The firm retained the name Henry Holt and Company until it acquired Rinehart and Company and John C. Winston and Company in 1959, when its name was changed to Holt, Rinehart and Winston.

Henry Holt, son of Dan and Ann Eve (Siebold) Holt, was born in Baltimore, Maryland, on 3 January 1840 and died in 1926. He graduated from Yale in 1862 and the Columbia University Law School in 1864. While at Yale he had been impressed by a remark by the librarian, Professor Daniel C. Gilman: "If you find on a book the imprint of Ticknor and Fields it is probably a good book." A clerk of George Palmer Putnam, a former classmate at Yale, remembering the inclination toward publishing that this remark had aroused in Holt, introduced him in 1863 to Putnam, who had just suffered the loss of a partner. Putnam proposed that Holt share an investment with him in an elaborately illustrated edition of Washington Irving's Sketch Book. Holt also bought a third interest in The Rebellion Record, edited by Frank Moore. During his spare time he translated the About novel, which led to his association with Leypoldt. Holt achieved modest distinction as an author in addition to his work as publisher with a number of articles on copyright for The Forum both before and after the passage of the 1891 copyright law, two novels, Calmire--Man and Nature (1892) and Sturmsee--Man and Man (1895), Talks on Civics (1901), On the Cosmic Relations (1914), and Garrulities of an Octogenarian (1923). Henry Holt was married in 1863 to Mary Florence West, who died in 1879.

160

His son of this marriage, Roland, was born on 18 December 1867. Holt married Florence Tabor in 1886. His son of this marriage, Elliot, joined the firm on his return from World War I.

Henry Holt's role in his firm was multifaceted, involving acquisitions, supervision of production and sales, and editing. For his American Science Series, for example, he engaged in lengthy editorial correspondence with authors, and when the popular novelist Anthony Hope sent Holt the first draft of what was to be a best-seller, Rupert of Hentzau (1898), Holt suggested that sales would be twice or three times greater if Hope changed the ending so that "they lived happily ever after." After 1900 Holt spent more and more time on his own writing and in magazine editing. From 1890 to 1899 he was the publisher of The Educational Review, with Nicholas Murray Butler as editor. The first issue of The Unpopular Review, under Holt's personal supervision, appeared December 1913, its name changed in 1919 to The Unpartizan Review. Holt died on 13 February 1926 at the age of eighty-six.

Leypoldt and Holt's first book was Eichendorff's Memoirs of a Good-For-Nothing. It was followed by books by Théophile Gautier, George Sand, Turgenev, Heine, Schiller, and uniform editions of Thackeray and Kingsley. Despite the prestige of the authors, the firm barely kept alive because these publications did not prove profitable. The concern's imports and its foreign language textbooks enabled it to survive. Serving as sales agents for the Tauchnitz Collection of British authors was also profitable. When Hippolyte Taine's History of English Literature appeared in England in translation, Holt was asked in 1871 about the possibility of publishing it in the United States. Although dubious, he undertook publication in two volumes. Approximately 7,000 sets were sold in three years at considerable profit. Subsequent editions continued to sell well into the end of the century. Taine, happy to receive royalties on a book he could not copyright, royalties four times his return from the British edition, decided to have Holt publish his French Revolution. In 1873 Holt published his A Tour Through the Pyrenees, illustrated by Gustave

Doré, as a gift book for the Christmas trade, priced at $10.00 a copy. In 1875 Holt brought out a handsome, uniform edition of Taine's writings in twelve volumes.

The publication of Taine's work illustrates the fulfillment of a major Holt objective: to publish trade editions of significant and worthwhile books. Another example was the publication of John Stuart Mill's Autobiography, even though Mill's other works, when published by others, had poor sales. An admirer of Mill, Holt sought to publish a uniform edition of his works and offered to buy the plates of Mill's other works from various publishers. The result was a thirteen-volume edition of the nontechnical works.

In 1876 Holt, in common with other publishers of the day, attempted to sell books by subscription. Agents were offered 40 percent of the selling price. The first such publication, An Abridgement of the Debates of Congress for 1874-5, was followed by Goodholme's Domestic Cyclopedia: A Family Record and a two-volume History of Yule. Charles Holt actively promoted the sale of the Cyclopedia, offering aggressive agents as much as 55 percent, but none of the subscription books sold well enough to encourage Holt to continue this aspect of the business.

A major achievement of the firm, and one that related it to publishing for mass enjoyment, was the publication of the Leisure Hour Series. Early in his career Holt conceived the idea of publishing a series of novels, attractive in appearance, at relatively low prices. After a number of experiments with design, in 1872 he began the publication of Turgenev's Smoke and Fathers and Sons, About's The Man With the Broken Ear, the book Holt had translated and that had been refused for publication by Leypoldt (perhaps it was the spirit of whimsy that led Holt to dedicate it to Leypoldt), and three other novels in sixteenmo. The original $1.00 price was soon raised to $1.25. In 1877, faced with the competition of cheap paperbacks, the price was reduced to $1.00. On the flyleaf of each volume appeared the words "A collection of Works whose character is light and entertaining, though not trivial. While they are handy for the pocket or the satchel, they are not, either in contents

162

or appearance, unworthy of a place on library shelves."
With the reduction in price Publishers' Weekly (3 October
1877) commented, "How very cheap this is the readers of
these pleasantly familiar books, now found on everybody's
table, may reckon for themselves: anybody who wants more
for his money simply can't get it. The books run as high
as 500 close pages, 'Clarissa Harlow', for instance,
reaching 515, while the average number of pages is about
340 . . . Of the clever dress and handy shape of these
books it is late in the day to speak."

The series was superior in content and format to
comparable series by other publishers. Madison quotes
the New York Tribune of June 1873 as expressing the hope
that the series was profitable. "The approval of their
own conscience may be enough for these meritorious publishers, but good pecuniary returns for an enterprise so
praiseworthy would exercise a wholesome moral influence
upon the book trade generally. They have not printed an
objectionable book as yet, and not one which was not
worth reading." Four years later, on 3 March 1877, the
Tribune called the series "one of the most popular series
in the higher class of cheap literature." The most popular book, Mrs. Alexander's Wooing O'T, reached a sale of
20,000. Turgenev's novels sold only 2,500 copies upon
publication and thereafter at the rate of 1,000 per year.
Far From the Madding Crowd and A Pair of Blue Eyes by
Thomas Hardy reached a sale of between 7,000 and 8,000
copies. By 1880 over one hundred volumes had been published and by 1888 there were over two hundred titles
in the series.

Among the seventy titles in the series in 1876,
there were two by About, four novels by Mrs. Alexander,
six by Berthold Auerbach, one by Bjornstjerne Bjornson,
two by Gustave Freitag, five by Thomas Hardy, six by
Mrs. C. Jenkin, six by Ivan Turgenev, and five by
Theodore Winthrop. Winthrop, the only American in the
series, had a sale of 1,000 to 1,200 copies per novel
each year. Seven volumes of Shakespeare's plays and the
novels of Robert Louis Stevenson were published in later
years. Translations of French, German, Russian, and
Scandinavian literature took second place to English
novels.

Henry Holt and Company

In the absence of international copyright laws, American publishers felt free to produce pirated editions of European works. Among leading houses such as Appleton, Harper, Lippincott, Putnam, and Scribner, a "courtesy of the trade" principle enabled a publisher who expressed an interest in a foreign book, a copy of which he possessed, to have priority and exclusivity with publication. Holt had occasion to ask his fellow publishers to desist from publishing a work for which he claimed prior commitment. In addition, the publisher had first call upon the subsequent works of an author he had previously published. To illustrate, in February 1873, according to Madison, Holt asked Harper to desist from publishing Hardy's A Pair of Blue Eyes because Holt was then publishing his Under the Greenwood Tree and felt he should have the opportunity, if he so chose, to publish the former. Harper agreed. When in 1874 James R. Osgood started to publish Far From the Madding Crowd, Holt, realizing that Osgood was unaware of Holt's prior claim, volunteered to assume the amount already spent on plates. Osgood refrained from publication and an amicable arrangement was made.

Although there was no legal obligation to pay foreign authors royalties, leading publishers did pay the usual 10 percent to popular English novelists. Thus Holt paid Hardy for the ten novels he published and helped Hardy place articles in American periodicals. In a trip to England in 1878, Holt visited him. Mrs. Alexander, the popular English novelist, also benefited from the ethical practices of Holt although in her case the royalties were sent to a third party with whom she had contractual arrangements.

The success of the Leisure Hour Series tempted Holt to compete with the pirates whose titles were available at 10 cents a copy. Using many of the titles of the Leisure Hour Series, the firm inaugurated a Leisure Moment Series in 1883 to sell at 20 to 35 cents a copy. The books were printed in clear type on good paper and were sewn with thread instead of being wired, as were most of the cheap publications. This series contained Hardy and Turgenev novels, Dostoievsky's Buried Alive, and several of Mrs. Alexander's works. A bookseller

commented in Publishers' Weekly (7 June 1884) that "the
admirably edited and well made Leisure Moment Series of
Messrs. Henry Holt and Co., is or could be, largely sold
by every intelligent bookseller in the country." Some
hundred titles were issued by 1888.

Less successful was the Leisure Season Series of
novels launched in 1886, published at 50 cents and bound
in flexible covers, advertised as "a new invention . . .
convenient for travelers . . . and at the same time better able than paper covered books to resist such wear."
Only five novels were issued before the series was abandoned. After the 1891 copyright law was passed, English
novels were not as readily available, and the Leisure
Hour and Leisure Moment Series were abandoned.

One of the firm's most creative acts was the launching of the American Science Series in 1874, at a time of
scientific ferment. Fourteen volumes were published,
representing the work of leading American scientists:
Astronomy by Simon Newcomb in collaboration with Edward J.
Holden; Political Economy by Francis A. Walker, president
of the Massachusetts Institute of Technology; The Human
Body by H. Newell Martin; and a landmark work, Psychology
by William James, first assigned in 1878 and completed in
two volumes in 1890. Since despite its critical acclaim
the work was too long and expensive for class use, in
1891 James prepared the Briefer Course, which sold 47,531
copies in the first ten years as compared with 8,115
copies in twelve years for the earlier work.

The next decade saw publication of Fanny Kemble's
Memoirs, John Stuart Mill's Dissertations and Discussions
in five volumes, H. G. Wells's The Time Machine, and
Anthony Hope's best-seller The Prisoner of Zenda. Although Holt took a less active part in the firm after
1900, he still exercised control.

During the nineteenth century, especially during
the 1870s and 1880s, Henry Holt and Company,[1] a firm
dedicated to publishing books of quality for light and
serious reading, attempted with considerable success in
its Leisure Hour Series to make the best of English and
European fiction available in fine format at reasonable
prices for a wide readership. Many of the same titles
were sold at cheaper prices in the Leisure Moment Series

Henry Holt and Company

in a vain effort to compete with pirates and cheap book
publishers. By paying royalties to foreign writers and
by advocacy of the International Copyright Law the firm
raised the ethical and professional level of publishers.
It managed to accomplish this at the same time that it
provided reading matter for mass consumption.

David S. Edelstein

References and Note

"The Bookmakers, Reminiscences and Contemporary Sketches
of American Publishers," New York Evening Post
(23 December 1875), facsimile reproduction in the
R. R. Bowker Library, New York.

Henry Holt, Garrulities of An Octogenarian (Boston and
New York: Houghton Mifflin Company, 1923).

Raymond H. Shove, Cheap Book Production in the United
States, 1870 to 1891 (Urbana: University of
Illinois Library, 1937).

Charles A. Madison, The Owl Among Colophons: Henry Holt
as Publisher and Editor (New York: Holt, Rinehart
and Winston, 1966).

[1]There is a Holt Archive at Princeton University Library,
and company records are deposited in the offices
of Holt, Rinehart and Winston, 383 Madison Avenue,
New York.

24 Hurst and Company

Hurst and Company (1871-1919), publishers, specialized in cheaply printed and bound books for widespread sale. In its various series hundreds of titles were published, one alone--the Argyle Series--containing over 300. As Hurst and Company, the business was established in 1871 at 122 Nassau Street in New York. By 1900 it had moved to 135 Grand Street with a branch in Pulaski City, Virginia, and by 1919 its address was 354 Fourth Avenue, New York.

Major Authors: George Louis Buffon, M. Lafayette Byrn, Virginia Wales Johnson.

Major Series: Cameo Edition, Nassau Edition, Arlington Edition, Bijou Hand Books, Magnet Hand-Books.

Thomas D. Hurst was born in England in 1843 and died 2 February 1924. After migration to the United States he set up an electrotyping business which he sold to a former employee, F. A. Ringler, before embarking as a publisher. As his sons George and Richard grew to maturity, they joined their father in the firm. One important employee, J. H. Fletcher, retired in 1883.

From its inception in 1871 the firm specialized in cheap editions of standard works, clothbound editions known as cheap twelvemos. To print the firm's books, Hurst founded the Argyle Press, from which flowed the cheap publications bearing the Hurst imprint. It was in the print shop of the Argyle Press that the famous pirated edition of the Encyclopedia Britannica was published by Henry G. Allen and his associates.

One of the most popular of the Hurst series was the Cameo Edition, "comprising all the Best Works of the Great Poets." By 1880 there were twenty-two volumes in this series at 30 cents per copy by Felicia Hemans, Robert Southey, Sir Walter Scott, Alexander Pope, and John Milton. The Cameo edition was advertised as "tastefully printed and bound in the best English cloth."

167

(Courtesy Edward T. LeBlanc, *Dime Novel Round-Up*)

In actuality, the printing and the paper were of poor quality. According to John Tebbel, "Even among the re-printers, Hurst did not stand out as a bookmaker."

Hurst and Company in 1880 also launched its Arlington Edition of British classics, consisting of standard popular works in twelvemo running from 400 to 800 pages. Each volume had several full-page illustrations, and was advertised as "Elegant in Style, Moderate in Price, Type Large, Paper Fine, Binding Excellent." Among the titles were Robinson Crusoe, Arabian Nights' Entertainment, Pilgrim's Progress, Dante's Inferno, and The Complete Works of Robert Burns. Eventually there were over three hundred volumes, bound in fairly substantial covers, in the series. Although advertised at $1.00, in reality they sold at retail for much less.

Many of the Arlington Edition titles were also sold in the cheaper Nassau Edition, described as "at once the Best and cheapest edition ever published." In fact the volumes were neither; Hurst books were never known for their quality and there were competing paperback editions that sold for as little as 10 cents, whereas the bound copies of the Nassau Edition were advertised at 30 cents.

In its Library of Choice Romance, Fiction and Adventure the firm turned out a series of paperbacks at 10 cents a copy. They bore such titles as The Cabin Boy; A Tale of the Wide Ocean; Captain Doe; The Mountain Chief; and Clerk Barton's Crime; or, the Adventures of a Night and A Tale of New York Life, High and Low by Steele Pen. These books belong to the "dime novel" category which was already past its heyday.

In the same class was the Popular Series of Fiction, Fancy and Fact, on sale for 15 cents each or ten for $1.00. Among the first seventeen volumes of the series were Spirit Eye, The Indian Captive; Inez, The Forest Bride; Dare-Devil Dick; or, The Curse of Gold, and Mercedes; or, the Outlaw's Child.

The Bijou Hand Books, with twelve volumes published by 1880, was another Hurst production. Selling for 15 cents a copy, this series dealt largely with the social amenities. There were two True Politeness volumes, A Handbook of Etiquette for Ladies and a similar one for "gentlemen," The Marriage Looking Glass, A Hand-Book for

169

Newly Married Couples, Hand-Books of Conversation and
Table Talk, The Ball-Room Companion, and Lover's
Companion.

The Magnet Hand-Books were described as "the very
best ever issued upon the various subjects which they
treat. Each volume is complete and perfect, and thoroughly practical. Each book contains 100 pages large
12mo, well printed and bound in handsome illuminated
covers for sale at 25¢ each." Titles included How to
Write a Letter, Hunters' and Trappers' Guide, Tricks and
Diversions with Cards, the Practical Magician and Ventriloquists' Guide, Parlor Pastimes; or The Whole Art of
Amusing, Personal Beauty, or the Whole Art of attaining
Bodily Vigor, Physical Development, Beauty of Feature
and Symmetry of Form with the Science of Dressing with
Taste, Elegance and Economy.

Hurst and Company entered the field of juvenile
literature with gift books for children, such as The
Christmas Stocking by "Cousin Virginia" [pseudonym of
novelist Virginia Wales Johnson] at $1.00, and Flowers
from Fairy Land. Another series offered at 30 cents
ABC Made Easy or Little Lessons for Little Children.

The American Popular Dictionary Containing Every
Useful Word to be found in the English Language was advertised for sale at 50 cents "strongly bound in cloth,"
containing "a vast amount of absolutely necessary information upon science, mythology, biography, American history, constitutions, laws, land titles, cities, colleges,
army and navy, rate of mortality, growth of cities, in-
solvent and assignment laws, debts, rates of interest
and other useful knowledge being a perfect library or
reference in one handy volume." Hurst also promoted the
sale of its American Diamond Dictionary of the English
Language, which was offered for 50 cents as "the cheapest book in the World."

Other popular reference works published by Hurst
were Chambers's Information for the Millions, containing
a description of products from tea and coffee to elec-
tricity, 360 pages "in English cloth" for $1.00 The
"Perfect" Shakespeare was priced at $1.50, as was the
Stanhope Edition of Shakespeare. Buffon's Natural History, 600 pages, was priced at $1.00 as was Crabbs's

170

Handy Cyclopedia or an Explanation of Words and Things
Connected with all the Arts and Sciences.

A prolific Hurst author, M. Lafayette Byrn, M.D.,
produced a whole "Library of Medical and Higienic [sic]
Knowledge at Trifling Cost." The first in the series
was How to Live a Hundred Years, A Practical and Reliable Guide to Health and Longevity with plain and specific instruction for Improving the Memory. Other
titles, all sold at 15 cents each, were The Secret
Beauty; or How to be Handsome; A Scientific Treatise
on Stammering and Stuttering; and The Art of Beautifying and Preserving the Hair. Common Complaints and How
to Cure Them, part of another series by the same author,
was advertised at 25 cents.

Despite a notice in the American Bookseller to the
effect that the firm was dissolved 10 January 1883, by
1 September 1883 announcement was made of Fletcher's
retirement from the firm which "continues under the same
style." In 1890 John Lovell, the outstanding publisher
of cheap books, conceived the idea of a giant combine of
cheap book publishers to eliminate cutthroat competition.
He organized the United States Book Company, which
Madeleine Stern in Imprints on History called "one of
the most amazing and significant events in the annals
of American publishing." A considerable number of publishers entered the combine, including Hurst. As Publishers' Weekly (March 1890) put it: "Most important
of all . . . Hurst & Co. have finally been induced to
come into the arrangement." The new company acquired
use of the plates of competing publishers. When as a
result of overexpansion and poor management the United
States Book Company failed in 1893, the Hurst plates
reverted to the original firm, which again became active.
George Hurst, returning from a European trip in 1895,
set up as an independent publisher at 114 Fifth Avenue,
producing an edition of Oliver Wendell Holmes's The
Autocrat. The author's son sued for copyright infringe-
ment. The Supreme Court, in Oliver Wendell Holmes, Jr.
v. G. D. Hurst, ruled that since The Autocrat had appeared
in a periodical in installments prior to copyright and
book publication, it was in effect, in the public domain.

171

Hurst and Company

.   In an effort to extend the geographical distribution of its books, Hurst and Company appointed the Chicago firm of Reilly and Britton, founded in 1902, as its sales representative in the Middle West and Far West. When the A. C. Gunter Publishing Company went bankrupt in New York in 1908, Hurst and Company took over its books.

Hurst and Company was a major publisher of cheap books cheaply produced in the last three decades of the nineteenth century and the early years of the twentieth. Through its Arlington Edition and cheaper Nassau Edition of classics, its Cameo Edition of poetry, its dime novels and handbooks, the firm played a significant role among publishers of widely distributed, low-priced books.

David S. Edelstein

References

Publishers' Trade List Annual (New York: F. Leypoldt, 1880).

Publishers' Weekly, 105 (9 February 1924): 432.

Raymond H. Shove, Cheap Book Production in the United States, 1870 to 1891 (Urbana: University of Illinois Library, 1937).

John Tebbel, A History of Book Publishing in the United States Vol. II (New York: R. R. Bowker Company, 1975).

25 M. J. Ivers and Company

M. J. Ivers and Company (1886-1908?), published cheap
fiction, dime novels, and jokebooks. The firm's first
listing in the American Catalogue appears in 1886, when
it was located at 379 Pearl Street in New York. It remained at this address until its dissolution in 1908.

Major Authors: Mrs. Margaret Argles, Ada Ellen
Bayly, Charlotte Braeme, Marie Corelli, H. Rider Haggard,
Mrs. Annie Hector, Mrs. E. D. E. N. Southworth, Robert
Louis Stevenson.

The Ivers firm apparently began publishing in 1886
with the first number of its American Series of cheap
fiction. In 1898 the firm, under the proprietorship of
James Sullivan, purchased the assets of the Beadle &
Adams Company. Ivers continued several of the Beadle
Series until 1908, when the company was dissolved.

Ivers published several jokebooks in the early
years of this century, each in cheap paperback editions--
The Automobile Joker (1906); The College Joker (1907);
and Matt Sullivan's "Coon Yarns" (1903)--none selling
for more than 12 cents. Ivers began a Standard Language
Series, but apparently only one number was produced, a
German Self-Instructor (1886), paperback, 10 cents.
The company likewise published Luther Cushing's Manual
of Parliamentary Practice (1887).

The remainder of the firm's publications (nearly
150 titles, in addition to the continuation of several
of Beadle's series) were in cheap fiction. Its American
Series proved to be its most popular line. Comparable
to Munro's Library and Lovell's Household Library, this
paperback series specialized in women's romances, while
occasionally including more substantive authors. Ivers
offered several notable "extras" (priced at double the
usual 25 cents) to its regular catalog in this series:
Telemachus Timayenis and Mrs. Humphry Ward were accorded
this special treatment, and Marie Corelli made her

M. J. Ivers and Company

American debut in 1887 with Ivers's publication of
Thelma. The next year the firm published another
Corelli best-seller, A Romance of Two Worlds.

A particular Ivers favorite was H. Rider Haggard;
between 1887 and 1890 twelve of his novels appeared in
the series (as did novels by Hardy, Verne, Stevenson,
and the younger Dumas). The heart of the series, however, was the woman novelist, particularly Mrs. Margaret
Argles, Ada Ellen Bayly, Charlotte Braeme, Rosa Nouchette
Carey, and Mrs. Annie Hector. Such titles as Argles's
The Troublesome Girl, Braeme's Lord Lisle's Daughter, and
Carey's Wee Wife earned the series a good measure of popularity. The firm published a limited successor (the Union
Series) to the American Series in 1896 and 1897, high-
lighted by the appearance of several of Mrs. E. D. E. N.
Southworth's novels.

After the firm purchased Beadle & Adams's stock
and plates in 1898, most of its attention and energy
was devoted to dime novels. That year Ivers began
monthly issues of Beadle's Dime and Half-Dime Library
and in 1900 published sixty-four of Edward Wheeler's novels in twelvemo pamphlets of the nickel Deadwood Dick
series. Ivers also continued sixty-four of the Beadle's
Boys Library series, twelve numbers of the Popular Series of Fiction, Fancy and Fact, and one hundred numbers
from Beadle's Frontier Series. Although Johannsen sug-
gests that the firm ceased publishing in 1905, Charles
Bragin lists the final Ivers publication (of the Frontier
Series) in 1908. Both agree that the company's assets
were sold to the Arthur Westbrook Company, which briefly
continued the series.

If Ivers is to be remembered, it must be for the
American Series and the various Beadle and Adams dime
novels, as well as for the introduction of Corelli's
work. The firm's publication of many popular authors
in paperback editions, and the continuation of the dime
and half-dime novels remain significant events in American publishing history.

Timothy K. Conley

174

M. J. Ivers and Company

References

Albert Johannsen, The House of Beadle and Adams and Its Dime and Nickel Novels: The Story of a Vanished Literature (Norman: University of Oklahoma Press, 1950-1962).

Frank L. Schick, The Paperbound Book in America: The History of Paperbacks and Their European Background (New York: R. R. Bowker Company, 1958).

Charles M. Bragin, Bibliography [of] Dime Novels 1860-1964 [Dime Novel Club Issue 63] (New York: Charles Bragin, 1964).

175

(Courtesy Edward T. LeBlanc, *Dime Novel Round-Up*)

26 Laird and Lee

Laird and Lee (1883-1928) published dictionaries and
reference books (many for schools), popular fiction,
children's books, and adventure books such as the
Pinkerton Series. Founded in Chicago in 1883 by
Frederick C. Laird and William H. Lee at Lake and
South Water streets, the firm in 1899 moved to 263-265
Wabash Avenue, in 1910 to 1732 Michigan Avenue, and
later to 2001 Calumet Avenue. After the death of Lee
in 1913 it was taken over by the public administrator
and then became a division of Laidlaw Bros., Inc., 328
South Jefferson Street, itself a division of Albert
Whitman & Company of 560 West Lake Street. The Laird
and Lee imprint was still occasionally used as late as
1974 by Albert Whitman and also by what had then become
the Laidlaw division of Doubleday & Company, Inc., at
River Forest, Illinois.

Major Authors: B. Freeman Ashley, Opie Read,
H. A. Stanley, Emile Zola.

There is little factual biographical information
about Frederick C. Laird and William Henry Lee. The
latter, who never referred to his early years or answered
any questions about them, was called the most mysterious
publisher in Chicago. He was supposed to have been born
near Philadelphia and to have been a body servant of a
Confederate officer during the Civil War, which led to
the assumption that he was black although he looked
white. He came to Chicago in the early 1880s, was well
educated, and spoke several foreign languages. His only
admissions of an autobiographical nature were that he
had once been a waiter, a clerk, a book agent, and a
commercial traveler. He never married. At his death,
30 June 1913, he left no relatives and his estate, valued
at $200,000, was turned over to the public administrator.

In 1883 the founders each made an initial investment of $1,000 in the firm and were quickly able to

develop a successful business. The first Laird and Lee
"best-seller" was one of Emile Zola's novels. Later publications that had enormous sales records for their period were The Jucklins by Opie Read (1895), Conklin's
Handy Manual (two million copies), Uncle Jeremiah and
His Family (400,000), The World's Fair Viewbook and If
Christ Came to Chicago by William T. Stead (1900) (each
selling over 300,000 copies). In September 1888 the
firm obtained an injunction against the rival Chicago
publisher, the Rand McNally Company, to restrain it from
publishing Zola's Dream. This suit was not successfully
settled until January 1892. By 1899 Laird and Lee was
the third-ranking Chicago publishing house, producing
thirteen new titles compared to the sixty issued by
Herbert Stone & Company and the eighteen published by
Rand McNally. Laird and Lee dictionaries were published
in many sizes, with numerous foreign language ones in
"vest pocket" sizes. By 1913 the firm was reputed to
have the finest collection of dictionary plates of all
sizes in the country. Much of the Laird and Lee popular
fiction appeared with cloth bindings, including such
titles as Opie Read's A Tennessee Judge, A Kentucky
Colonel, and The Jucklins, as well as Edmondo de Amicis's
The Heart of a Boy, all best-sellers for many years. The
Pinkerton Series conformed to the paperbound style of
rival adventure publications, and included such titles
as Life for a Life, Saved at the Scaffold, and The $5,000
Reward by A. F. Pinkerton, who also wrote under the name
"Dyke Darrell."

Frederick C. Laird withdrew from partnership in the
firm 19 June 1894, at which time Lee bought his interest
for $60,000.

Laird and Lee, whose house motto was "Perseverance
and Excellence," was a typical publisher of its day,
turning out a mixture of popular fiction and reference
books for wide distribution.

William B. Liebmann

Laird and Lee

References

Publishers' Weekly, 84 (19 July 1913): 121.

John Tebbel, A History of Book Publishing in the United
     States Vol. II. (New York: R. R. Bowker Company,
     1975).

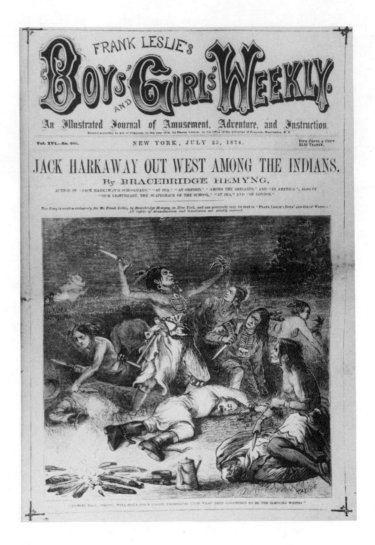

(Courtesy Edward T. LeBlanc, *Dime Novel Round-Up*)

27 The Frank Leslie Publishing House

The Frank Leslie Publishing House (also known as Frank
Leslie's Publishing House) (1854-1905), periodical and
book publishers, reprinted serials from Leslie periodicals in book form and was innovative in directing its
publications at the reading public that traveled the
nation's expanding network of railways. The firm published approximately thirty periodicals and eighty-six
books and pictorials. Frank Leslie began publishing
at 10 John Street, New York, in 1854. He moved several
times by 1864. In 1856 he was located at 12 Spruce
Street; in 1859 at 13 Frankfort Street; in 1860 at 19
Chatham Street; in 1863 at 72 Duane Street. In 1864
the firm was located in a five-story building at 537
Pearl Street, where it remained until 1878 when it
moved to Park Place (corner Park and College Place).
Subsequent moves were made in 1889 to 110 Fifth Avenue
(the Judge Building) and in 1898 to 141-143 Fifth Avenue.
       The Frank Leslie Publishing House was personally
directed by Frank Leslie until his death in 1880, when
the business was bequeathed to his widow, Miriam, who
changed her name legally to Frank Leslie in 1881 and
conducted all its operations. Between 1889 when the
firm was incorporated, and 1905 when it was out of existence, certain changes in management occurred, details
of which appear below.
       Major Authors: Mary Elizabeth Braddon, Frederick
John Fargus, Charles Gayler, Bracebridge Hemyng, Isa
Craig Knox.
       Frank Leslie was born Henry Carter in Ipswich,
England, in 1821 and died in New York City in 1880. He
adopted the name Frank Leslie because of his father's
hostility to his interest in taking up a career in pictorial art. As Frank Leslie he was employed on The
Illustrated London News, where he learned techniques
of pictorial printing. He was early married to Sarah

181

Ann Welham and had three sons, later divorcing. In 1848
Leslie emigrated to the United States where he worked
for P. T. Barnum and was managing foreman of Barnum and
Beach's Illustrated News. Leslie also served as wood
engraver in Frederick Gleason's Publishing Hall, Boston.
In January 1854 he began publishing on his own by launching a periodical in New York, Frank Leslie's Ladies Gazette of Fashion.

Mrs. Frank Leslie was born Miriam Florence Follin
in New Orleans in 1836 and died in New York City in 1914.
After an early marriage in 1854 to David Charles Peacock
and an annulment, she was married in 1857 to the archeol-
ogist Ephraim George Squier, who in 1861 became editor
of Frank Leslie's Illustrated Newspaper. In 1863 Miriam
Squier began her official association with the Frank
Leslie Publishing House, becoming editor of Frank Leslie's
Lady's Magazine. In 1865 she edited Frank Leslie's Chimney Corner, and in 1871 Frank Leslie's Lady's Journal.
She divorced Squier in 1873 and the following year married Frank Leslie, who had been divorced in 1872. She
continued her association with the Leslie Publishing
House after her marriage to Leslie, coupling her editorial work with a brilliant social life. Following a
spectacular transcontinental railroad journey with Leslie
and his entourage in 1877, she wrote California: A Pleasure Trip from Gotham to the Golden Gate (1877). In 1880
she inherited the Frank Leslie Publishing House.

Leslie's first periodical, Frank Leslie's Ladies
Gazette of Fashion, was successfully edited by the novelist Ann Stephens. On 15 December 1855, Leslie began publication of Frank Leslie's Illustrated Newspaper, which
would endure under Leslie management until 1889 and under
other publishers until 1922. That weekly made Leslie a
power on New York's Publishers' Row. With its graphic
illustrations of murders, assassinations, prizefights,
and fires, the weekly appealed to mass interest in violence, and with Harper's Weekly it dominated the field
of illustrated journalism for years. By the ingenious
device of dividing a woodblock into small sections so
that a number of engravers could work on the same picture simultaneously, before the wooden squares were
screwed together, Leslie completed huge double-page

engravings in a single night instead of the customary
two weeks.

In time the Leslie line of periodicals was ex-
panded to include weekly and monthly story papers, joke
papers, news sheets, pictorials. Among them were Frank
Leslie's Illustrirte Zeitung, a German language paper
(1857-1889); Frank Leslie's Budget of Fun (1859-1896);
Jolly Joker (1862-1878); Frank Leslie's Ten Cent Monthly,
later Frank Leslie's Pleasant Hours (1863-1896); Frank
Leslie's Chimney Corner (1865-1885); Frank Leslie's
Children's Friend, later Frank Leslie's Boy's & Girl's
Weekly, consisting mainly of dime novels (1866-1884);
Once a Week, later Frank Leslie's Lady's Journal (1871-
1881); Frank Leslie's Popular Monthly (1876-1905); Frank
Leslie's Sunday Magazine (1877-1889). Frank Leslie's
periodical publications led him naturally into book publication. It was a simple matter to reprint novels separately after they had appeared as serials in his
periodicals. Similarly, an illustrated supplement to a
periodical could be reprinted in the form of a separate
pictorial.

After publishing a few almanacs and minor picto-
rials--Frank Leslie's Christmas Pictorial (1856); Great
Eastern Steamship Pictorial (1858); Pictorial History of
the Harpers Ferry Insurrection (1859)--Leslie began book
publishing in earnest with his Pictorial History of The
War of 1861 and Frank Leslie's Pictorial History of the
American Civil War, edited by E. G. Squier, between 1861
and 1862. Consisting of thirty-three numbers, the Pictorial History of the American Civil War strongly resembled a serial. In 1862 Leslie published two more war
pictorials, Incidents of the Civil War in America and
Frank Leslie's Pictorials of Union Victories. Many of
Leslie's publications suggested a transition stage between periodical and book.

In 1863 and 1864 Leslie launched his first major
series of cheap fiction: Frank Leslie's Series of New
Novels, which consisted of six escapist romances:
Annette; or, The Lady of Pearls by Alexandre Dumas, Jr.
(1863); three pirated fictional effusions by the popular
and prolific Mary Elizabeth Braddon: Aurora Floyd
(1863), Lady Audley's Secret (1863), and Eleanor's

<u>Victory</u> (1864); <u>Living or Dead</u> by Frederick John Fargus (1864), and <u>The Half Sisters</u> by Isa Craig Knox (1864).

The remainder of Leslie publications during the 1860s consisted of pictorials on current events such as <u>Frank Leslie's Pictorial Life of Abraham Lincoln</u> (1865); <u>Frank Leslie's Atlantic Telegraph Cable Pictorial</u> (1866), and <u>Frank Leslie's Illustrated History of the Great National Peace Jubilee</u> (1869), along with a few almanacs-- <u>Frank Leslie's New England Almanac</u> (1866); <u>Frank Leslie's Lady's [Illustrated] Almanac</u> (1866-1868), and <u>Frank Leslie's Comic Almanac</u> (1866-1895).

By the 1870s the Frank Leslie Publishing House had so expanded that thousands of dollars were spent each week to pay the firm's three hundred to four hundred employees. During that decade the house reached its quantitative zenith as publisher of books and periodicals. At first it published a miscellaneous selection geared to a general readership. In 1870 Leslie produced two works for children, <u>Master Mouse's Supper Party</u> and <u>The Nursery Picture-Gallery and Child's Own Picture Book</u>. The following year the firm issued an elaborate travel book, <u>Mountains and Lakes of Switzerland and Italy</u> by Jerome J. Mercier, and reprinted the popular <u>Mrs. Beeton's Book of Household Management</u>. In 1874 <u>Frank Leslie's Chimney Corner Cookery Book</u> appeared, and in 1876 C. Edward Lester's <u>Lives and Public Services of Samuel J. Tilden and Thomas A. Hendricks</u>.

In 1876 Frank Leslie returned to the series idea he had first attempted in 1863 and 1864, producing four different series of cheap reprints, all of which, whatever the individual format of the volumes, seemed to suggest the nature of a magazine. Indeed many of the volumes were actually reprints of stories that had run in Leslie journals. Most of the books in these series were designed as railroad literature--books to be read on the railroad. All were published between 1876 and 1877, when Leslie was acutely aware of and enthusiastic about the expansion of the nation's railways. With a journalistic entourage he and his wife made a flamboyant transcontinental journey by rail in 1877, accounts of which appeared in <u>Frank Leslie's Illustrated Newspaper</u>. Leslie was keenly alive to the need for

184

appropriate reading matter for the masses of people enjoying train travel in the 1870s.

Leslie began his cheap series of the seventies with his Chimney Corner Series (1876-1877), the title of which was adopted from his periodical, Frank Leslie's Chimney Corner. This series consisted of five melodramatic novels: reprints of Living or Dead by Frederick John Fargus and of The Half Sisters by Isa Craig Knox, as well as Wife in Name Only by Charlotte Mary Braeme, and two anonymous romances: A Russian Bullet and a Broken Heart and Woman's Victory. All these novels were duodecimos, bound in boards, and priced at 50 cents each.

At the same time Leslie launched his Chimney Corner Series he published another series entitled Frank Leslie's Popular Library. This included four popular romances: Michael Strogoff by Jules Verne; Fritz, The Emigrant and Montague: or, The Belle of the Matinee, both by Charles Gayler; and Reaping the Whirlwind by Mary Cecil Hay. The books in the Popular Library series were octavos, illustrated, bound in heavy covers, and priced at 25 cents.

Between 1876 and 1877 Frank Leslie's Publishing House also issued the Boys Library Series or Frank Leslie's Popular American Tales for Boys. This consisted of eight paper-covered books for boys, of which five were authored by Samuel Bracebridge Hemyng, the firm's star writer of juveniles and a member of the transcontinental railway excursion of 1877. The Boys Library Series, designed for boys at home or on trains, included the following stories by Bracebridge Hemyng: Jack Harkaway in America; Jack Harkaway out West among the Indians; Red Dog, Blue Horse, and Ghost-that-Lies-in-the-Woods; Jack Harkaway and his Friends in Search of the Mountain of Gold; Jack Harkaway and the Secret of Wealth. In addition, the series offered Lone Wolf, the Apache Chief and Elinor's Chase. A Story of the Pawnee Range, both by W. O. Stoddard, and Three Yankee Boys, and Three Yankee Boys Afloat by Commodore Ah-Look of New Bedford [Edward Greey].

In 1877, at the height of his publishing career, Frank Leslie published his major series: Frank Leslie's Home Library of Standard Works by the Most Celebrated Authors. The Home Library was designed to provide reading matter for the general public and especially, despite its domestic heading, for all who traveled through the country on the growing network of railways. Books usually priced at $1.50 or $2.00 were furnished at 10 or 20 cents, and the standard authors were offered as traveling companions. Though the series boasted that its authors had been made famous by the test of time, it featured, among the more classic works of Charles Reade, Bulwer-Lytton, Victor Hugo, and Wilkie Collins, such less established but still delectable titles as Good-by, Sweetheart! by Rhoda Broughton, Mrs. Annie Edwards's A Vagabond Heroine, and Murphy's Master by James Payn. The price of the series depended upon size, double numbers fetching 20 cents and single numbers 10. A copy of Hannah by Miss "Muloch" (better known today as Dinah Craik, author of John Halifax, Gentleman) is one of the few volumes in this ephemeral series that has survived through the years. Appearing as it does, without hard covers, it strongly resembles Leslie's magazine serials, and it remains one of the few extant specimens of the type of novel purveyed by Leslie for readers en route in a Railway Age. Other books in that series included Elizabeth Lynn Linton's From Dreams to Waking, George Alfred Lawrence's Sword and Gown, William Black's In Silk Attire, and Granville de Vigne by "Ouida" [Marie Louise de la Ramée].

Nearly every book bearing the Leslie imprint was in the class of cheap railroad literature and was handled by the American News Company. Through that company's system, and with the development of railroads throughout the country, cheap popular books could be retailed at newsstands, station kiosks, and on the trains themselves, where train boys included books among the wares they offered. Leslie clearly understood the effect of railroads upon national literary consumption. Between 1876 and 1877, when railroad expansion was at a height, he tripled his book production of the preceding years, catering to the developing mass market for cheap reprints to read aboard trains.

The Panic of 1877 occurred just when the Frank Leslie Publishing House was overextended. With the general business depression, the circulation of Leslie periodicals fell off. A sumptuous pictorial, <u>Historical Register of the United States Centennial Exposition</u> (1876–1877), proved a heavy trade loss. In September 1877 Frank Leslie was forced to make an assignment of his property, for the benefit of his creditors, to Isaac W. England, publisher of the New York <u>Sun</u>. Leslie was to remain in the company as general manager. On 20 March 1879 he entered into a composition deed with his creditors who agreed to accept 50 percent of the balance of his debts in full settlement of the claims against him. By January 1880 he had paid 35 percent, leaving a debt of only $100,000. On 10 January 1880, however, Frank Leslie died, leaving his business and his debt to his wife.

Borrowing $50,000, Mrs. Leslie paid the last cent due the firm's creditors on 23 May 1881. On 4 June the Leslie property was transferred by the assignee to Mrs. Leslie, who promptly changed her name, at a special term of the Court of Common Pleas, to "Frank Leslie." Seizing upon the assassination of President Garfield as a news story of universal interest, Mrs. Leslie made a journalistic coup, retailing all the details of the crime in advance of other periodicals to the sensation-hungry readers of <u>Frank Leslie's Illustrated Newspaper</u>. Before the first installment of her $50,000 debt was due, Mrs. Leslie was able to pay the entire amount.

The new Frank Leslie reorganized every department of the publishing house until it became one of the most extensive mail-order businesses in the country. Its pressroom accommodated sixteen presses; some seventeen tons of paper were consumed each week; the establishment ranked third among the nation's ink consumers. Mrs. Leslie gave more attention to the firm's periodicals than to its book publications. Among the latter she issued the following miscellaneous titles: <u>Frank Leslie's Bubbles and Butterflies</u> (1881), designed for summer travelers, priced at 25 cents; <u>Frank Leslie's Holiday Book</u> (1881); <u>Queen Titania's Book of Fairy Tales</u> (1883), bound in an illuminated cover, priced at $1.00; <u>Amusing Adventures, Afloat and Ashore, of Three American Boys</u> by Henry Lyell (1886); <u>Prince Lucifer</u> by Etta W. Pierce (1890). The Frank Leslie Publishing House also continued the Leslie tradition of publishing pictorials by producing

187

the Pictorial History of President Garfield's Career
(1881); Pictorial History of the Life of James G. Blaine
(1893); Frank Leslie's Illustrated Famous Leaders and
Battle Scenes of the Civil War (1896).

In time, Mrs. Frank Leslie began to cut down on the
number of periodicals that had been launched by her husband. She eliminated the Lady's Journal in favor of the
Lady's Magazine, and finally merged that with the Popular
Monthly. By the end of 1885 she had only two weeklies
and four monthlies, centering her attention upon Frank
Leslie's Popular Monthly, which was sold by every train
boy on every railroad in the country. In January 1889
the Frank Leslie Publishing House was incorporated with
a million dollars of capital. The next month the Judge
Publishing Company, W. J. Arkell, President (later
Arkell Weekly Company and Leslie-Judge Company) purchased
the remaining Leslie weeklies.

After fifteen years at the head of the business,
Mrs. Frank Leslie in May 1895 leased her interest in the
Leslie publications to a syndicate managed by Frederic L.
Colver. In 1898 the syndicate formed a stock company of
which she became president. In 1900 Mrs. Leslie was
forced to retire because of economic conditions and personal differences. Ellery Sedgwick took her place as
editor of the Popular Monthly, which eventually was renamed The American Magazine. By 1903 the new management
bought the remainder of the Leslie holdings, and in 1905
the Frank Leslie Publishing House ceased to exist. The
Colver Publishing House had taken its place.

Mrs. Leslie, who in 1891 had married Oscar Wilde's
brother William Charles Kingsbury Wilde, was separated
from him two years later. After her forced retirement
she adopted the title Baroness de Bazus which she claimed
as a family title. She died in 1914, leaving a fortune
of two million dollars to further the cause of women's
suffrage.

The Frank Leslie Publishing House had its hand on
the public pulse. In its periodicals it supplied serial
stories graphically illustrated to entertain a host of
readers. At their peak the Leslie publications had a
combined circulation of 250,000. The individual books
issued by the house were a natural outgrowth of its

188

periodicals and often resembled them in appearance. The various cheap series that appeared over the Leslie imprint were aimed primarily at the large readership that developed concurrently with the mushrooming of national railroads. In this it was innovative, catering to the vast numbers who found leisure for books while traveling the railroads that crisscrossed the country.

Madeleine B. Stern

References

Madeleine B. Stern, "The Frank Leslie Publishing House," Antiquarian Bookman 7 (16 June 1951): 1973-75.

Madeleine B. Stern, Purple Passage: The Life of Mrs. Frank Leslie (Norman: University of Oklahoma Press, 1953; reprinted, University of Oklahoma Press, 1970, in hardback and paperback). This work contains, pp. 189-98, a checklist of Leslie publications.

Madeleine B. Stern, Imprints on History: Book Publishers and American Frontiers (Bloomington: Indiana University Press, 1956; reprinted, New York: AMS Press, 1975).

(Courtesy Edward T. LeBlanc, *Dime Novel Round-Up*)

28   A. K. Loring

A. K. Loring (1859-1881), proprietor of a circulating
library, bookseller and publisher, was one of the principal pioneer cheap book publishers and was the first
major publisher of the works of Horatio Alger, Jr. The
firm published about two hundred titles in various editions. It began business as Loring's Select Library at
319 Washington Street, Boston, operating as a circulating
library and bookstore. Between 1861 and 1864 George W.
Dillingham was an assistant. In 1863 the firm began publishing at the same address. For a short period in 1870,
while awaiting completion of new offices at the corner
of Bromfield and Washington streets, it moved, first to
35 School Street and then to 205 Washington. During the
next decade A. K. Loring remained at the corner of
Bromfield and Washington streets (369 Washington Street),
combining publishing activities with the operation of a
coffeehouse (between 1875/76 and 1881) located at 1
Bromfield. In 1881 he was located at 542 Washington.
     Major Authors: Louisa May Alcott, Horatio
Alger, Jr., John Habberton, Virginia F. Townsend,
Mrs. A. D. T. Whitney.
     Aaron K. Loring was born in Sterling, Massachusetts,
in 1826 and died in 1911. He served his apprenticeship
as clerk and junior partner in the Boston publishing firm
of Phillips, Sampson and Company. After the dissolution
of that firm he entered business in his own right in 1859
as Loring's Select Library.
     Loring's Select Library lent books for circulation
at 2 cents per volume per day. It also offered at cheap
prices the surplus books withdrawn from circulation.
According to a Catalogue of the library preserved at the
Boston Public Library, its purpose was "to provide ample
supplies of all books of sterling interest and merit,
that will be enjoyed by the great mass of readers, as
soon as they are published." Thus Loring aimed from the

start at cheap prices and a mass readership. The purpose
of Loring's Select Library was identical with the purpose
of A. K. Loring in his publishing enterprises. Through
his library experience Loring developed the ability to
gauge public taste, an ability he put to good use as a
publisher.

A. K. Loring entered the publishing field in 1863
with Faith Gartney's Girlhood by Mrs. A. D. T. Whitney.
Sometime during the following year, in an undated letter
to another of his authors, Louisa May Alcott (now at the
Alderman Library, University of Virginia), Loring formu-
lated his publishing demands and credo: "I judge a book
by the impression it makes and leaves in my mind, by the
feelings solely as I am no scholar.--A story that touches
and moves me, I can make others read and believe in.--
What I like is conciseness in introducing the characters,
getting them upon the stage and into action as quickly
as possible.--Then I like a story of constant action,
bustle and motion.--Conversations and descriptive scenes
are delightful reading when well drawn but are too often
skipped by the reader who is anxious to see what they do
next, and its [sic] folly to write what will be skipped
in reading. The books you have read and admired, the
poetry you love, the music that has enchanted, Paintings
and Sculpture admired, the heroic words uttered by earnest thinkers who sway the world rightly introduced add
greatly to the enjoyment of the story as they revive and
refresh the memory of every reader. . . . I like a story
that starts to teach some lesson of life [and] goes
steadily on increasing in interest till it culminates
with the closing chapter leaving you spell bound, enchanted and exhausted with the intensity with which it
is written, the lesson forcibly told, and a yearning
desire to turn right back to the beginning and enjoy
it over again. . . . Stories of the heart are what
live in the memory and when you move the reader to tears
you have won them [sic] to you forever."

In essence, Loring's literary requirements were
the same as those of mass readers in search of entertainment: a story of action that carried a moral lesson and touched the heart. Those requirements are to
be found in most of the titles that bear the Loring

192

imprint. The firm's first publication, <u>Faith Gartney's
Girlhood</u> by Mrs. A. D. T. Whitney (1863), was a narrative
of New England village life for girls. The story, which
concerned Faith's domestic difficulties and her choice
between two lovers, became extremely popular. The same
year, 1863, Loring published an English import, <u>Pique.
A Novel</u> by Sarah Stickney Ellis, and <u>Twice Lost; A Novel</u>
by Menella Bute Smedley.

In 1864 Loring began his association with Horatio
Alger, Jr., publishing <u>Frank's Campaign; or, What Boys Can
Do on the Farm for the Camp</u>, a full-length Civil War
novel intended to show the part boys could play in over-
coming the Rebellion. For that book Loring allowed the
author ten free copies, a $50.00 advance, and a royalty
of 5 cents for each copy sold. With the publication of
<u>Frank's Campaign</u>, Loring's firm initiated a business re-
lationship with Alger that continued until 1880. During
those years Loring published thirty-six Alger titles and
became the first major publisher of that extraordinarily
popular author. <u>Frank's Campaign</u> became the first volume
of what was later dubbed the Campaign Series, which included two additional Alger stories, <u>Paul Prescott's
Charge</u> (1865) and <u>Charlie Codman's Cruise</u> (1866).

The combination of action, emotional appeal, and
moral lesson was nowhere better exemplified than in the
succession of Alger titles that appeared over the Loring
imprint. In 1866 the firm published two other Alger stories, <u>Helen Ford</u> and <u>Timothy Crump's Ward; or, The New
Years Loan, And What Came of it</u>. The latter, published
anonymously in hard covers and in paper wrappers as a
volume in Loring's Railway Companions Series, has become
one of the scarcest and most sought-after of the Algers.

In 1868 Loring published one of the most popular
and characteristic Alger narratives and began grouping
Alger titles in appropriately named series. "Ragged
Dick; or, Street Life in New York" had been serialized
the year before in the juvenile magazine <u>Student and
Schoolmate</u>. Manly, self-reliant, self-supporting from
age seven, Ragged Dick performs an act of kindness and
courage for which he is rewarded by being helped onto
the great American road that leads to fame and fortune.
Perceiving in the rags-to-riches story not merely a tale

of action with a moral lesson, but an inspiring reflection of American rugged individualism, A. K. Loring published Ragged Dick; or, Street Life in New York in 1868.
The book was so popular that the publisher made a liberal
offer for a series of six volumes on a similar subject,
incorporating a similar theme, set against New York street
life. The result was the Ragged Dick Series, which exalted the legend of rags-to-riches on the sidewalks of
New York, and deeply appealed to the nineteenth-century
masses. The series included Fame and Fortune; or, The
Progress of Richard Hunter (1868), Mark, The Match Boy;
or, Richard Hunter's Ward (1869), Rough and Ready; or,
Life Among the New York Newsboys (1869), Ben, The Luggage
Boy; or, Among the Wharves (1870), Rufus and Rose; or,
The Fortunes of Rough and Ready (1870).

In time half a million readers testified to the
popularity of the Alger books, which Loring priced at
$1.25 per copy and published in a variety of aptly named
series. In 1869 the Luck and Pluck Series was introduced, which, according to Alger bibliographer Ralph
Gardner, depicted "robust lads" who "left the farm to
seek fortune . . . and--with luck and pluck--prospered,
returning in time to . . . save the old homestead from
the clutches of the villainous squire." The series--a
double series--made its bow with Luck and Pluck; or,
John Oakley's Inheritance (1869) and included seven more
volumes: Sink or Swim; or, Harry Raymond's Resolve
(1870), Strong and Steady; or, Paddle Your Own Canoe
(1871), Strive and Succeed; Or, The Progress of Walter
Conrad (1872), Try and Trust; or, The Story of a Bound
Boy (1873), Bound To Rise; or, Harry Walton's Motto
(1873), Risen From The Ranks; or, Harry Walton's Success
(1874), Herbert Carter's Legacy; or, The Inventor's Son
(1875).

In 1871, the place of Ragged Dick and Harry Walton
was taken by Tattered Tom, who lent his name to the Tattered Tom Series (also a double), which included Tattered
Tom; or, The Story of a Street Arab (1871), Paul the Peddler; or, The Adventures of a Young Street Merchant
(1871), Slow and Sure; or, From the Street to the Shop
(1872), Phil, the Fiddler; or, The Story of a Young
Street Musician (1872), Julius; or, The Street Boy Out

West (1874), The Young Outlaw; or, Adrift in the Streets (1875), Sam's Chance; and How He Improved It (1876), The Telegraph Boy (1879).

Still another Alger series--the Brave and Bold Series--was begun in 1874 with Brave and Bold; or, The Fortunes of a Factory Boy. This was followed by Jack's Ward; or, The Boy Guardian (1875), Shifting For Himself; or, Gilbert Greyson's Fortunes (1876), Wait and Hope; or, Ben Bradford's Motto (1877).

When Loring noted that Alger's popularity was increasing in the West but declining in the East, he advised his star author to reverse his procedure and write stories about the West for boys in the East. The result was the Pacific Series, in which the theme remained constant while the background altered. Its titles included The Young Adventurer; or, Tom's Trip Across the Plains (1878), The Young Miner; or, Tom Nelson in California (1879), and The Young Explorer; or, Among the Sierras (1880). In addition, Loring published two other Alger works: a collection, Grand'ther Baldwin's Thanksgiving; With Other Ballads and Poems (1875), and a collaboration between Alger and his sister, Olive Augusta Cheney, Seeking His Fortune, and Other Dialogues (1875).

The publishing desiderata which Alger's books embodied so well had been outlined by Loring in a letter to Louisa May Alcott. In 1865 the firm published her novel Moods, which she based upon Emerson's comment that "Life is a train of moods like a string of beads." In explaining to Alcott his demands as a publisher, Loring also offered editorial advice, suggesting that Moods be cut to about 286 pages. As a result, Alcott eliminated ten chapters from her story. In return for the right to publish, Loring offered her ten free copies, 10 cents on each clothbound copy sold, and 5 cents on each in paper. In 1870, without consulting Alcott, the firm published another edition of Moods. The author received from the publisher $286.90 and later $700.00.

In line with most publishers who aimed at a mass market, A. K. Loring published several series, among them Loring's Tales of the Day, which consisted of sixteenmos priced at 10, 25, or 50 cents, published during the late 1860s and the 1870s. The series included

195

several works by Louisa May Alcott all published in 1868: Kitty's Class Day, Aunt Kipp, Psyche's Art, and an omnibus collection of those Proverb Stories printed from the plates of the separate stories.

Other Loring series were entitled Books for Young Ladies, a paper-covered Railway Library, Standard English Novels, Select Novels, Popular Books. Loring's Select Novels consisted of thirty paperbound titles priced at 50 cents each. Among the firm's popular fiction publications for mass consumption were Erring, Yet Noble. A Tale of, and for Women by Isaac George Reed, Jr. (1865); Simplicity and Fascination: Tale of the English Yeomanry by Anne Beale (1866); the stories of Edmund Yates: Broken to Harness (1866), Forlorn Hope: A Novel (1867), Running the Gauntlet: A Novel (1866); Linnet's Trial by Menella Bute Smedley (1867); Victory Deane. A Novel by Cecil Griffith Beckett (1872). One of Loring's most successful works of fiction was John Habberton's Helen's Babies, with Some Account of Their Ways, . . . Also a Partial Record of Their Actions During Ten Days of Their Existence, by Their Latest Victim (1876). This was produced in cloth at $1.00 and in paper at 50 cents. A charming account of the antics of two small boys, the story was immediately popular.

Numerous sentimental stories for girls by Mrs. A. D. T. Whitney appeared over the Loring imprint, among them Hitherto. A Story of Yesterdays (1869), Patience Strong's Outings (1869), and Mother Goose for Grown Folks (1870). During the late 1860s and into the 1870s the firm developed a strong line of juveniles. It produced the Breakwater Series by Virginia Frances Townsend, which included The Boys from Bramby (1868), Joanna Darling; or, The Home at Breakwater (1868), Hope Darrow. A Little Girl's Story (1869), and Max Meredith's Millennium (1870). Two other popular juvenile authors published by Loring were George Macdonald, represented by David Elginbrod (1869) and Robert Falconer (1870), and "Laura Caxton" [Elizabeth B. Comins], represented by Marion Berkley: A Story for Girls (1870) and The Hartwell Farm (1871).

The how-to book was also published by Loring with an aim at mass consumption. In this category of home

196

manuals were included numerous books by Eliza Warren,
such as How I Managed My House on £200 A Year (1866);
Maria Massey Barringer's Dixie Cookery (1867); the
gardening guides of Charles Barnard, for example Gardening for Money (1869) and A Simple Flower Garden for
Every Home (1870); Edward Mitchell's $5000 A Year, and
How I Made It (1870); Seranus Bowen's Dyspepsia (1877).
   Around 1875/1876, Loring opened a coffeehouse at
1 Bromfield Street, combining his Select Library and his
publishing activities with the new enterprise. Despite
the success of Habberton's Helen's Babies (1876),
Loring's combined operations did not long survive. The
depressed state of the trade, caused in part by a pleth-
ora of cheap books on the market, contributed to the
failure of his firm. On 15 June 1881 the Loring bankruptcy was announced, with gross liabilities placed at
$28,514.75 and gross assets at $19,304.36. The Loring
plates were sold to various publishers, the stereotype
plates of the Alger publications going to Porter &
Coates. Loring's career as a publisher ended. After
1882 A. K. Loring made sporadic but unsuccessful attempts
to resume business as a stationer, bookseller and library
proprietor. He died at the Home for Aged Men, Boston,
26 September 1911.
   As a general publisher of cheap books the firm of
A. K. Loring provided entertainment for the masses of
readers. As the first major publisher of Horatio
Alger, Jr., it also helped glorify the image of the
nineteenth-century American self-made man and rugged
individualist and helped shape the rags-to-riches legend.
Both the image and the legend appealed strongly to a mass
readership during the period the firm flourished.

   Madeleine B. Stern

References

"Aaron K. Loring," Publishers Weekly, 80 (30 September
      1911): 1284.

   197

A. K. Loring

Madeleine B. Stern, <u>Imprints on History: Book Pub-</u>
<u>lishers and American Frontiers</u> (Bloomington:
Indiana University Press, 1956; reprinted,
New York: AMS Press, 1975).

Ralph D. Gardner, <u>Horatio Alger; or, The American Hero</u>
<u>Era</u> (Mendota, Illinois: Wayside Press, 1964;
reprinted, New York: Arco Publishing Company,
1978).

John Tebbel, <u>A History of Book Publishing in the United</u>
<u>States</u> Vol. I (New York: R. R. Bowker Company,
1972).

29   John W. Lovell

John W. Lovell (1876-1893), book publisher and book trust
organizer, gave unprecedented impetus to the printing and
distribution of cheap books. He was among the first American publishers of Rudyard Kipling and James M. Barrie.
His firm published several thousand titles in various editions. In 1876 he began publishing in copartnership with
his father and G. Mercer Adam as Lovell, Adam & Company,
and shortly after, with the admission of Francis L.
Wesson, as Lovell, Adam, Wesson & Company, at 764 Broadway, New York. In 1877 the copartnership was dissolved
and in 1878 John W. Lovell became an independent publisher at 24 Bond Street, New York, later moving to 16
Astor Place. In 1881 he failed, but reorganized the next
year as John W. Lovell Company at 14 Vesey Street. Lovell
established a subsidiary firm in New York and Boston with
his brother under the style of Frank F. Lovell & Company;
he opened a branch in Chicago and, in 1888 in London at
2 Dean's Yard, Westminster. In 1890 Lovell organized the
United States Book Company at 150 Worth Street, New York,
a giant trust which went into bankruptcy in 1893 when
Lovell's career as a major publisher ended.

> Major Authors: James M. Barrie, Charlotte Mary
Braeme, Henry George, Rudyard Kipling, Mrs. Humphry Ward.

> John Wurtele Lovell was born in Montreal in 1851
and died in 1932. The son of John Lovell, founder of the
Lovell Printing and Publishing Company of Montreal, he
was apprenticed at age thirteen to his father to learn
the printing trade. In 1873 he managed his father's
Lake Champlain Press at Rouses Point, New York, on the
Canadian border. That plant printed the sheets of British copyright works in the United States and circulated
them in Canada through the Montreal firm. As manager of
the Rouses Point branch, which soon became the largest
New York State printing and publishing establishment
north of Albany, John W. Lovell gained enough experience

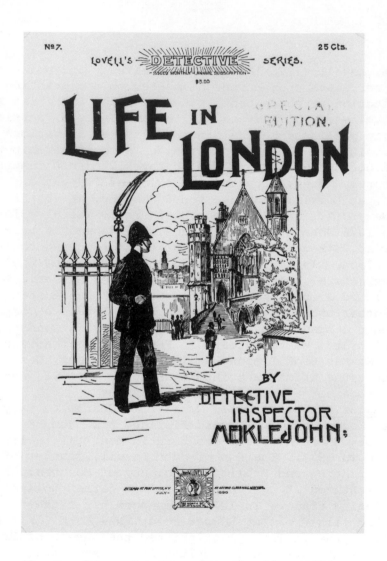

(Courtesy Edward T. LeBlanc, *Dime Novel Round-Up*)

to organize his own publishing firm. Having married and
declared his intention of becoming an American citizen,
he formed a copartnership, Lovell, Adam & Company, in
1876, with G. Mercer Adam of the Toronto wholesale
bookseller-publishers Adam, Stevenson & Company.

From the start Lovell recognized the importance of
coupling cheap retail prices with wide distribution among
the masses of readers. This was evident even during his
brief period as a copartnership. Lovell, Adam & Company
reprinted British copyright books in cheap editions, and
Lovell, Adam, Wesson & Company reissued English and foreign classics and published the Lake Champlain Press
Series. The firm made use of the elder Lovell's estab-
lishments in Montreal and Rouses Point to expedite their
operations.

In 1878, as an independent publisher, Lovell, taking
advantage of the absence of an international copyright
law, became a large-scale pirate of reprints. The times
were ripe for his aggressive methods. Although production
costs had fallen after the Panic of 1877, established publishing houses still upheld exorbitant prices, thanks to
a courtesy agreement among the principal publishers that
secured them the exclusive right to reprint certain English or foreign books. Faced with that situation, Lovell
determined to break up the prevalent exclusivity, make
inroads upon the sales of long-established publishing
houses, and also bring within reach of the masses as much
cheap literature as possible. To accomplish this he pirated reprints.

Lovell began with Charles Knight's Popular History
of England (1878) and went on with inexpensive editions
of Dickens, Thackeray, Coleridge, and Milton. A variety
of cheap reprint series rolled from his presses: Popular
Twelvemos, Standard Histories, Caxton Classics, Lovell's
Editions of the Poets--all aimed at a mass market. Lovell
made new electrotype plates of books at his father's plant
in Rouses Point, and promised to pay authors a 10 percent
royalty in return for the right to reprint. It was
charged, however, that Lovell's promises of royalty payments were not fulfilled, and it was observed that he
was printing cheap, unauthorized editions of works whose
worth and popularity had been tested by authorized

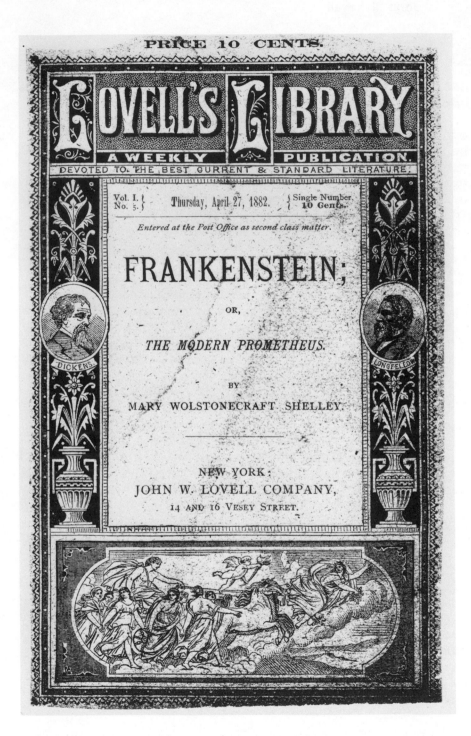

PRICE 10 CENTS.

LOVELL'S LIBRARY

A WEEKLY PUBLICATION.

DEVOTED TO THE BEST CURRENT & STANDARD LITERATURE.

Vol. I.
No. 5. } Thursday, April 27, 1882. { Single Number, 10 Cents.

Entered at the Post Office as second class matter.

FRANKENSTEIN;

OR,

THE MODERN PROMETHEUS.

BY

MARY WOLSTONECRAFT SHELLEY.

NEW YORK:

JOHN W. LOVELL COMPANY,

14 AND 16 VESEY STREET.

(Courtesy Edward T. LeBlanc, *Dime Novel Round-Up*)

publishers. Partly as a result of his unsavory reputation at this time, Lovell failed in business in 1881.
In 1882 he reorganized as the John W. Lovell Company.

The John W. Lovell Company became one of the largest distributors of popular and important books at cheap
prices in the history of American publishing. It began
its wholesale operations in 1882 with Lovell's Library,
a series of paper-covered books priced at 10, 20, or 30
cents. Lovell's Library, which included fiction, history, biography, and travel, exerted a strong influence
through the 1880s upon the reading habits of the masses.
Among its most popular titles were Thackeray's Vanity
Fair (1883); Bunyan's Pilgrim's Progress (1883); Longfellow's Poems and Voices of the Night (1885); the romantic novels of Charlotte Mary Braeme, better known
under the pseudonym "Bertha M. Clay": Love Works Wonders
(1884), Love's Warfare (1886), Diana's Discipline (1889);
and the sentimental narratives of Mrs. Margaret Wolfe
Hungerford, who wrote under the pseudonym "The Duchess":
Airy Fairy Lilian (1883), and Dick's Sweetheart (1885).

Among the nonfiction works in Lovell's Library one
of the most interesting was Social Solutions (1886) edited
by Edward Howland and translated by Marie Howland from the
French of Jean Baptiste André Godin. That work, which
formed a manual for organized labor and opposed the wages
system, was published in twelve semimonthly numbers at 10
cents each or $1.00 complete. While it may not have en-
tertained the masses as much as it instructed them,
Social Solutions presented an interesting variation in
cheap series publications, for it was paged continuously
from beginning to end and was literally a paperbound book
in parts.

New numbers of Lovell's Library were published
weekly, later triweekly. Moreover, Lovell was able to
obtain a second-class postal rate for his publications
and so could distribute them at the same price as newspapers. Occasionally his firm published a work in two
editions, cloth and paper. By 1890 Lovell's Library included nearly 1,500 numbers. Lovell himself came to be
known as "Book-A-Day Lovell." He boasted a yearly sale
of seven million cheap books, carried four million in

stock, and for a time actually did publish a new book
each day. In 1884 Lovell added a periodical to his list,
Tid-Bits, a cheap illustrated miscellany filled with jokes
which continued, in an improved style and with a different
name, until 1890.

In 1888 the John W. Lovell Company expanded further
with the purchase, for a quarter of a million dollars, of
all the plates and stock of the Munro Library. Lovell's
various series were augmented with Lovell's American
Authors' Series, Lovell's American Novelists' Series,
the Foreign Literature Series edited by Edmund Gosse,
the Rugby Series, the Universal, the Franklin, the Red
Line, and others. To expedite his grand scale operations,
Lovell formed a subsidiary firm with his brother, Frank F.
Lovell & Company in Boston and New York. Another brother,
Charles W. Lovell, was president of a bookbinding firm,
the Lovell Manufacturing Company. Lovell established a
Chicago branch and in 1888 opened a London office.

Lovell's London representative, Wolcott Balestier,
had edited the Lovell magazine Tid-Bits. His first act
as Lovell's London representative was to obtain from
Mudie's Library a copy of the popular novel Robert Elsmere
by Mrs. Humphry Ward, and mail it to Lovell. As a result
Lovell became the first American publisher of Mrs. Humphry
Ward, to whom he paid $500.00 for the right to reprint.
His edition of Robert Elsmere appeared in 1888. Through
Balestier, Lovell was also among the first American publishers of Rudyard Kipling, whose Soldiers Three appeared
over the Lovell imprint in 1890, and of James M. Barrie,
whose Little Minister was published by him in 1891. By
offering payment to British authors Lovell obtained the
use of advance sheets of their forthcoming books. Instead
of pirating English books he now published authorized editions by arrangement with their writers, and distributed
vast quantities of cheaply priced literature, sometimes
in their first American editions, for mass consumption.

Despite his early piracies, Lovell was deeply interested in the advancement of labor. He added to his
numerous series Lovell's Political and Scientific Series,
with books published weekly or monthly at from 10 to 35
cents. No. 1 in that series was Henry George's Progress
and Poverty (1883), priced at 35 cents. Lovell also

204

published the book as No. 52 in Lovell's Library, priced
at 20 cents. He thus became the first American publisher
to produce a popular-priced edition of Progress and Poverty, whose anticipated sale was 250,000 copies. Although
that influential book on the single tax which inveighed
against private property in land was designed less to
entertain than to instruct and sway the laboring masses,
the details of its publication throw light upon Lovell's
general methods as well as upon his reputation, accomplishments, and relations with authors.

According to Henry George, Jr., in The Life of Henry
George, "The English cheap edition of 'Progress and Poverty' was doing so well that the author was set on a
cheap American edition. He thought of importing a dupli-
cate set of the English plates, but abandoned this to put
the book in the hands of John W. Lovell, a publisher of
standard books in cheap form, who had just started a serial library, with a complete book in each number. They
were paper covered, compact, attractive volumes. 'Progress and Poverty' . . . was sold for twenty cents [in
Lovell's Library]. . . . Mr. George was to get ten per
cent. royalty, the same as from Appleton for the better
edition; but this in effect amounted to very little, for
the author gave away so many copies and made such large
personal discounts to those who bought quantities for
educational purposes, that the Lovell edition brought
small return to him, considering the great sale."

On his side, Lovell outlined his publishing plans
to Henry George in a detailed letter dated 28 November
1882, now in the New York Public Library's Henry George
Collection:

> We will publish in 'Lovell's Library' your work
> Progress and Poverty, making the price 20¢ retail.
> We will make new electrotype plates at our own ex-
> pense and in consideration of this we are to have
> the right to continue the publication of the work
> in the Library on the following conditions
> That we pay to you 10% of the retail price,
> that is (2¢) two cents per copy for every copy
> sold of the work.

205

That we furnish to you all copies you may require for your own use, or for sale to any person or persons, except booksellers, (our agreement with the Am[erican]. News C[ompan]y who handle the Library gives them the exclusive sale to the Book and News Trade), at the lowest price we sell to the Am. News Co.

. . . we will publish the work only in the 'Library' form and continue to do so, unless we receive instructions from you or your permission to publish in some other form.

Other titles of political and labor interest published during the 1880s included Edward Kellogg's Labor And Capital (1884), A. J. Starkweather and S. Robert Wilson's Socialism (1884), Albert K. Owen's Integral Co-Operation (1885), as well as Marie Howland's novel, Papa's Own Girl (1885), which concerned a socialistic home in France.

Lovell's personal interest in theosophy, a mystical faith that upheld the universal brotherhood of man, induced him to publish another series for mass consumption, Lovell's Occult Series. Priced at 50 cents in paper and $1.00 in cloth, its titles appealed to readers interested in psychic research and doubtless afforded entertainment to the more skeptical. The first volume in that monthly series was The Blossom And The Fruit (1889) by Mabel Collins, a strange tale mysteriously narrated to its author, who claimed to be able to leave her physical body at will. Other titles in the Occult Series included Clothed With the Sun (1889) by Anna B. Kingsford, The Idyll Of The White Lotus (1890) by Mabel Collins, Magic White and Black and The Talking Image of Urur (1890), both by Franz Hartmann. With the theosophist Ursula Gestefeld, Lovell organized a satellite firm in 1892, Lovell, Gestefeld & Company, which published occult, labor, and feminist books.

According to the report of a seance of 19 October 1890 at which John W. Lovell was present, the medium saw

enormous piles of paper, and different countries;
France, England, and others, all round this. Mr.
Lovell is inside of this, and they all go up to
him; and the spirit says, "he will control them
all. A second Archimedes."
    They show a great roll of paper, and they say
that is the lever. . . . The spirit now turns
to Mr. Lovell and says, You will receive, through
spirit power, knowledge of the planets; which you
will give to the world; and would you have more?
    . . . If you only make all the countries bow
to this one:--and you, you, will make them by
this work you have begun.

The medium's remarks might be construed as a vision of the
gigantic book trust organized by Lovell the same year,
1890. In the absence of an international copyright law,
competition in cheap reprints had by then increased to
such an extent that price-cutting was the order of the
day. Lovell proposed to consolidate all the publishers
of cheap reprints into a combine that would stabilize
prices, stop huge discounts, pool profits, and end ruinous
competition. If publishers refused to consolidate volun-
tarily, Lovell bought them out, purchasing or renting the
plates of his competitors. He accumulated plates from
Worthington; W. L. Allison; DeWolfe, Fiske; Hurst & Company; Pollard and Moss, and others, until he controlled
more than three-quarters of the paper-covered books published by the trade and more than half of the clothbound
books.
    Lovell's giant combine, which aimed at controlling
the entire output of cheap literature in the United
States, was incorporated under New Jersey law as the
United States Book Company in July 1890. Although the
United States Book Company lasted only until 1893, it
was the parent organization of many satellite firms including Lovell, Coryell & Company, Wayside Publishing
Company, Seaside Publishing Company, National Book Company, International Book Company, Empire Publishing Company, and others. As a result of the passage of the
International Copyright Act (1891) and the Panic of 1893,

the gigantic, overextended combine called the United
States Book Company, which proliferated so many cheap
reprint houses, went into bankruptcy in 1893, and
Lovell's career as a publisher ended.

Subsequently John W. Lovell tried to obtain a
controlling interest in Godey's Lady's Book, and became
a member of the firm of Lovell Brothers, printers, on
Lafayette Place, New York. He did some desultory publishing, an edition of Longfellow's Psalm of Life appearing over the imprint of the Lovell Company in 1900.
The same year he filed a petition in bankruptcy. His
remaining years were spent partly in real estate
development.

Lovell's obituaries refer to him accurately as
the speed king of publishers, founder of Lovell's Library, book trust magnate who introduced Kipling and
Barrie to the American masses. He was a grandiose
schemer who distributed cheap books to entertain and
instruct the millions in vaster quantities than ever
before. He was also the organizer of one of the largest
and most audacious book trusts in publishing history.
Lovell's grand-scale methods foreshadow assembly lines,
as his book trust foreshadows the publishing mergers of
the twentieth century. He was perhaps more important
for his approach to publishing and for his publishing
techniques than for the specific titles he published.

Madeleine B. Stern

References

Raymond H. Shove, Cheap Book Production in the United
    States, 1870 to 1891 (Urbana: University of
    Illinois Library, 1937).

Madeleine B. Stern, Imprints on History: Book Pub-
    lishers and American Frontiers (Bloomington:
    Indiana University Press, 1956; reprinted, New
    York: AMS Press, 1975).

John W. Lovell

Frank L. Schick, The Paperbound Book in America: The History of Paperbacks and Their European Background (New York: R. R. Bowker Company, 1958).

John Tebbel, A History of Book Publishing in the United States Vol. II (New York: R. R. Bowker Company, 1975).

No. 6. LOVELL'S ILLUSTRATED SERIES.

The Little Minister

BY

J. M. BARRIE

AUTHOR OF
"A WINDOW
IN THRUMS,"
ETC

NEW YORK
LOVELL, CORYELL & COMPANY
43, 45 and 47 East Tenth Street

(Courtesy Edward T. LeBlanc, *Dime Novel Round-Up*)

30 Lovell, Coryell & Company

Lovell, Coryell & Company (1892-1904) was a prolific subsidiary of the United States Book Company set up by John W. Lovell to publish his better-made books, mostly novels, in varied series. Its output reached some 800 titles in 1892, with the list of authors published reading like a Who's Who of English literature. The firm began a general publishing business around 1 April 1892 at 43, 45, and 47 East 10th Street, New York, between University Place and Broadway, its stock, along with that of other subsidiaries, being moved to the United States Book Company offices at 5 and 7 East 16th Street on 1 May 1893. In February 1894 Lovell, Coryell & Company moved to the Cammeyer Building at the corner of Sixth Avenue and 20th Street, No. 310-318, where it proudly advertised that it would carry full lines of stock under one roof, some one and a half million books on one floor. From 1896 to 1898 it was part of the American Publishers Corporation, and from 1898 to 1899 it was part of the Publishers' Plate Renting Company, with which it shared offices. In April 1902 the enterprise, now Coryell & Company, opened the "City Hall Bookstore" in the Stewart Building at 61 Chambers Street near Broadway, opposite City Hall Park, its last move except for liquidation procedures, which took place in Room 813, 309 Broadway.

Major Authors: James M. Barrie, Marie Corelli, A. Conan Doyle, Alexandre Dumas, Rudyard Kipling, John Morley, William Norris, Mrs. Margaret Oliphant.

Vincent M. Coryell (died 193?), president of Lovell, Coryell & Company, and later of Coryell & Company from 1892 to 1904, became a broker in books and plates in 1904 upon the demise of his company, with an office in Room 112 at 97 Nassau Street. Four years later he opened an office at 119 West 23rd Street as a special agent for P. F. Collier and broker in publishing and other business property. Cutler mentions having had a personal interview

211

with Coryell around 1930 in preparation for his bibliography of Barrie.

The East 10th Street firm of Lovell, Coryell & Company began a general publishing business in the spring of 1892, specializing in well-made, inexpensive reprints of many of the classic titles made popular by John W. Lovell and the United States Book Company, including their standard sets, poets, standard twelvemos, Universal series, Illustrated Series of American Novels, and others. Although the parent United States Book Company was involved in business troubles and lawsuits, Lovell, Coryell & Company was able to carry on, turning out what for the time was high-grade work, advertising "gilt top presentation sets," "de luxe editions," limited in number and on fine paper, some with autographs, at prices of from $5.00 to $12.00. Some of the authors honored by de luxe editions were Henry Irving, James M. Barrie, Henrik Ibsen, James M. Whistler.

An interesting sidelight on this period appears in George T. Dunlap's memoirs The Fleeting Years. Dunlap was a traveling salesman for the United States Book Company in the early '90s; when this company went into receivership in 1893, Dunlap went to work for Lovell, Coryell & Company for several years. Eventually he became a partner, with Alexander Grosset, in the publishing house of Grosset and Dunlap.

The ubiquitous series published by Lovell, Coryell & Company were extensive. In 1894 the Publishers' Trade List Annual devoted some thirty-six pages to the listing and advertising of this company, presenting standard sets of Brontë, Scott, and others; the New Oxford series of two-volume sets "handsomely bound in best silk vellum cloth with gilt top," Eliot, Dickens, and others at 60 cents; one hundred volumes in the New Oxford twelvemos fiction series at 50 cents; ten sets of the Century series of two volumes, featuring Darwin, Spencer, Austen, and Ruskin at $1.00; one hundred volumes of fiction, essays, and poetry at 75 cents, also in the Century series; fifty volumes of classics at $1.50, in a half-morocco, gilt top edition; presentation sets, bound in cloth with gilt tops, of Brontë, Irving, Thackeray and others; Grace Greenwood's illustrated stories for

212

children at $1.25; Library of Masterpieces of English
Literature, $3.50 to $7.00; Modern Fiction, the best
English and American novels in cloth, twelvemo, at $1.00;
Modern Fiction illustrated, slightly higher.

In the attempt to reach everyone, several paperback
series were published quarterly, including novels by
Americans Amelia Rives and W. H. Bishop; the Belmore series priced at 50 cents, modern English and American novels; and an illustrated paper of old favorites at 50
cents. As was common during this period, many of the
titles published were pirated, even though an international copyright law had been passed in 1891.

In 1895 Lovell, Coryell & Company was stressing
novels by Edward W. Townsend, Eleanor Merron, Hall Caine,
Dane Conyngham, E. S. Van Zile, Raymond Raife, and others;
these novels were billed as "earnest, strong, vivid,
clear-cut, clever, clean" and sold for $1.00 to $1.75 in
cloth and 50 cents in paper.

In the spring of 1896 Lovell, Coryell & Company became a part of the American Publishers Corporation which
was handling the intricate affairs of the defunct United
States Book Company; the next year the Lovell, Coryell
name was dropped. In 1898 the American Publishers Corporation also failed; it was succeeded by the Publishers'
Plate Renting Company, which went out of business the next
year, scattering the plates among many publishers. By
spring of 1902 the Publishers' Plate Renting Company was
auctioning off at 61 Chambers Street the last of its
plates, some sixty sets of well-known authors.

Meanwhile in April 1902, Coryell & Company had
opened the City Hall Bookstore at the same address, 61
Chambers Street, and was hawking as of old the "greatest
writers in the English language" on special paper, with
line cuts and steel and wood engravings, two-color bindings with headbands and plenty of gilt, "very chaste in
style . . . that no one need be ashamed to have in his
library," at a moderate price. The sets included the
complete works of Carlyle, Cooper, Dickens, Dumas,
Fielding, and others. In June 1903, Coryell & Company
was receiving bids for some of its plates, and by fall
its voluntary liquidation was announced, with a closing
sale of library editions of some thirty-five multivolume,

213

illustrated, standard sets, including Macaulay, McCarthy, Plutarch, Prescott. In February 1904 some three hundred sets of remaining plates were sold, and by May the final business of Coryell & Company was being taken care of by former president Vincent Coryell, according to Publishers' Weekly (7 May 1904), "from eleven A.M. till twelve at noon daily" in an office at 309 Broadway.

Lovell, Coryell & Company was the longest lived of the subsidiaries of the United States Book Company. By its publication of fine authors in inexpensive editions it helped to form the taste of the middle class, encourage the creation of good literature, offer recreation for the masses, and develop best sellers. Through its publishing of quality works in what was for the time a quality format, all done up inexpensively, the firm reached a vast audience.

Irene P. Norell

References

Publishers' Trade List Annual (New York: R. R. Bowker Company, 1892-1902).

Bradley D. Cutler, Sir James M. Barrie, a Bibliography (New York: Greenberg, 1931).

Raymond H. Shove, Cheap Book Production in the United States, 1870 to 1891 (Urbana, Illinois: University of Illinois Library, 1937).

Madeleine B. Stern, Imprints on History: Book Publishers and American Frontiers (Bloomington: Indiana University Press, 1956; reprinted, New York: AMS Press, 1975).

John Tebbel, A History of Book Publishing in the United States, Vol. II (New York: R. R. Bowker Company, 1975).

31 F. M. Lupton Publishing Company

F. M. Lupton Publishing Company (circa 1882–circa 1910) published over 850 titles in various editions of cheap twelvemos and other reprints. Its founder, Frank M. Lupton, beginning with his Leisure Hour Library, devised successful promotional techniques to sell his mass-produced books to a mass audience. By 1888 the firm was located at 63 Murray Street, New York, in 1890 at 106–08 Reade Street, in 1894 at 72–76 Walker Street, and on 1 May 1899 the company was relocated at 52–58 Duane Street on the southeast corner of Duane and Elm streets. In 1903 the firm's address was the Lupton Building, 23–27 City Hall Place. Although Lupton started his publishing business in the early 1880s, the F. M. Lupton Publishing Company was incorporated to manufacture, deal in, print, bind, publish, and sell books in 1892. Directors were Walter S. Trigg, Thomas H. Marshall, Stuart H. Moore, Albert B. Beers, and August Schlegel. By 1903 the name of the firm was changed to the Federal Book Company.

Major Authors: Emerson Bennett, Frances Hodgson Burnett, John Habberton, Caroline Lee Hentz, Emma Southworth, Ann S. Stephens.

Frank Moore Lupton was born in Mattituck, Long Island, 21 February 1854, and died 6 October 1910. His family was one of the oldest and best known among the farming community at the east end of Long Island. He was educated at a private school at Cutchogue until he was fifteen, when he was apprenticed to learn the printer's trade in the office of the Suffolk Weekly Times at Greenport. The next year he moved to New York City, where he worked for five years in the printing concern of S. W. Green, located at the corner of Frankfort and Jacob Streets. In 1875 Lupton became associated with Stuart H. Moore and J. Victor Wilson in publishing a monthly journal, the Cricket on the Hearth. Four years later he founded his own business, which published monthly literary

Special Number.
Price, 25 Cents.
THE LEISURE HOUR LIBRARY.
No. 308.
PUBLISHED WEEKLY.   BY SUBSCRIPTION, PER YEAR, 50 CENTS.   NOVEMBER 10TH, 1900.
Entered at the New York Post Office as Second-Class Matter.

The GUNMAKER of MOSCOW

By Sylvanus Cobb, Jr.

(Courtesy Edward T. LeBlanc, *Dime Novel Round-Up*)

periodicals, originally the Fireside and Home, and later
the People's Home Journal and Good Literature.

Lupton was a very energetic man, well known for his
business and philanthropic enterprises. In addition to
his work with the F. M. Lupton Publishing Company, he
published the Ladies' World with a partner, S. H. Moore,
under the firm name of S. H. Moore & Company; he was
owner of William J. Brown & Company, a printing and binding
establishment; and he was part owner of the Manhattan
Typesetting Company. In 1905 he donated $30,000 to the
town of Mattituck for a building which housed a meeting
hall and the public library. With its Italian gardens,
his Brooklyn mansion at 839 St. Mark's Avenue was a show-
place. Due to overwork, ill health, and melancholia,
Lupton ended his life by cutting his throat. His estate
was worth more than a million dollars at the time of his
suicide.

Although other associates joined the business, the
F. M. Lupton Publishing Company continued to reflect the
early printing and merchandising methods of its founder.
The Lupton slogan, "Publishers of Popular Books for the
Masses," expressed the essence of Lupton's promotional
practices. He pioneered with his publication of the Leisure Hour Library, a series of novels that were cheaply
constructed and cheaply sold. The sales of the Leisure
Hour Library increased until they aggregated more than a
million copies each month.

Popular works appearing over the Lupton imprint
were precursors of the do-it-youself books in vogue today: The Standard American Poultry Book: A Guide to
Profitable Poultry Keeping (1886), The National Farmer's
and Housekeeper's Cyclopaedia (1888), and The American
Domestic Cyclopaedia: A Volume of Universal Ready Reference for American Women in American Homes (1890). With
544 pages and 189 illustrations, the Domestic Cyclopaedia
was a carefully detailed, useful handbook for homemakers.

By 1894 the Publishers' Trade List Annual contained
a thirty-page Lupton catalog. It advertised a variety of
series--the Lenox and the Princeton Twelvemos, the Avon
and the Stratford, the Hammock and the Souvenir, the
Elite and the Bijou--all usually selling for as little
as 25 or 50 cents. Costing 60 cents were the National

F. M. Lupton Publishing Company

Twelvemos, copyright works by popular American authors such as Mrs. C. A. Warfield and Eliza Dupuy. These books, the advertisement asserted, had "never heretofore been sold in cloth at less than $1.50." British classics by Dickens and Thackeray could be had for only 25 cents, and an illustrated, eight-volume set of the works of Shakespeare for $7.50.

In 1897 the firm hired as its sole manager J. M. Ruston, formerly connected with one of its competitors, Hurst & Company. Ruston promoted a series with flower covers--The Golden-rod: "An entirely new line, consisting of the selected works of over fifty well-known and popular authors including, Rudyard Kipling and A. Conan Doyle." The Violet Series, with dainty, illuminated covers selected especially for women readers, included Camille and many "charming novels" by women authors, such as My Sister Kate by Charlotte M. Braeme and the perennial favorite, Charlotte Temple by Susannah Rowson. Editions in the flower series sold for 10 cents as the firm joined the intense competition of the time.

Soon after the turn of the century, Lupton devoted his energies once again to publishing magazines and periodicals. Following Lupton's death in 1910, the stock company was turned over to the management of his son-in-law, Charles Courtenay Hoge.

The F. M. Lupton Publishing Company successfully published inexpensive books, most of which were reprints. The firm made its niche in publishing history on the strength of its mass publishing and merchandising techniques.

Marie Olesen Urbanski

References

Publishers' Trade List Annual (New York: R. R. Bowker Company, 1880-1910).

F. M. Lupton Publishing Company

William S. Pelletreau, <u>History of Long Island</u>, III
(New York and Chicago: Lewis Publishers, 1903).

Charles E. Craven, <u>A History of Mattituck</u> (Long Island:
Published for the Author, 1906).

<u>New York Times</u> (7 October 1910): 5.

Raymond H. Shove, <u>Cheap Book Production in the United
States, 1870 to 1891</u> (Urbana: University of
Illinois Library, 1937).

Madeleine B. Stern, <u>Imprints on History: Book Pub-
lishers and American Frontiers</u> (Bloomington:
University of Indiana Press, 1956; reprinted,
New York: AMS Press, 1975).

219

(Courtesy Edward T. LeBlanc, *Dime Novel Round-Up*)

32　George Munro

George Munro (1864-1893) published dime novels about the
frontier, cheap story papers, and a series of inexpensive
reprints of foreign novels. The company published over
three hundred ten-cent novels and more than three thousand
quarto and pocket-size books in various editions. Begun
late in 1862 as a partnership, Irwin P. Beadle and Company, at 137 William Street, New York, the house became
George Munro and Company when Beadle left in 1864. In May
1868 the name was changed to George Munro, and the offices
were moved to 118 William, and to 84 Beekman in 1870. By
1883 Munro had offices, presses, and storage in the eight-
story Munro Building 17-27 Vandewater Street, and a nine-
story building at 43-51 Rose Street. The firm's Fireside
Companion Series and Seaside Library were housed there.
George Munro retired 1 April 1893, and the business was
continued by his sons George W. and John as George Munro's
Sons until dissolved in 1906.

　　　Major Authors: Edward S. Ellis, Harlan P. Halsey,
J. Milton Hoffman, L. Augustus Jones, George G. Small,
Louis Vincent.

　　　George Munro was born in West River, Nova Scotia,
on 12 November 1825, and died 23 April 1896 at Pine Hill,
New York. He learned printing as an apprentice at the
Pictou Observer, and taught at the Free Church Academy in
Halifax while completing his study of theology. He never
served as a minister. In 1856 he went to New York City
and was employed first by the American News Company and
then by Beadle and Adams, at whose office, according to
Edward Ellis (as quoted by Rogers in "Munro's Ten Cent
Novels"): "One day Mr. Beadle pointed out an employee to
whom he was paying $16 a week. 'He is from Nova Scotia,'
he said, 'and the best thing about him is that he is absolutely satisfied with his situation. He will never ask
for an advance in wages, nor seek any other situation.'"
Little more than a month later, according to Ellis, that

221

employee, George Munro, became Irwin P. Beadle's partner in publishing dime novels.

In January 1863 the two established Irwin P. Beadle & Company in the old Beadle & Company office on William Street. They began with the publication of the first of a series: Irwin P. Beadle's Ten Cent Song Books. Munro and Beadle placed the likeness of a ten-cent postage stamp on the front cover in unveiled imitation of the dime used by Beadle & Adams on its covers. The latter firm sued Munro & Beadle in New York Superior Court, but lost. Munro and his partner were allowed to use the cover design.

The firm began a series of novels called Irwin P. Beadle's Ten Cent Novels. Only five numbers carried that title. With Number 6, published 27 February 1864, it was changed to Munro's Ten Cent Novels following the retirement of Irwin P. Beadle. Number 1 in the series was The Hunters, or Life on the Mountain and Prairie by Capt. Lathan G. Carleton, a pseudonym of Edward S. Ellis. He went on to write at least 90 of the 354 novels in the series, which were published approximately every two weeks to Number 345, and monthly to the last issue in August 1877.

In 1867 Munro began The New York Fireside Companion (1867-1903), an inexpensive family paper featuring stories and entertainment. The Old Sleuth serials by Harlan P. Halsey began with Old Sleuth Detective (1872). More than one hundred other titles followed in what was called the Old Sleuth Library. The detective stories had many imitators, including Munro's former employer, and in 1888 Munro sued Beadle & Adams to restrain that firm from using the word sleuth in its titles. Beadle & Adams won the initial decision, but the house was barred in 1890 from using the word in titles or authors' names.

In 1877 Munro began the Seaside Library, a series of cheap reprints of English works in paper-covered pamphlets which could be mailed at newspaper rates. The first numbers were East Lynne, John Halifax, Jane Eyre, A Woman-Hater, The Black Indies, The Last Days of Pompeii, and Adam Bede, priced at 10 cents each. Since the United States and England had no copyright agreement, no compensation went to the authors. With the huge success of the

George Munro

Seaside Library, Munro dropped his 10-cent novel series in 1877.

Munro retired from publishing in April 1893. The firm was carried on by his sons as George Munro's Sons until its dissolution in May 1906. Upon his death in April 1896, George Munro's estate was estimated at ten million dollars.

George Munro's family story papers and Seaside Library brought entertainment and quality literature to large numbers of readers at cheap prices. The firm's popular fiction, beginning as frontier tales and ending as detective adventures, reflected and catered to the changing tastes of nineteenth-century American readers.

Michael B. Goodman

References

"Death of George Munro," The New York Times (25 April 1896): 1.

Charles M. Harvey, "The Dime Novel in American Life," Atlantic Monthly, 50 (July 1907): 37-45.

Edmund Pearson, Dime Novels; or, Following an Old Trail in Popular Literature (Boston: Little, Brown and Company, 1929).

Albert Johannsen, The House of Beadle and Adams and Its Dime and Nickel Novels: The Story of a Vanished Literature (Norman: University of Oklahoma Press, 1950-1962).

Denis R. Rogers, "Munro's Ten Cent Novels," Dime Novel Round-Up, Supplement 2 (October 1958): 1-40.

(Courtesy Edward T. LeBlanc, *Dime Novel Round-Up*)

33 Norman L. Munro

Norman L. Munro (1873-1894) published story papers, cheap detective novels, and inexpensive reprints. The firm was begun by Norman L. Munro and Frank Tousey in 1873 at 163 William Street, New York, with publication of The New York Family Story Paper, which continued weekly until 1921. In 1876 Tousey left the firm. Munro moved to 28-30 Beekman Street in 1875, and to the Munro Building 24-26 Vandewater Street in 1883. Fires in 1887 and 1893 partially destroyed the offices there. The first of 131 issues of Our Boys of New York appeared in 1883. It featured installments of Old Cap Collier stories, over seven hundred of which appeared in the Old Cap Collier Library. Munro's wife Henrietta continued the firm after his death in 1894.

    Major Authors: Thomas C. Harbaugh, George G. Small, Edward Ten Eyck.

    Norman L. Munro was born in Millbrook, Nova Scotia, in 1844, and died 24 February 1894. At twenty-five he came to New York to work for his brother George Munro, determined to learn the publishing business and to set aside enough money to start his own firm. On 18 September 1873, the first day of the Panic, he published the first number of his New York Family Story Paper. He and his wife Henrietta had two children, Norma and Henry.

    Munro's first publishing venture, after leaving his brother, proved his most sustaining money-maker. Shortly after his Family Story Paper was established, he began a series directed toward a different audience. The first number of The Boys Own Story Teller (23 August 1875) differed from George Munro's Girls and Boys of America series. Ross Craufurd described it in Dime Novel Round-Up (February 1979) as "heady, stimulating, almost intoxicating stuff . . . stories of brash boys making their way through brash, gusty times." After a dozen issues Munro changed the format to a sixty-four page biweekly magazine

225

priced at 10 cents. It featured short stories, novel-
ettes, and serials, but ran only nine numbers. With
Number ten it was changed to the eight-page, 5-cent Our
Boys of New York.

In 1876 Munro's partner Frank Tousey, nephew of
the American News Company's Sinclair Tousey, left with
his money to start a new firm. He also took writer
George G. Small with him. Tousey's New York Boys Weekly
featured a full front-page illustration, which Munro soon
imitated. In September Tousey began another competitive
paper. Shortly afterward Munro declared bankruptcy and,
according to Craufurd, "ceded the Boys of New York, Our
Boys, and his 138 issues of the New York Boy's Library to
Tousey and Small." In July 1878 Tousey merged his New
York Boys Weekly with the Boys of New York; and Our Boys
was incorporated with the Young Men of America. Tousey
thought he would also acquire the Family Story Paper, but
Munro retained it and used it to rebuild his fortune.

The Our Boys series provided ammunition for the at-
tackers of the immorality of dime novels. Serials with
titles such as The New York Jack Shephard, the Boy Highwayman, Behind the Bars, or the Boy Convict, and Jack the
Joker, or the Irish Robber's Apprentice were charged with
leading young boys to ruin.

In 1883 Norman Munro began the Old Cap Collier series, using several authors, most with pseudonyms, for
the more than seven hundred numbers. The first in the
series was by W. I. James: Old Cap Collier, or "Piping"
the New Haven Mystery. Pearson in Dime Novels notes that
the story had its basis in the mysterious death of Jennie
E. Cramer in 1881. Many of the early entries in the series were similarly based on actual cases. Toward the end
the quality of contents as well as the paper and illustrations deteriorated. I. S. Cobb in A Plea for Old Cap
Collier tried in the early 1920s to rescue the detective
from oblivion and erase the tainted reputation of the dime
novel as a corrupter of youth.

Munro also published Munro's Pocket Magazine, a
book-sized, 350-page monthly. Each issue contained a complete novel, several serial chapters, short stories, poems, and gossip. The firm also published Munro's Library,
which consisted of complete, unabridged editions of

Dickens and Eliot on fine white paper in clear readable
type priced at from 10 to 20 cents. Munro was concerned
with typographical appearance and accurate proofreading.

Shortly after his death an unidentified newspaper
of June 1895 described him as "the originator of the publication of standard and popular works of fiction in
cheap form." Actually, Norman L. Munro was more imitative
than innovative. With most of the cheap book and story
paper publishers of the nineteenth century, he provided
exciting narratives and standard works at reasonable
prices for a large reading public.

Michael B. Goodman

References

"Contribution to Trade History, No. XXIV: Norman L.
Munro," American Bookseller, 19 (1886): 103-104.

Charles M. Harvey, "The Dime Novel in American Life,"
Atlantic Monthly, 100 (July 1907): 37-45.

I. S. Cobb, A Plea for Old Cap Collier (New York:
Doran, 1921).

Edmund Pearson, Dime Novels; or, Following an Old Trail
in Popular Literature (Boston: Little, Brown and
Company, 1929).

Albert Johannsen, The House of Beadle and Adams and Its
Dime and Nickel Novels: The Story of a Vanished
Literature (Norman: University of Oklahoma Press,
1950-1962).

Ross Craufurd, Bibliographic Listing. OUR BOYS and NEW
YORK BOYS WEEKLY: The Great Tousey-Munro Rivalry
(Fall River, Mass.: Edward T. LeBlanc, 1979).

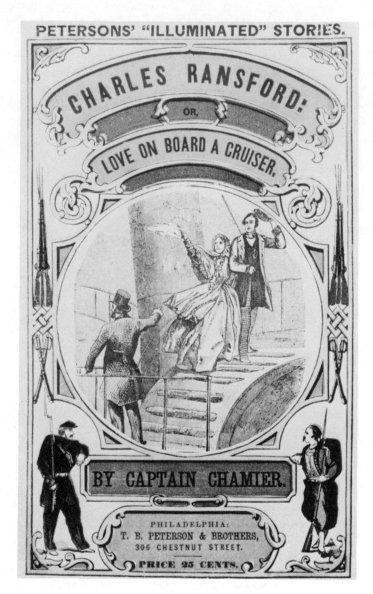

(Courtesy Edward T. LeBlanc, *Dime Novel Round-Up*)

34   T. B. Peterson & Brothers

T. B. Peterson & Brothers (1845-1896), publishers of romantic and sensational fiction, also specialized in cookery books. The firm published over one thousand titles
in various editions. In 1845 T. B. Peterson established
himself as a bookseller and news agent at 98 Chestnut
Street, Philadelphia, publishing his first publication
the following year. At 98 Chestnut (renumbered 102
Chestnut in 1854) he conducted his wholesale and retail
publishing and bookselling business until it outgrew its
original quarters. In 1858 Peterson moved to a larger
store at 306 Chestnut and, in the same year, took his
brothers, George W. and Thomas, into partnership. The
firm was then styled T. B. Peterson & Brothers, a name
retained despite the death of George W. Peterson in 1861.
The business prospered at 306 Chestnut under the direction of the senior partner. When T. B. Peterson died in
1890, Thomas Peterson continued the business as T. B.
Peterson & Brothers Ltd. for a few more years. In 1896
the sale of stock and stereotype plates took place and
the firm was dissolved.

    <u>Major Authors</u>: Charles Dickens, Eliza Ann Dupuy,
Caroline Lee Hentz, Mrs. E. D. E. N. Southworth, Mrs. Ann
Sophia Stephens, Mrs. Henry Wood.

    Theophilus Beasley Peterson was born in Philadelphia
on 14 January 1823 and died in that city on 30 December
1890. He was descended on his father's side from the
original Swedish immigrants whose settlements on the
Delaware River antedated that of William Penn, and on his
mother's side from an old New England family. From an
early age Peterson displayed the familial traits of self-
reliance, courage, and enterprise. At thirteen he decided
that the routine of school life was too distasteful to be
pursued, so he left it to seek his fortune in the world
of business. He spent the next eighteen months as a
clerk, first in a dry goods store and later in a shipping

house, but found neither position sufficiently challenging. His next choice was a trade, and he entered a stereotyping foundry where he learned the arts of type-setting and stereotyping. He became so proficient in these skills that in 1843 he was offered the position as foreman of the Saturday Evening Post, then edited by George R. Graham and Theophilus's older brother, Charles Jacobs Peterson. Though the position was a responsible one, Theophilus was determined to have his own business. After two years with the Saturday Evening Post he had saved $300.00 and decided to resign. He set himself up as a bookseller and news agent at 98 (later 102) Chestnut Street with capital stock of less than $100.00 after initial expenses were paid.

Adopting the motto, "small profits and quick sales," Peterson dealt only in books, chiefly fiction, which could be sold at very low prices. He was a shrewd judge of the popular market and within the first year did remarkably well. He quickly realized that current publishing practices were not meeting the demand for cheap popular fiction and decided to try his hand at publishing as well as bookselling. His first venture was a reprint of Lady Charlotte Bury's sensational novel, Ensnared or The Divorced, as it was called in some editions. It had been published as a three-decker, selling at $7.50, but Peterson priced his one-volume edition, published in 1846, at 25 cents. Sales were so successful that Peterson resolved to stereotype all the popular foreign and American fiction he could obtain and sell at the lowest possible prices.

He wasted no time putting his plan into action. Catalogs of his publications soon listed the works of the most celebrated and popular writers from all over the world. E. L. Bulwer, Wilkie Collins, Charles Dickens, G. P. R. James, Captain Marryat, Sir Walter Scott, and Mrs. Henry Wood were among the English writers, while Alexandre Dumas, George Sand, Eugène Sue, and Emile Zola represented the French, in translation. The firm's list of American authors included T. S. Arthur, Emerson Bennett, Eliza Ann Dupuy, Caroline Lee Hentz, George Lippard, Charles J. Peterson, Mrs. E. D. E. N. Southworth, and Mrs. Ann Sophia Stephens. By 1858 Peterson's

230

business, having outgrown its original quarters, moved to a larger store at 306 Chestnut Street. The new shop was well suited to the activities of the publishing and book-selling firm. The spacious front on the ground floor was devoted to the sale of books, both Peterson's and other publishers', at wholesale and retail prices, while the other departments of the business filled the remaining four floors. In the same year Theophilus took his brothers George W. and Thomas, who had served their apprenticeship with him as clerks, into partnership, changing the firm's name to T. B. Peterson & Brothers.

By that time the firm ranked among the major publishing houses in Philadelphia. Edwin T. Freedley included it in his 1858 listing of Philadelphia and its Manufactures, stating that T. B. Peterson possessed stereotype plates of 600 different books, principally novels, and sold an average of 50,000 volumes annually. Freedley also asserted that Peterson had invested $50,000 in Charles Dickens alone and was the sole publisher of the complete works of Dickens in the United States. Peterson was, in fact, the "official" publisher of Dickens by 1853. He had purchased the copyrights and stereotype plates of all of Dickens's works that had been published by Carey, Lea & Blanchard, Stringer and Townsend, Jasper Harding, and Harper & Bros. He also negotiated a lucrative agreement with Harper & Bros. for Dickens's later works. Harper and Peterson shared the cost of procuring advance proof sheets of Dickens's stories from his London publisher. Harper & Bros. would manufacture the plates and illustrations, run the story in its magazines, and then turn the plates and illustrations over to the Philadelphia firm so Peterson could publish the story in book form. In all, Peterson published over twenty different editions of Dickens's novels, ranging in price from 25 cents to $2.00.

But it was in the romantic and sensational fiction produced by American authors that Peterson found his bonanza. His editions of the temperance tales of T. S. Arthur, the adventurous accounts of Emerson Bennett, and the sensational and historical novels of George Lippard met with great success. His most popular authors were

231

T. B. Peterson & Brothers

Mrs. Emma Dorothy Eliza Nevitte Southworth and Mrs. Ann
Sophia Stephens.

Mrs. E. D. E. N. Southworth's first novel, Retribution, had appeared in the Washington National Era in 1849
and was later published in book form by Harper & Bros.
It was well received and brought Mrs. Southworth to the
attention of Henry Peterson, Theophilus's cousin, who was
then editor of the Saturday Evening Post. Soon the National Era and the Saturday Evening Post were publishing
her novels serially, while Appleton & Company and Carey &
Hart produced them in book form. The Saturday Evening
Post ran her tale The Lost Heiress but she had some dif-
ficulty finding a book publisher to take it up. One
afternoon late in 1854 she presented herself in T. B.
Peterson's shop with the manuscript in hand. Peterson's
astute sense of popular taste was aroused. He agreed to
publish the book and signed Mrs. Southworth to a long-
term contract for her future books. Peterson also bought
the copyrights and plates of her earlier stories from
their original book publishers. While The Lost Heiress
was in press, Peterson expended great sums of money advertising it. The experiment was a success, for the novel
sold well and renewed the demand for Mrs. Southworth's
early writings.

Soon after Peterson became Mrs. Southworth's publisher he learned that Robert Bonner, proprietor of the
New York Ledger, was running one of her stories for which
Peterson owned the copyright. An irate letter to Bonner
brought apologies and the explanation that he had picked
up the story from an English newspaper which had published
it as an original work. Peterson accepted Bonner's state-
ment and allowed him to continue the story in the Ledger.
Later, Mrs. Southworth and Bonner concluded an agreement
that gave Bonner exclusive serial rights for her novels
while Peterson remained her book publisher. The arrangement was not without its problems. When Bonner published
The Hidden Hand in 1859 he sensed that it would be an extremely popular story. So he purchased the copyright and
refused to release the novel to Peterson despite appeals
and protests. Bonner ran the story three times in the
Ledger before it finally appeared in book form, published
by one of Bonner's sons. Mrs. Southworth did, however,

make quite a fortune for Peterson. Her novels went
through several editions before the uniform set of forty-
three volumes was launched by T. B. Peterson & Brothers
in 1877.

Mrs. Ann S. Stephens's literary reputation was well
established when she became associated with Peterson's
house. She had begun her literary career in 1834 as editor of The Portland Magazine, published by her husband.
The couple later moved to New York where Mrs. Stephens
became a contributor and associate editor of The Ladies
Companion. Nearly every number of the magazine contained
one of her stories emblazoned on the first page, and soon
the editors of other literary journals were vying for her
stories. When, in 1841, George R. Graham and Charles J.
Peterson sought contributors for Graham's Magazine, their
list included such eminent authors as Longfellow, Bryant,
Cooper, Poe, and Mrs. Stephens. In the following year
Charles J. Peterson commenced publication of his own journal, in competition with Godey's Lady's Book, and attracted Mrs. Stephens to his staff. Her association with
Peterson's Magazine was to continue for the next forty
years. After her serials and their sequels appeared in
his "lady's magazine," Charles Peterson would turn the
stories over to his brothers, whose quarters at 306 Chestnut Street he shared, for publication in book form. The
mutually productive family arrangement resulted in a uniform fourteen-volume edition of Mrs. Stephens's works in
1869, and a new twenty-three volume set that was being
printed when Mrs. Stephens died in 1886.

T. B. Peterson & Brothers did not neglect the other
literary ladies whose novels were so popular in circulating libraries. Eliza Ann Dupuy and Caroline Lee Hentz
met with great success under Peterson's system, as did
their British counterpart, Mrs. Henry Wood. Peterson paid
liberally for advance sheets of Mrs. Wood's stories, publishing thirty-three of them, including her famous East
Lynne. The firm also made a specialty of cookery books
and had a dozen best-sellers in this field alone.
Francatelli's Modern Cook, which offered the most approved
methods of English, French, German, and Italian cookery,
Miss Leslie's and Mrs. Hale's were among the most popular.

T. B. Peterson & Brothers

By 1874 T. B. Peterson & Brothers was among the largest publishers of cheap books in the United States with over one thousand titles in plates. A few years earlier Peterson had closed the retail department of the business, selling the books from other publishers at extra discounts. Thereafter the business was confined to the manufacture and sale of the firm's own publications. Circulating libraries and bookstalls in railway stations were important outlets for Peterson's books, but his monopoly was soon challenged by the competition of the Seaside and other cheap libraries. In 1880 T. B. Peterson & Brothers was forced into bankruptcy, but an agreement with its creditors allowed the firm to remain in business. Peterson continued to direct the business until a few weeks before his death on 30 December 1890. It did well under his guidance, although price-cutting and pirating among the cheap book publishers remained a problem. After T. B. Peterson's death, his brother Thomas ran the business until 1896 when the stock and plates were sold.

T. B. Peterson was regarded by his colleagues as a publisher of enterprise and integrity. In 1875 the New York Evening Post deemed him worthy of a sketch in its series, "The Bookmakers." That opinion was reiterated sixteen years later when Peterson's death was announced to the publishing world. Publishers' Weekly styled him one of the "self-made men" of the American book trade. Specifically, T. B. Peterson initiated the practice of publishing catalogs with biographical sketches and portraits of his principal authors, an idea adopted by other publishers. In general, his firm's success demonstrated how popular tastes could be exploited and illustrated the potential of advertising in the sale of books.

Marie E. Korey

234

T. B. Peterson & Brothers

References

"The Bookmakers. Reminiscences and Contemporary Sketches
of American Publishers. XIX. T. B. Peterson &
Brothers," New York Evening Post (24 February 1875).

"Obituary. Theophilus B. Peterson," Publishers' Weekly
(10 January 1891): 27-28.

Complete in one Number.   Price, 5 Cents.

The Nickel Library

5 CENTS · UNITED STATES OF AMERICA

Entered according to Act of Congress by PICTORIAL PRINTING CO. in the office of the Librarian at Washington, D. C., in the year 1877.

SERIES ONE.   CHICAGO.   NUMBER EIGHT.

DUNCAN,
:OR:
THE GIANT OF THE WOODS.

BY C. LEON MEREDITH.

THE GIANT AND THE THREE HURONS.---See page 19.

CHAPTER I.
THE PIONEER'S HOME.

It was the hour of night-fall. The beech and maple trees of the primitive forest threw out long shadows across the little clearing where stood the cabin of Joel Spencer, one of the first pioneers who ventured the establishment of a home west of the Allegheny river.

It was the hour when the whip-poor-will begins its monotonous cry, and the nocturnal birds come forth with their hoots and cries—the hour by far the most lonesome and solemn of all the day to the human inhabitant of the wilderness.

In the doorway of the cabin sat the sturdy woodman and his wife. Both were a little past the meridian of life, but each remained

(Courtesy Edward T. LeBlanc, *Dime Novel Round-Up*)

35   Pictorial Printing Company

Pictorial Printing Company (1874-1893) entered the serial publishing field in 1876 and earned a place in popular publishing history with its Nickel Library, featuring stories of Indians, the frontier, and the West. This was the first weekly in octavo to offer complete original stories at 5 cents. The original partners were Albert Sibley and John McGreer. Late in 1875, George E. Blakelee became secretary and treasurer and brought with him his general literary monthly In-Door and Out. In January 1876 its first number under the new partnership appeared. The firm's address was 74-76 Randolph Street, Chicago. It also published The Illustrated Literary Monthly, The Parlor Library, and The Weekly Novelist, a 5-cent, eight-page story paper. In March 1881, when G. P. Bassett and Frank L. Waite bought the company, Sibley and Blakelee left, forming the Novelist Publishing Company, Chicago, which continued to publish The Nickel Library and The Weekly Novelist. On 3 June 1882 the firm moved to 20 Rose Street, New York, and continued to publish various "libraries," including a War Library whose 413 numbers were devoted to tales of the Civil War. In 1885 Sibley moved to 18 Rose Street, and in 1888 Blakelee moved to 24 Rose. Early in 1893 the house's publishing activities ended.

Major Authors: George E. Blakelee, T. C. Harbaugh, William H. Manning, James Milford Merrill, St. George Rathborne.

From November 1868 to August 1874 George Blakelee was owner and editor of the Ohio Farmer of Cleveland. After selling it he moved to Indianapolis where, in January 1875, he founded In-Door and Out, a 15-cent literary monthly. After he became a partner in the Pictorial Printing Company this magazine was published by his new firm until May 1879.

Pictorial Printing Company

On 20 June 1877 appeared the initial number of The
Nickel Library, a series of 32-page octavo nickel novels--
the first of a genre that was to flood the country during
the next thirty-five years. The first number was Rainbow.
A Romance of Frontier Life by C. Leon Meredith [George
Blakelee]. The first four numbers were published monthly
until 6 October 1877 when, with number 5, The Young Gold
Hunters. A Tale of the Black Hills by Marline Manly
[St. George Rathborne] it became a weekly. The Nickel
Library ended with number 920, 4 March 1893.

St. George Rathborne joined the firm as editor in
1878. He was a prolific contributor to The Nickel Library, furnishing sixty-three stories under various pen
names: twenty by "Marline Manly" and thirteen by "Harry
St. George." Blakelee himself contributed twenty stories
under the pseudonym C. Leon Meredith; T. C. Harbaugh supplied twenty stories under his own name and twenty-two
under the pen name Major A. F. Grant. As "Capt. Mark
Wilton," William H. Manning contributed thirty-nine stories. Another important author was James Milford Merrill
with thirty stories, nineteen by "Morris Redwing."

In all, seventy-five different authors wrote the 359
original stories in The Nickel Library. Reprints began
with number 298, and from then on were interspersed with
original stories until number 419, after which all stories
were reprints. Most of the Nickel Library authors supplied such publishers as Beadle & Adams, Frank Tousey,
and Street & Smith. An outstanding feature of the library
was its covers, in a style peculiarly appropriate to the
tales of woods and wilds, trappers and redskins, pioneers
and bordermen that they encased.

On 16 September 1882, a few months after the Novel-
ist Publishing Company moved to New York, the first number
of The War Library appeared, consisting of quarto pam-
phlets usually of 24 pages, priced at 10 cents, subtitled
"Original Stories of Adventure in the War for the Union."
The authors were, for the most part, the Nickel Library
mainstays. The stories, the majority representing the
Union point of view, included Fighting Joe Hooker; or, The
Battle Above the Clouds by Marline Manly [St. George
Rathborne]; Black Cudjo; or, A Thrilling Story of the Fort
Pillow Massacre by Lieutenant Keene [Rathborne]; Libby

Prison; or, In the Shadow of Death by Colonel Oram Eflor
[Maro Rolfe]; The Girl Guerilla; or, The Secret League of
Gray by J. M. Merrill; Lincoln's Spy; or, The Loyal Detective by Major A. F. Grant [T. C. Harbaugh]; and The Sky
Scouts; or, Ballooning for the Union by Colonel Oram Eflor
[Rolfe]. The series of 413 numbers, of which some 200
were reprints, ended 9 August 1890. With its details of
generals and campaigns, battles and skirmishes, naval encounters and espionage, The War Library provides a colorful panorama of the Civil War.

Late in 1885 Albert Sibley moved to 18 Rose Street
along with The War Library. On 18 October 1885 he started
The American Library, which was similar in format and
price to The War Library and included some 30 numbers.
Before it ended The Saturday Library was launched, ending
with number 231, 24 May 1890. Both libraries featured
detective stories, miscellaneous adventure stories and,
in the case of The Saturday Library, comic stories. Half
the numbers were reprints. Other Sibley libraries were
The Camp Fire Library, 95 numbers (1887-1888) and The
Cricket Library, 16 numbers (1888).

In his Bibliography of Dime Novel Publications,
Charles Bragin arbitrarily ascribes the Novelist Publishing Company publications to Street & Smith. There is no
evidence to support this attribution, which may have been
suggested by the similarity in the firms' addresses,
Street & Smith offices at 31 Rose Street being diago-
nally opposite Sibley and Blakelee.

George Blakelee continued in business as the Nickel
Library Company. On 18 September 1886 he published the
first number of the Little Chief Library, a spin-off of
The Nickel Library, its 296 numbers containing many
Nickel Library stories under new names and with new by-
lines. The last number of the Little Chief Library
appeared in April 1892 and was followed 11 May by the
first number of Border Boys Library, also largely made
up of reprints from The Nickel Library. The last number
known is 26, dated 2 November 1892. Albert Sibley turned
over his publications to his brother Charles D. Sibley
and nephew Charles S. Sibley, who continued to publish
libraries of reprinted stories.

Pictorial Printing Company

The Nickel Library exerted a powerful influence upon competing publishers. Its 5-cent price impelled Beadle & Adams to follow suit with the Half-Dime Library, begun 15 October 1877. Frank Tousey altered his 10-cent New York Boys Library, acquired from Norman L. Munro, into The Five Cent Wide Awake Library, begun 6 September 1878. Both libraries lasted until the turn of the century when the 5-cent colored-cover weeklies dominated the field. The Pictorial Printing Company's pocket-sized Nickel Library inspired several imitators.

Although generally unknown today except to a few collectors, the Pictorial Printing Company and its successor the Novelist Publishing Company were important contributors to the development of popular publishing during the nineteenth century. The Pictorial and Novelist publications offer an impressive body of reading matter relating to the West and the Civil War which found warm public acceptance over a period of fifteen years.

Ross Craufurd

Reference

Albert Johannsen, <u>The Nickel Library</u> (Fall River, Mass.: Edward T. LeBlanc, 1959).

36   Pollard & Moss

Pollard & Moss (1879-1889), subscription book publishers, mostly reprinted cheap editions of standard and illustrated works. The firm began publishing at 47 John Street, New York, and in May 1888 moved to 42 Park Place and 37 Barclay Street. The business was terminated in 1889 with the assignment of the firm.

Major Series: Echo Series; P & M Series.

The partnership was established in 1879 with a formal agreement between Martha B. Pollard of Riverdale, New York, and Charles Moss of New York City. Mrs. Pollard's interests were represented in the firm by her husband, who left the employ of D. & J. Sadlier when that publishing firm, specializing in Catholic books, experienced financial difficulties.

Like the firm of Belford, Clarke & Company, Pollard & Moss specialized in the reprinting of cheap editions of standard works. Its books were produced in series: the Echo Series of popular novels in paper covers priced at 25 and 50 cents, and its P & M Series of clothbound twelvemos. The latter have been described by Shove as of the "'cheap and nasty' variety," in which the firm "followed the practice of printing at the back of the volume a few pages of another novel in the series." Publishers' Weekly of 7 December 1889, commenting on Pollard & Moss's "not unexpected" failure of 1889, asserted that the firm was "so far outside the lines·of the 'regular' trade that we have found it almost impossible to get bibliographical record of their books each year, despite every effort on our part to do so."

Pollard & Moss was apparently too preoccupied with lawsuits to supply bibliographical information to Publishers' Weekly. In the course of its reprint activities, particularly in the early years of the business, the firm was noted for its involvement in extensive litigation with the original publishers of some of the works in its series.

241

Pollard & Moss

The first and best known of the lawsuits in which Pollard & Moss was involved concerned one of the earliest publications of the firm--a collection of works by Washington Irving no longer under copyright, which it published under the general title, Irving's Works. In an attempt to deal with the problem of unauthorized publishing, G. P. Putnam's Sons, Irving's publisher, and the author's nieces to whom his literary property had been bequeathed, joined in a suit against Pollard & Moss. The main issue was the claim by the plaintiffs that the rights of an author and his heirs to his works continued indefinitely under common law. The suit also attacked the use of the term Works by the reprinters, as implying Complete Works (which they were not) and claimed that the publication of books in any form but that authorized by the author damaged the reputation of the author and the value of the literary property. Putnam's suit was unsuccessful and the decision served merely to encourage unauthorized reprint activities in general.

Pollard & Moss, however, was not always successful in legally defending its reprinting activities. In December 1884, in a suit filed by Cassell & Company, a New York City court issued an injunction aimed at preventing Pollard & Moss from publishing an edition of Dante's Inferno translated by Cary and illustrated by Gustave Doré.

Regardless of the firm's fortunes in litigation, Pollard & Moss faced increasing financial difficulties in the 1880s. As Shove puts it, "Selling publications at a fraction of their published price did not prove to be profitable." The assignment of the firm in 1889 involved liabilities estimated at $100,000. Much of the remaining stock of the firm's publications was subsequently distributed by the United States Book Company.

Although Pollard & Moss was active for a decade as a reprinter of cheap books, the firm is of less interest for its publications than for its involvement in litigation--one of the less fortunate side effects of the ubiquitous effort to provide cheap books for the masses.

Jacob L. Chernofsky

242

Pollard & Moss

References

George Haven Putnam, Memories of a Publisher, 1865-1915
    (New York: G. P. Putnam's Sons, 1915).

Raymond H. Shove, Cheap Book Production in the United
    States, 1870 to 1891 (Urbana: University of
    Illinois Library, 1937).

37 Porter & Coates

Porter & Coates (1867-1904), publishers of cheap juveniles
in series (especially those of Horatio Alger, Jr.), general books, and textbooks, became the second largest publishing house in Philadelphia, surpassed only by
Lippincott. It grew out of the bookselling establishment
styled Davis & Porter founded in 1848 by Charles H. Davis
and Robert Porter. With the entry of Henry T. Coates into
the firm in 1866, the house was restyled Davis, Porter &
Coates. With Davis's retirement in 1867 the firm became
Porter & Coates. In that same year G. Morrison and
Benjamin Coates, Henry's father and uncle, became special
partners. Several years later Morrison Coates became a
senior partner. After his death in 1893 and the retirement of Porter in July 1895, the firm name was changed to
Henry T. Coates & Co., the name under which it continued
bookselling and publishing activities until the early
twentieth century. The firm was located at the corner of
9th and Chestnut streets, 822 Chestnut, until December
1898 when it moved to new quarters a block away at 1222
Chestnut.

    <u>Major Authors</u>: Horatio Alger, Jr., R. M. Ballantyne,
Harry Castlemon (pseudonym of C. A. Fosdick), Margaret
Hosmer, Holm Lee (pseudonym of Harriet Parr).

    Robert Porter was born in Wilmington, Delaware, in
1842 and died 10 October 1899. He worked in George S.
Appleton's bookstore on Chestnut Street in Philadelphia
before establishing his own business with Charles H. Davis
in 1848. He became the second traveling salesman in the
publishing industry at a time when most publishers sold by
auction or by mail order. In 1876 he and Henry T. Coates
were appointed to the committee arranging the booksellers'
Centennial exhibit in Philadelphia. In July 1895, at the
age of fifty-three, he retired from the firm.

    George Morrison Coates, father of Henry T. Coates,
was born in Philadelphia on 20 August 1817, the

great-great-grandson of Thomas Coates, one of the early
Quaker merchants of Philadelphia. He died 21 May 1893.
At the age of twenty-two he went into the dry goods business, then became a successful cloth merchant until he
was wiped out in the Crash of 1857. Thereafter he and his
brother Benjamin went into the wool business as Coates
Brothers at 127 Market Street. Both he and Benjamin became special partners in the publishing firm of Porter &
Coates in 1869 and Morrison later became a general partner. He left the wool business completely in 1881 to
devote himself to the book business. Coates, who was married to the former Anna Troth, was an active civic worker
and served as a director of the Pennsylvania Railroad and
as a Republican presidential elector in the elections of
1864, '68, and '72.

Benjamin Coates, who had invested in the firm in
1869, was a wool merchant. He died on 7 March 1887.

Henry Troth Coates, the second of Morrison Coates's
six children, was born 29 September 1843. He attended
Haverford College and married Estelle Barton Lloyd on 15
June 1874. In addition to his business, he was also a
writer and editor. Among his works were genealogical
studies of the Coates family and a popular series called
the Fireside Encyclopedia of Poetry that was in its thirty-
first edition by 1895.

As booksellers, Porter & Coates specialized in art,
trade, and rare books, many in fine bindings, and published catalogs of their stock. In August 1869 the art
focus was enhanced by the opening of an art gallery above
the store. The publishing firm was widely known for its
general and juvenile books. One way the business grew
was through acquiring other publishers' rights. For example, in August 1869 Porter and Coates bought the stereotype plates of the defunct Davis & Bro., and in 1873 it
acquired the popular series of Schwartz novels from Lee &
Shepard. In 1881 it bought the stock, stereoplates, and
copyrights of Horatio Alger's books from the bankrupt
Boston publisher A. K. Loring.

Even before buying the Alger rights the company was
publishing books in series for families. For example, by
mid-1869 it had published twenty-three volumes in the
Waverley Novels series ($1.50 in cloth), followed by a

246

ten-volume series of thirty-twomo books of English and
American poetry. Its Christmas advertising included notices for Mrs. Hosmer's Little Rosie (75 cents) and Little
Lennie ($1.00) series. The Parlour Poetic Library was
offered in three prices according to binding style:
cloth, half leather, or "Turkey morocco antique." One
book on horses, although not in a series, contained "pho-
tos from life," obviously taking advantage of a new technology. Other popular series were French Fairy Tales and
Grimm's German Popular Tales and Household Stories. The
house also published toy books and colored primers and became a large publisher of textbooks in 1880.

In March 1870 Porter and Coates prepared a series of
six handbooks devoted to language (a book of synonyms),
manners, flower arrangement, letter writing, and a volume
called the Pocket Lawyer. The same month it published a
facsimile of the English edition of the Bab Ballads. The
series Knight's Half-Hours with the Best Authors was reported to have sold 1,500 copies, equaling 9,000 volumes.
Other series appealing to various segments of the family
were the Famous Fairy Library, the Ladies' Historical Romance series, the Holiday Library, and the At Home and
Abroad series. The Alta series of twelvemos on good paper, clothbound, was very popular. By 1886, 101 volumes
had been published in this 35-cent series. A slightly
more expensive group, selling for $1.25 per volume, was
the International Series, advertised as "cheap, substantial and elegant!" in their large twelvemo format and
"smooth English cloth" binding. The same books in wrappers sold for $1.00. For a period around 1873 the Porter
& Coates books were printed at the Caxton Press.

In the late 1870s Porter & Coates began publishing
series of books by Harry Castlemon: The Boy Trapper,
Frank Nelson, Rod and Gun, and Roughing It. Most of
these were of only two or three volumes each. By Christmas 1882 the publishers took out a full-page advertisement in the American Bookseller to advertise eight series
by Horatio Alger and six by Castlemon. Although each series could be bought as a set for $3.75 to $7.50, each
individual volume was for sale separately for $1.25. Most
of the Alger books were reprints of the Loring titles.
The American Catalogue listing for the period 1876-1884

247

shows Porter & Coates as publishers of thirty-three Alger
books, most of them dated 1882 and marked "new issue."
The price of $1.25 was maintained at least through 1900.

The firm published only one magazine, House and Garden, which was begun by three Philadelphia architects in
1901.

On 25 October 1902 Coates sold the retail book business to the John Wanamaker department store, and in 1903
the stationery division and manufacturing plant went to
the G. W. Jacobs Company. The publishing business of
approximately one thousand titles, plates, stock, and
copyrights was sold to John C. Winston in November 1904,
thereby turning Winston, previously a publisher of Bibles,
into one of the country's largest publishers of juveniles.
Thus between 1902 and 1904 Porter & Coates divested itself
of its retail book business, its stationery and manufacturing plant, and its stock and copyrights.

During the latter half of the nineteenth century
when it flourished as Porter & Coates the firm was one
of the largest, most dynamic publishers of cheap juveniles.
Its series reached a wide audience and contributed
strongly to mass entertainment.

Anna Lou Ashby

References

Publishers' Trade List Annual (New York: R. R. Bowker
     Company, 1874).

Raymond H. Shove, Cheap Book Production in the United
     States, 1870 to 1891 (Urbana: University of
     Illinois Library, 1937).

Madeleine B. Stern, Imprints on History: Book Pub-
     lishers and American Frontiers (Bloomington:
     Indiana University Press, 1956; reprinted, New
     York: AMS Press, 1975).

Porter & Coates

Frank Luther Mott, A History of American Magazines, 1885–1905 (Cambridge: The Belknap Press of Harvard University Press, 1957).

Charles A. Madison, Book Publishing in America (New York: McGraw-Hill Book Co., 1966).

"Boston" Christmas Card designed by Lizbeth B. Humphrey. Louis
Prang & Co.
(Courtesy Jack Golden Collection)

38   Louis Prang & Co.

Louis Prang & Co. (1860–1897), publisher of many and varied interests, was considered by its peers to be the greatest color lithographer of the time. The firm started in business in Boston at 34 Merchants Row, then moved to 159 Washington Street in 1861. By 1867 business had developed at such a pace that a new building was erected at 286 Roxbury Street, and in 1881 additions nearly doubled its space and facilities. In 1882 the Prang Educational Company was formed as a separate entity to facilitate the expansion of educational publishing. For the next fifteen years business continued to prosper, but by 1897 adverse conditions prompted the merger of Louis Prang & Co. with the Taber Art Company of New Bedford, Massachusetts. Prang devoted his remaining years to the Prang Educational Company, which was sold to the American Crayon Company in 1918.

Major Business Activities: Publishers of greeting cards, juvenile literature, periodicals, art and educational material; chromolithographers for popular and commercial consumption of prints, calendars, advertising trade cards, posters, and catalogs.

Louis Prang was born in Breslau, Germany, on 12 March 1824 and died at the age of eighty-five on 15 June 1909 in a Los Angeles, California, sanatorium. The second of six children, he was carefully trained by his father (part owner of a calico-printing firm), and by the age of twenty had acquired a thorough knowledge of chemistry, color mixing, designing, engraving, and printing. As the protégé of a wealthy Bohemian manufacturer, he spent four years enhancing his technical training by visiting important calico-printing plants throughout Europe, with the ultimate objective of becoming superintendent of his Bohemian factory. The revolution of 1848 put an end to these plans. Active participation in the revolution, which was short-lived, forced him to flee

251

Stock Card published for centennial of 1876. Louis Prang & Co. Note use of
black background as originated by Prang.
(Courtesy Jack Golden Collection)

Germany, and after a brief stay in Switzerland he arrived in this country on 5 April 1850, landing in New York City.

After a short association with Rosenthal, Duval & Prang in Philadelphia (1855-1856), he settled in Boston where he first worked for Gleason's Pictorial, and later for John Andrew, an English engraver and printmaker.

He was married twice. On 1 November 1851 he married Rosa Gerber (1825-1898), a Swiss girl he had met in Paris. They had one child, Rosa, who married Karl Heinzen (who later came to work for Prang). His second marriage, to Mary Dana Hicks, a widowed art teacher who came to work for Prang in 1880, took place on 5 April 1900.

In July 1856 he formed a partnership with Julius Mayer, and as Prang & Mayer opened an office at 17 Doane Street. As the business prospered, they moved to 14 Kirby Street, then finally to 34 Merchants Row. Prang produced the artwork, polished the stones, and Mayer did the printing on a handpress. In 1860 he bought out his partner and moved from Merchants Row to 159 Washington Street in 1861.

Just prior to the outbreak of the Civil War, his business suffered an initial and discouraging setback, but within twenty-four hours after the attack on Fort Sumter, Prang had lithographed and placed on sale at all Boston newsstands a black-and-white map of Charleston Harbor. It was an immediate success, selling 40,000 copies at 25 cents each. Throughout the war he continued publishing maps and plans of all the battles, as well as several pieces of sheet music related to the war.

To satisfy the new craze for collecting album cards, one of the popular pastimes in the Victorian era, he published three sets of popular Civil War generals, political, and naval personalities, twenty-four cards to a set, each selling for 30 cents. In a similar style (2 3/8 by 4 1/4) he produced two sets (twelve to a set) of humorous war scenes by Winslow Homer, Life in Camp, which was followed by a large (11 by 14) and more elaborate set of Campaign Sketches, sold in sets of six at $1.50 per set.

253

Louis Prang & Co.

Of all the album card publishers, Prang produced the greatest variety. In addition to nine different sets of wildflowers, there were mosses, butterflies, birds, animals, and two sets of American Childhood. In 1864 he published Views on the Hudson, White Mountain Scenery, Pilgrim's Progress, and subsequently the popular Views of Niagara Falls, Street Scenes in New York, and Views in Central Park. In 1868 there were twenty-six different sets on the market, as well as a wide variety of friendship, congratulation, and reward of merit cards.

An interesting comment on his album cards appeared in a Philadelphia newspaper, quoted in the January 1868 number of Prang's Chromo: "The Album Pictures, of which an almost infinite variety are made, 'form an event' in the history of popular pictures. During the past four years, many hundred thousand packs of them, twelve in a pack, have been sold; and the demand is still so great, that from four to six presses are still kept constantly running on them . . . Very few households are now without a specimen of these or of the Sunday-school cards, which are filling a great demand and have had an incredible sale."

Prang's love for color printing prompted his return to Europe in 1864 to examine the latest developments of the art. In a speech on color lithography before the Grolier Club on 7 January 1897, he told his audience, "I was drawn toward this art just forty years ago, by seeing a very good German color print, representing a Venetian carnival scene. This happened during the first week of my lithographic career and I made a vow then and there that prints of this quality should be done in America and that they must be done in my establishment." He returned from Europe not only with a staff of skilled artists and craftsmen, but with a firm grasp of the technology necessary to realize his lifelong ambition--to equal, if not surpass, the finest color reproduction on the continent.

In 1866 he produced his first "chromo," the name Prang coined for color lithography. With the belief that the public would pay $6.00 for such prints, he advertised in the popular weeklies the need for "raising the

254

standards for better art in the home." Skeptical at
first, public response became overwhelming with the
introduction of A. F. Tait's Group of Chickens, followed
by his Group of Ducklings. Prang's Chromo for Christmas
1868 lists forty-one full-size chromos, among which were
two by Eastman Johnson, The Barefoot Boy and The Boyhood
of Lincoln, as well as twenty-eight half chromos,
slightly smaller in size. By 1871 he had published well
over a hundred chromos, and continued to add new ones
each year until 1897 when, rather than compromise quality, he discontinued publishing them due to the influx
of cheaper reproductions.

In addition to chromos and album cards, Prang had
also been publishing a select group of juveniles, toy
books, and games. Among these were two series of toy
books, the Doll series (books die-cut in the shape of a
doll) and the Christmas Stocking Library. Each sold for
25 cents. Little Red Riding Hood, Robinson Crusoe, Goody
Two-Shoes, Cinderella, and King Winter comprised the Doll
Series, and A Visit from St. Nicholas, with thirteen
illustrations by Thomas Nast, was one of the six in the
Christmas Library. One of the finest of his juveniles
was A New Version of Old Mother Hubbard by Ruth Chesterfield, splendidly illuminated as never before attempted
in children's literature. Slate Pictures (to teach drawing to children), magic and rebus cards, several humorous
books, illuminated bookmarks, marriage certificates and
eight children's games completed his firm's output.

By 1867 business had grown so dramatically that it
was necessary for Prang to erect a new building at 286
Roxbury Street, to house his forty presses and seventy
workmen. In January 1868, Prang started to publish a
quarterly magazine, Prang's Chromo. It not only served
as a company catalog, but contained articles pertaining
to chromolithography, pertinent comments and testimoni-
als from newspapers and prominent people here and abroad
as well as announcements of new items. Prang was a re-
cipient of many distinguished awards during his lifetime.
He received the Medal of Progress at the Vienna World's
Fair in 1873, two bronze medals at the 1876 Centennial
Exhibition in Philadelphia, and a silver medal at the
1878 International Exposition in Paris. Among his other

awards were silver and gold medals at the Barcelona Exposition in 1888, the gold medal at the Paris Exposition of 1889, and a medal and diploma at the 1892 Columbian Exposition in Chicago.

Called the "Father of the American Christmas Card," Prang distributed his first cards in England in 1873 and introduced them in this country a year later. With typical Victorian sentimentality, but with an elegance uniquely Prang's, these early cards showed the customary Santa Claus, reindeer, and Christmas tree, in addition to a generous helping of his favorite roses and floral bouquets. Eventually Prang introduced a complete line of cards including birthday, Easter, New Year's cards, and valentines. Their success was phenomenal. By 1881 he was reputed to be printing over five million cards a year for distribution here and abroad, and employing about three hundred people.

Ever the innovator, and firm in the belief that he was raising the level of popular taste, he inaugurated the first of four successive competitions, inviting prominent American artists to design his 1880 Christmas card line. The awards, prizes of $1,000, $500.00, $300.00, and $200.00, were given to Rosina Emmet, Alexander Sandier, Alfred Fredericks, and Anna G. Morse, respectively. The New York Evening Post made the following comment on his second contest in February 1881: "It is easy to see that art is advancing in this country, when Elihu Vedder makes our Christmas cards." Vedder had won first prize that year. Exhibitions of the cards were held each year, and were so well received that at the close of the fourth and last contest in 1884, the collection was shown by invitation at the Museum of Fine Arts, Boston, and the Art Institute of Chicago.

As distinctive and popular as the Prang cards were, the cost of production, with the use of seven or more zinc plates (Prang had substituted zinc for litho stones for nearly all his work in 1873), made them more expensive than that of his competition. When cheaper German cards flooded the market in the early 1890s, Prang's high quality cards went into a sharp decline. By 1897 he retired from the greeting card business completely.

Louis Prang & Co.

The growth of American industry in the 1870s and the perfection of color lithography prompted the introduction of the trade card as a means of advertising. An article in the May 1885 number of The Paper World claimed that trade cards were introduced in this country in 1876 by Field, Leiter & Company, Chicago merchants. The cards, first imported from France, had such spectacular success (store sales doubled within a week) that rival firms began using them to advertise and "like wildfire the craze spread over the country." Every lithographer was swamped with work, new firms came into the business, and production soared into the millions.

But in the very next number of The Paper World Prang took exception with a letter to the editor, to set the record straight. "The first series of Chromo Cards . . . was designed and printed by our firm in 1873, advertising our exhibit at the Vienna International Exhibition. We opened a special agency for these advertising cards in New York in 1874, and during this and the following year the sprouting of the 'card craze' as you have it, began. The year 1876 saw it in full bloom with us; we already made millions of cards." In addition to trade cards, the stamp of Prang excellence appeared on vast quantities of other commercial printing as well, including countless labels, calendars, almanacs, booklets, catalogs, and posters.

In 1874 an Educational Department was established within the company to assume publication of an Art Education Series under the direction of Professor Walter Smith, State Director of Art Education in Massachusetts. From 1874 to 1876 Prang published a series of manuals and textbooks for drawing in public schools, a booklet by Grace Carter, Plant Forms Ornamentally Treated, and probably one of the rarest and most beautifully lithographed teaching sets, Aids to Object Teaching consisting of twelve chromo illustrations of trades and occupations.

Through the years Prang published a miscellany of books for artists, craftsmen, and architects, and books on his lifetime infatuations, flowers and natural history. The better known titles include The Theory of Color in its Relation to Art and Art Industry by Koehler and

257

Louis Prang & Co.

Pickering (1876), <u>Prang's Standard Alphabets</u> (1878), <u>Art in The House</u> by Jacob von Falke (1879), and an American edition of <u>Architecture, Sculpture and Industrial Arts</u> by S. R. Koehler (1879). In the early 1870s came the highly popular <u>Prang's Natural History Series for Children</u> in six volumes; a four-volume set on <u>Native Flowers and Ferns of the United States</u> by Thomas Meehan was published 1878-1880, and a beautiful set of twelve chromolithographs for <u>Mushrooms of America</u> by Julius Palmer, Jr., in 1885.

In 1880 a widowed art teacher from Syracuse entered Prang's employ to write how-to books and books on the training of teachers for public school positions, in which Prang had also become involved. She became director and editor of the Prang Educational Company in 1882, which was formed to concentrate on art education exclusively, a rapidly expanding field in public schools. Among the many manuals and books on the industrial arts published were <u>The Use of Models</u> (1886), <u>A Teacher's Manual for the Prang Course in Drawing</u> (1890), <u>Art Instruction in The Primary School</u> (1890), <u>Lessons in Pencil Drawings from Nature</u> (1894). Other instruction books included <u>Progressive Studies in Water Color Painting</u> (1890), <u>Studies in Composition and Color</u> (1902), and <u>The Textbook of Art Education</u> (1904).

In his earlier years Prang had produced many spectacular chromolithographs, such as the series on the natural wonders of Yellowstone Park, fifteen plates after watercolors by Thomas Moran, and the Yosemite Valley after a painting by Thomas Hill, but nothing could compare with his crowning achievement as a lithographer, the monumental set of ten large volumes published by D. Appleton & Company in 1897, the <u>A. T. Walters Collection of Oriental Ceramic Art</u>. According to Prang, it took the better part of five years to complete the chromolithography for the project, after three artists had worked seven years producing the painting from which the reproductions were made. It was well worth the price of $500.00. The set included 116 chromolithographs and 437 black-and-white illustrations, many of the plates requiring from twenty to forty-four separate stones. The project was an unparalleled technical and artistic masterpiece.

The golden age of stone lithography was coming to an end. The great market for chromos for the home disappeared with the changing times. In August 1897, Louis Prang & Company and the Taber Art Company were consolidated as the Taber-Prang Art Company. The Prang Educational Company continued until it was sold to the American Crayon Company in 1918.

Prolific and innovative in the annals of publishing, Louis Prang was a great lithographer, originator of the advertising trade card, father of the American greeting card industry, and creator of magnificent chromos and books that set new standards of publishing while they catered to developing public taste during the latter part of the nineteenth century.[1]

Jack Golden

References and Note

"Prang, Picture and Poesy," The Paper World, 7 (October 1883): 5.

"The Advertising Card Business," 10 (May 1885): 4.

Louis Prang, "Origin of Holiday and Advertising Cards," The Paper World, 10 (June 1885): 20.

"Louis Prang, Boston, Mass., U.S.A." The British Lithographer, 1 (August-September 1892): 5-6.

Gleeson White, Christmas Cards and Their Chief Designers (London: The Studio, 1895).

Louis Prang, "Color Lithography," Transactions of the Grolier Club, Part III (1899): 182-94.

Louis Prang & Co.

Ruth Webb Lee, A History of Valentines (Wellesley
    Hills, Mass.: Lee Publications, 1952).

George Buday, The History of the Christmas Card
    (London: Spring Books, 1964).

Dr. Larry Freeman, Louis Prang: Color Lithographer,
    Giant of a Man (Watkins Glen, N.Y.: Century
    House, 1971).

Katherine Morrison McClinton, The Chromolithographs
    of Louis Prang (New York: Clarkson N. Potter,
    1973).

Sinclair H. Hitchings, "Fine Art Lithography in Boston:
    Craftsmanship in Color, 1840-1900," Art and Com-
    merce: American Prints of the Nineteenth Century
    (Charlottesville: University Press of Virginia,
    1978).

[1]There are Prang collections in the Boston Athenaeum,
    Boston Public Library, New York Public Library,
    Hallmark Historical Collection in Kansas City,
    and American Antiquarian Society.

39   James Redpath

James Redpath (1863-1864) published book series designed
to instruct and reform as well as to entertain the masses
of readers in camp and at home during the Civil War. He
published about twenty-five titles in various editions,
all from his publishing office in Room 7 of the Washington Building, 221 Washington Street, Boston.

Major Authors: Louisa May Alcott, William Wells
Brown, Wendell Phillips, James Redpath.

James Redpath was born in Berwick-on-Tweed, Scot-
land, in 1833 and died in New York in 1891. Around 1850
he emigrated with his family to Allegan, Michigan. He
worked in a printing office in Kalamazoo and later moved
to Detroit, where his writing attracted the attention of
Horace Greeley, who offered him a position on the Tribune.
Redpath traveled through the South for that paper, became
its special correspondent on Kansas affairs, and was im-
plicated in John Brown's Harpers Ferry raid. After visiting Haiti, he established the Haytian Bureau of
Emigration in Boston, and in 1861 founded a weekly newspaper, Pine and Palm, to encourage the emigration of
blacks to Haiti. Redpath edited A Guide to Hayti and
also compiled Echoes of Harper's Ferry and The Public
Life of Capt. John Brown, all three volumes published in
Boston in 1860 by Thayer and Eldridge. When Thayer and
Eldridge failed, Redpath decided to publish books in his
own right.

Redpath began publishing in 1863 with a series entitled "Books for the Times," directed principally to a
readership of civilians at home. Several of the books
in that series were antislavery in nature: The Black Man
by William Wells Brown, which contained biographical
sketches of fifty-eight distinguished blacks, by a black
writer; The Public Life and Autobiography of John Brown
by Redpath himself, a work that examined the career of
the fallen martyr; The Speeches, Lectures, and Letters of

261

(Courtesy Edward T. LeBlanc, *Dime Novel Round-Up*)

Wendell Phillips, the antislavery orator; Toussaint L'Ouverture: A Biography and Autobiography by John R. Beard; Hospital Sketches by Louisa May Alcott, which presented the often entertaining and amusing aspects of her experiences as a Civil War nurse; Results of Emancipation by Augustin Cochin. Also in the series Books for the Times, Redpath published (and probably wrote) the anonymous Shall We Suffocate Ed. Green? By a Citizen of Malden (1864), directed against capital punishment.

Redpath published the volumes in his Books for the Times series in editions that would have a wide popular appeal. Hospital Sketches was priced at 50 cents, The Black Man and The Public Life and Autobiography of John Brown at $1.00 each, the biography of Toussaint L'Ouverture at $1.25. The Speeches, Lectures, and Letters of Wendell Phillips was offered in three separate editions at three different prices: a luxurious Library Edition at $2.25, a Trade Edition in cloth and boards at $1.50, and a People's Edition in paper at $1.00.

Besides offering liberal terms to agents for the distribution of his publications, Redpath advertised them in the Boston Almanac and American Publishers' Circular, and made arrangements with publishers in New York and Philadelphia to supply the trade with his Books for the Times series.

That Redpath published books with speed and lived up to his monetary promises to authors is borne out by his relations with one of his authors, Louisa May Alcott. Alcott's letters from the Union Hotel Hospital in Georgetown, where she had served as a nurse, were published under the title "Hospital Sketches" in The Commonwealth between 22 May and 26 June 1863. In June 1863 Redpath requested permission to reprint "Hospital Sketches" in book form. The author was promised 5 cents on each copy sold of an edition of 1,000; the publisher was to retain 10 cents on each copy, out of which he was to pay for the cost of the book and give something to charity. According to Alcott's journal entry for August 1863, Redpath carried on the publishing of the work "vigorously, sending letters, proof, and notices daily, and making all manner of offers, suggestions, and prophecies concerning the success of the book and its author." On 25 August

263

1863 the author received a copy of the 102-page eighteenmo, which she described in her journal as "a neat
little affair." By September Redpath began making payments to her for Hospital Sketches, which eventually
amounted to $200.00--a figure that represents payments
on all editions. He also requested another book from the
author.

 After the success of Books for the Times, Redpath
in 1864 launched another series. Books for Camp and
Home, also called Books for the Camp Fires, was aimed
not only at readers on the home front, but at soldiers
in the field. The series was lower-priced than Books for
the Times, and meant to attract a wider readership. On
1 March 1864 Redpath advertised the new series as "of a
much higher class than the dime publications now in the
market."

 The volumes in the Books for Camp and Home series
were bound in green paper covers ("greenbacks") and contained from 96 to 124 pages each. The first book in the
series was published 23 January 1864. This was another
work by Louisa May Alcott, On Picket Duty, and Other
Tales, a collection of entertaining short stories that
included "On Picket Duty," "The King of Clubs and the
Queen of Hearts" on the gymnastic craze of the times,
"The Cross on the Old Church Tower," and "The Death of
John." The second book in the series was Clotelle, A
Tale of the Southern States by William Wells Brown, a
novel that combined the sure-fire ingredients of entertainment and moral righteousness. The next three books
in the series were reprints of books by foreign authors:
Balzac's Vendetta; Swift's Gulliver's Travels . . . to
Lilliput; and Hugo's Battle of Waterloo. An army edition of Louisa May Alcott's Hospital Sketches was published in paper and priced at 25 cents, the author
receiving a royalty of 10 percent. Legends of the Infancy and Boyhood of Jesus Christ followed. In the
latter it was announced that "The flattering reception
of the first five numbers of these [Books for] the Camp
Fires, by the trade, the press, and the people, [indi-
cates] that a higher style of literature than has hitherto been issued [in the] cheapest form, will find a
ready support for them." The publisher quoted the

following laudatory opinions of the press: "They will
be welcome visitors in the camp, and the friends of our
patriotic soldiers should endeavor to supply them with
a copy." "Our soldier boys will find them just the
thing to beguile an otherwise tedious hour." Redpath's
Books for the Camp Fires were sold through all newsdealers as well as to the trade and to retailers at a
rate of $60.00 per thousand. Advertised as "the cheap-
est books of real merit in the market," they gave pleasure and enlightenment to soldiers in the field.

In addition to his two series, Redpath published
works of a more general nature, among them Croquet
by Captain Mayne Reid, The Rose Family, a fairy tale by
Louisa May Alcott, Breakfast in Bed by George Augustus
Henry Sala, The Morals of Epictetus and Spiritual Torrents by Mme. Jeanne Marie de la Motte Guyon. These
ranged in price from 25 cents to $1.00.

On 15 April 1864, Redpath published his last advertisement in the American Publishers' Circular, ending
his short but effective career as publisher. He became
an army correspondent in the South for a newspaper syndicate, and before returning north he organized South
Carolina's school system. In 1868 he established the
Lyceum Bureau in Boston, which continued under his management until 1875. In 1880 he went to Ireland as special
correspondent of the New-York Tribune, and the following
year he published Talks About Ireland. In 1883 he addressed a mass meeting of newsdealers in New York, and
subsequently morning papers were sold at stands at established rates. He founded Redpath's Weekly and became
managing editor of The North American Review before his
death in 1891.

Despite the quantitative paucity of his publications and the short period in which he was active as a
publisher, James Redpath must be credited with two important innovations: raising the literary and moral
tone of the cheap book, and making a direct attempt to
supply soldiers in camp with appropriate reading matter.
These he accomplished in his two series, Books for the
Times and Books for the Camp Fires, which provided to a

265

James Redpath

large readership at home and in the field books of merit that instructed while they entertained.

Madeleine B. Stern

References

Louisa May Alcott, Autograph Letters to James Redpath [1863], in the New York Historical Society.

Charles F. Horner, The Life of James Redpath and The Development of the Modern Lyceum (New York & Newark: Barse & Hopkins, [1926]).

Madeleine B. Stern, Imprints on History: Book Publishers and American Frontiers (Bloomington: Indiana University Press, 1956; reprinted, New York: AMS Press, 1975).

40   Roberts Brothers

Roberts Brothers (1863-1898) of Boston published about
1,300 works from its founding until its purchase by
Little, Brown and Company. The firm started at 143
Washington Street and operated from there until 1885
when it moved to 3 Somerset Street. Its success was not
due to its founder, the English-born Lewis Roberts, but
to a man whose name never appeared on the title page--
Thomas Niles, Jr., who became a partner in 1872. Iron-
ically, Niles both made and broke the firm; his literary
tastes gave Roberts Brothers its identity and success,
especially as a publisher of quality books. At his death
in 1894, however, the house, which had become a one-man
operation, floundered without direction before it was
purchased by Little, Brown and Company in June 1898.

> Major Authors: A. Bronson Alcott, Louisa May
Alcott, Philip G. Hamerton, Frederic Henry Hedge,
Jean Ingelow, Helen Hunt Jackson.

The first Roberts brother, Lewis Augustus, was
born in Ballingdon, England, on 6 December 1833 and died
23 January 1901. When Lewis was seven the family emigrated to New Bedford, Massachusetts, where they took up
farming. Lewis left for Boston in 1849 to seek his fortune. There he learned bookbinding and soon, with $500.00
borrowed from his father, he opened a store. Forming a
partnership with his brothers John and Austin, Lewis
opened a shop specializing in bookbinding and manufacturing blank books. This business--the first "Roberts
Brothers"--was moderately successful but, after surviving the financial panic of 1857, the struggling firm was
sold in 1859.

Lewis visited his homeland soon after the firm was
sold. There he discovered that photograph albums were
enjoying a widespread vogue. When he returned from England to Boston, he began importing these albums and, when
sales proved good, he began making them. His timing was

Robert Brothers' Establishment at 3 Somerset Street, Beacon Hill.
(Courtesy Joel Myerson)

excellent--the Civil War had introduced a demand for
photographs and, with it, a need for something in which
to preserve them. Lewis prospered and in 1861, with
Austin, he reestablished Roberts Brothers. (Austin
would withdraw in 1863, leaving Lewis as sole owner
until 1872.) Offices were set up on Washington Street,
a short distance from the famous Old Corner Book Store,
headquarters of the prestigious firm of Ticknor and
Fields. In 1862 Roberts Brothers advertised itself as
"Bookbinders and Photograph Album Manufacturers," but
by 1864 it had taken on a new identity, that of "Publishers and Booksellers and Manufacturers of Photograph
Albums." The new directions taken by Roberts Brothers
were mainly due to the efforts of one man, Thomas
Niles, Jr.

Niles was born 25 January 1825 in Boston and died
in 1894. After attending Boston Latin School, he went
to work in 1839 as a junior clerk at the Old Corner Book
Store, in the employ of William D. Ticknor and with
James T. Fields as a fellow worker. Eventually he became
responsible for handling most of the firm's correspondence, a job he later enjoyed doing at Roberts Brothers
until his death. Niles obviously thought his labors
would result in his being brought into the publishing arm
of the firm, for Fields had been made a junior partner in
William D. Ticknor and Company in 1843 and a full partner
(as the firm's new name, Ticknor and Fields, indicated)
in 1854. But in 1855 another clerk, James R. Osgood, was
brought in and Niles, a shy and reticent man, soon saw
that the more outgoing Osgood, not he, was being groomed
for better things, and he resigned.

Niles soon formed a partnership with John W.
Whittemore, a stationer, and Edward H. Hall, another
young man interested in publishing. The firm of
Whittemore, Niles, and Hall was a bookseller and stationery company. Its book list was undistinguished.
Like many small firms of the period, it specialized in
reprinting English works, since British sales could be
used to accurately forecast American sales, and in textbooks, which could be depended on for a regular income.
Perhaps its most distinguished title was a reprint of
Jared Sparks's edition of Benjamin Franklin's Works.

What satisfaction there must be in the habit of reading! The power to give one's self up graciously to a book is the wealthiest habit. I imagine, that one can acquire. It is fullness itself, or an endless and ever ready resource. — CHAUNCEY WRIGHT.

299 (Old No. 143) WASHINGTON STREET, BOSTON.
Winter of 1878-79.

MESSRS. ROBERTS BROTHERS'

GENERAL LIST OF WORKS.

The Books in this List, unless otherwise specified, are bound in Cloth. All of our Publications mailed, postpaid, on receipt of price.

Alcott (Louisa M.).
LITTLE WOMEN ; or, Meg, Jo, Beth, and Amy. With Illustrations. Two volumes. 16mo. $3.00.
HOSPITAL SKETCHES and CAMP AND FIRESIDE STORIES. With Illustrations. 16mo. $1.50.
AN OLD-FASHIONED GIRL. With Illustrations. 16mo. $1.50.
LITTLE MEN : Life at Plumfield with Jo's Boys. With Illustrations. 16mo. $1.50.
MY BOYS, &c. : Being the first volume of AUNT JO'S SCRAP-BAG. 16mo. $1.00.
SHAWL-STRAPS : Being the second volume of AUNT JO'S SCRAP-BAG. 16mo. $1.00.
CUPID AND CHOW-CHOW, &c. : Being the third volume of AUNT JO'S SCRAP-BAG. 16mo. $1.00.
WORK : A Story of Experience. With Character Illustrations by Sol Eytinge. 16mo. $1.75.
EIGHT COUSINS ; or, The Aunt-hill. With Illustrations. 16mo. $1.50.
SILVER PITCHERS, and INDEPENDENCE, a Centennial Love Story. 16mo. $1.25.
ROSE IN BLOOM. A Sequel to "Eight Cousins." 16mo. $1.50.

Abbott (E. A.).
HOW TO WRITE CLEARLY : Rules and Exercises on English Composition. 16mo. 60 cents.

Advertisement for General List. Roberts Brothers.
(Courtesy Joel Myerson)

Many of the books were poetry or juveniles, interests
later continued by Niles at Roberts Brothers. After
publishing about sixty titles, the firm fell victim to
the Panic of 1857 and was dissolved the following year.
Whittemore began his own company and published only textbooks; Niles and Hall joined Roberts Brothers.

Hall entered the employ of Roberts Brothers in 1862
and Niles the next year. On 1 August 1863 the American
Publishers' Circular and Literary Gazette ran a Roberts
Brothers' advertisement for eight titles, all juveniles,
six of them reprints. Over the next thirty years Roberts
Brothers, led by Thomas Niles, prospered, as it combined
quality production, literary excellence, low overhead
(the total staff probably never exceeded ten employees),
and shrewd marketing. Its success is all the more remarkable because it declined to rely on two standbys of the
publishing trade, textbooks and periodicals (except for
Edward Everett Hale's Old and New, published, probably
as a favor, between 1870 and 1874).

Niles continued to import the best English books
in sheets; it actually cost less (because of the cheap
English labor) to buy the printed pages and ship them to
America than it did to print the books in Boston. He
also capitalized on the Christmas trade, producing luxury
editions at high prices for the annual gift book market.
The firm's printing was done by the best firms in Boston:
Welch, Bigelow, and Company and John Wilson and Sons (and
later, its firm, the University Press in Cambridge). In
1866 Roberts married Niles's half sister, Alice, and when
their son was born, he was named Lewis Niles Roberts, ce-
menting families and friendships. More important, Niles
was made a full partner in Roberts Brothers in 1872. In
1885, the firm moved to 3 Somerset Street, near the top
of aristocratic Beacon Hill.

Niles made Roberts Brothers successful because he
signed the best available authors and because he early
saw the advantages of selling books in series. The series idea, especially, helped make enormous profits.
Some of the series, such as the Handy Volume Series (reprints of English titles), are of little note--critically
or financially--but others hit the mark. In 1878 Roberts
Brothers began publishing the No Name Series, original

271

works whose authors were not identified. This combination of good literature and mystery both entertained and
teased the public, and the series took off. Many of the
writers were novices, others well known, such as Louisa
May Alcott, Helen Hunt Jackson, and George Parsons
Lathrop, Hawthorne's son-in-law. Probably the most famous title in the series was A Masque of Poets (1878),
containing verses by Emily Dickinson and Thoreau, the
fourteenth and final volume of the first series of No
Name works. A second No Name series, with twelve volumes, began publication in 1879 and ran through 1882,
when a third series was begun, publishing eleven volumes
through 1887. The first volumes in the initial No Name
series sold about 20,000 copies each, though at the end
sales were down to 2,500 copies, a likely reflection of
the drop in quality as the series progressed. The Famous
Women Series, begun in 1878 and containing eighteen volumes by 1889, was also noteworthy. Others, such as the
Wisdom Series (anthologies), Town and Country Series
(light reading), and The American Tauchnitz Series (based
on the famous European series by Bernhard Tauchnitz), all
capitalized on the growing market in the late 1870s for
inexpensive and--with the last series--paper-covered
editions.

But Niles's real coup was in obtaining authors.
Most of New England's famous authors--Emerson, Hawthorne,
Holmes, Longfellow, Lowell, and Whittier--were published
by Ticknor and Fields, but Niles's list of writers certainly was the next best in the country. His American
authors included Thomas Gold Appleton (a Boston racon-
teur), Lydia Maria Child (the famous abolitionist and
anthologist), Edgar Fawcett (a popular novelist), Edward
Everett Hale (a Roberts Brothers author from 1870 on),
Lafcadio Hearn (Some Chinese Ghosts), Joseph Holt
Ingraham (whose three religious historical novels sold
over 500,000 copies), Helen Hunt Jackson (whose Ramona,
a sympathetic novel on the plight of the American Indian,
became a classic of its kind), Joaquin Miller (the bard
of the Sierras), Louise Chandler Moulton (poet, children's writer, and novelist), John Neal (his autobiography, Wandering Recollections of a Somewhat Busy Life),
and Epes Sargent (novels on spiritualism). Walt Whitman

272

was represented with After All, Not to Create Only (1871).

Niles made Roberts Brothers the publishing house of the Transcendentalists and their offspring (of a sort), the Free Religious Association, publishing works by Joseph Henry Allen, Cyrus A. Bartol, Charles T. Brooks, John White Chadwick, Ellery Channing, Christopher Pearse Cranch, Frederic Henry Hedge, Thomas Wentworth Higginson, Theodore Parker, Elizabeth Palmer Peabody, and F. B. Sanborn. Alfred P. Putnam's anthology, Singers and Songs of the Liberal Faith, also tapped the liberal Unitarian market. The sole Transcendental novel, Sylvester Judd's Margaret, was reprinted in 1870. Bronson Alcott was represented by Tablets (1868), Concord Days (1872), Table-Talk (1877), Sonnets and Canzonets (1882), and New Connecticut (1887). Moreover, Elizabeth Peabody's Record of a School (1836), about Alcott's progressive Temple School in Boston, was reprinted in 1874 as Record of Mr. Alcott's School, and a two-volume biography of him by Sanborn and William T. Harris appeared in 1893. Probably at Alcott's urging, Roberts Brothers reprinted Margaret Fuller's works in six volumes (including the two-volume Memoirs of Margaret Fuller Ossoli, edited by Emerson, William Henry Channing, and James Freeman Clarke) in 1874. In 1884 Roberts Brothers planned to reprint the Transcendentalists' journal, the Dial, but failed to get enough subscribers to justify the effort. Roberts Brothers even published works by and about the conservative Unitarians, including a collection of William Ellery Channing's sermons, The Perfect Life, and his correspondence with Lucy Aiken, and biographies of Channing, Orville Dewey, Ezra Stiles Gannett, and Samuel Joseph May.

Emily Dickinson's first book was published by Roberts Brothers in 1890. Although Niles was unenthusiastic about her poetry--he thought (according to Kilgour) her verses "are quite as remarkable for defects as for beauties and are generally devoid of true poetical qualities"--he published her Poems. Niles had, in a rare instance, misjudged the public's response, for the 480 copies of the first printing were soon exhausted and the book went through sixteen printings in eight years.

273

Poems, Second Series appeared in 1891 and sold 7,000
copies in three years. The interest in Dickinson soon
waned, however, and both the two-volume Letters of Emily
Dickinson (1894) and Poems, Third Series (1896) sold
barely enough copies to provide royalties.

Far and away Roberts Brothers' most popular author
was Bronson Alcott's daughter, Louisa May. Although
Niles had not been much impressed with the manuscript of
her Little Women, he did give it to his niece and other
children to read, for the confirmed bachelor mistrusted
his own judgment in this case and wished an opinion from
the book's intended audience. The children all responded
enthusiastically, and Niles decided in 1868 to go ahead
with publication. He never regretted his decision: Little Women sold 175,000 copies and Alcott's other books
another 325,000 copies by 1885. Between 1868 and 1888,
when Louisa May died, she published some twenty books
with Roberts Brothers, including the two volumes of Little Women (1868-1869), An Old-Fashioned Girl (1870),
Little Men (1871), and Work: A Story of Experience
(1873). And in 1889 Roberts Brothers published Ednah D.
Cheney's biography of Louisa May. (Niles even took two
of her nephews, Frederick Pratt Alcott and John Alcott
Pratt, to work at Roberts Brothers.)

Roberts Brothers also published original editions
of many popular and excellent foreign authors. English
writers published by the firm included Jane Austen (an
edition of her novels), Walter Besant (The French Humor-
ists), Philip G. Hamerton (single titles and his col-
lected works), Jean Ingelow (an enormously popular poet),
Richard Jefferies (The Story of My Heart), Walter Savage
Landor (Pericles and Aspasia and Imaginary Conversations),
Arthur Machen (The Great God Pan), George Meredith (an
edition of his novels that sparked his popularity in
America), Richard Monckton Milnes (Poetical Works),
William Morris (The Earthly Paradise and others),
Christina Rossetti (Poems and others), Dante Gabriel
Rossetti (Poems and Dante and His Circle), Olive
Schreiner (The Story of an African Farm), Robert Louis
Stevenson (Travels with a Donkey and Treasure Island),
A. C. Swinburne (Songs Before Sunrise), and Oscar Wilde
(Poems). Niles's ability to take on the controversial

pre-Raphaelites and Wilde is to his credit. Continental literature, too, received Niles's attention, and Roberts Brothers published translations of Goethe and other German authors, Balzac, Sainte-Beuve, and George Sand.

In 1894 Niles, now nearly seventy years old, took his first extended vacation since joining Roberts Brothers over thirty years earlier. He sailed for Europe on 17 March, going first to Italy. There, in the village of Perugia, he died of a heart attack on 18 May. Lewis Roberts (who had had progressively less and less contact with the business) and his son took over the direction of Roberts Brothers, but they could not have possibly hoped to replace Niles, with his literary taste and business sense. (Niles had, incidentally, done well for himself too; he left an estate of $600,000.) Although the firm continued to publish about fifty titles a year in 1895 and 1896, the number dropped to thirty titles in 1897, and only six titles were advertised in the first half of 1898. In June 1898, Little, Brown of Boston bought Roberts Brothers for an estimated $250,000 a bargain when one considers that Louisa May Alcott's novels alone would eventually return this investment. Two of Roberts Brothers' employees, Eugene Hardy and Frederick Pratt, continued to market editions of foreign authors as Hardy, Pratt, and Company, but their firm failed about 1905.

As Raymond Kilgour has written in <u>Messrs. Roberts Brothers Publishers</u>, Roberts Brothers was noted "for the quality, not the quantity" of its books. The firm's most distinguished--and best selling--author was Louisa May Alcott, and its list of publications by the Transcendentalists and their heirs was more extensive than that of any other publisher. During the latter part of the nineteenth century it supplied quality books to an appreciative readership.

Joel Myerson

Roberts Brothers

Reference

Raymond L. Kilgour, <u>Messrs. Roberts Brothers Pub-</u>
<u>lishers</u> (Ann Arbor: University of Michigan
Press, 1952).

41   Street & Smith

Street & Smith (1855-1960), published (through 1899) weekly publications, paperback book series, dime novels, a magazine, and later (starting in 1902), clothbound books. Major competitors included George P. Munro, Beadle & Adams, Norman L. Munro, and Frank A. Tousey. Operations began in 1855, when the firm occupied the two upper floors at 22 Beekman Street, New York. In 1865 Street & Smith bought its own building at 11 Frankfort Street; in 1869 it bought two adjacent buildings at 29 and 31 Rose Street. In 1897 it rented additional space at 2 Duane Street, which was the address of its printer, and also at 81 Fulton Street where it temporarily conducted part of its business under the name Howard, Ainslee & Co. In 1898--at which time there were 180 employees--it consolidated activities at 238 William Street, where it remained until 1905.

Major Authors: Horatio Alger, Jr., Annie Ashmore, Charlotte Mary Braeme [Bertha M. Clay], Frederick Van Rensselaer Dey, Theodore Dreiser, May Agnes Fleming, Mary J. Holmes, Col. Prentiss Ingraham, Edward Zane Carroll Judson [Ned Buntline], William G. Patten [Gilbert Patten, Burt L. Standish], Henry Wheeler Shaw [Josh Billings], Upton Sinclair, Ann S. Stephens, Edward Stratemeyer.

Francis Scott Street (1831-1883) was born in New York City, moving at an early age to New Brunswick, New Jersey. From early childhood he worked in a grocer's shop. Returning to New York, he found employment as a clerk at The Sunday Dispatch. Moving upward through the business departments, he was appointed office manager in charge of circulation and advertising. It was here that he met Francis S. Smith.

Francis Shubael Smith (circa 1819-1887) was raised in lower Manhattan, where his formal education ended after four years of grammar school. At thirteen he

THE BUFFALO BILL STORIES

A WEEKLY PUBLICATION — **DEVOTED TO BORDER HISTORY**

Issued Weekly. By subscription $2.50 per year. Entered as Second-class Matter at the N. Y. Post Office, by STREET & SMITH, 79-89 Seventh ave., N. Y.

No. 303   NEW YORK, MARCH 2, 1907.   **Price, Five Cents**

BUFFALO BILL AND THE WHITE SPECTRE

OR

THE MYSTERIOUS MEDICINE MAN OF SPIRIT LAKE

With wild cries of fright, the Arrapahoes fled in a panic from before the pointing finger of the white mystery.

(Courtesy Edward T. LeBlanc, *Dime Novel Round-Up*)

apprenticed himself as a printer on The Albion, a political weekly. His training completed, he worked as a
compositor on several newspapers, eventually moving to
The New York Tribune, where he also did some reportorial
work. He made two unsuccessful attempts at publishing
on his own before obtaining employment at The Sunday
Dispatch, first working in the composing room, then as a
reporter and story writer. He eventually became the publication's editor.

In 1855 Street and Smith took over ownership of The
Sunday Dispatch which, by then, had been renamed The New
York Weekly Dispatch. As in their previous positions,
Street handled business matters while Smith developed
editorial content. When Street died, Smith's son, Ormond
Gerald Smith (circa 1860-1933)--a recent graduate of
Harvard--bought Street's interest in the firm from his
estate. Another son, Gerald Campbell Smith (circa 1857-
1933) joined the firm later the same year. Ormond en-
tered the editorial department, while George concentrated
on business and advertising. When Francis S. Smith died,
Ormond became president and George became vice-president.
After careers that spanned nearly half a century, the
brothers died within eleven days of each other.

The Sunday Dispatch, which never achieved the success of such vigorous competitors as the New York Ledger,
Frank Leslie's Illustrated Newspaper, and The Weekly Sun,
was owned and edited as a sideline to his successful
printing establishment by Amos J. Williamson. In 1855,
with his publication's circulation below 24,000 and
steadily decreasing, Williamson decided to abandon publishing and concentrate on his lucrative printing business. He offered The New York Weekly Dispatch to his
two young executives who, according to Mary Noel, author
of Villains Galore, had less than $100.00 between them.
The price was $40,000 ($50,000, according to Quentin
Reynolds, author of The Fiction Factory). They made a
satisfactory arrangement, however, with Williamson assuring Street and Smith that he required no down payment,
that the two new partners could each draw a weekly salary
of $20.00 from the revenue--from which they would also
cover printing and editorial expenses--and they would

279

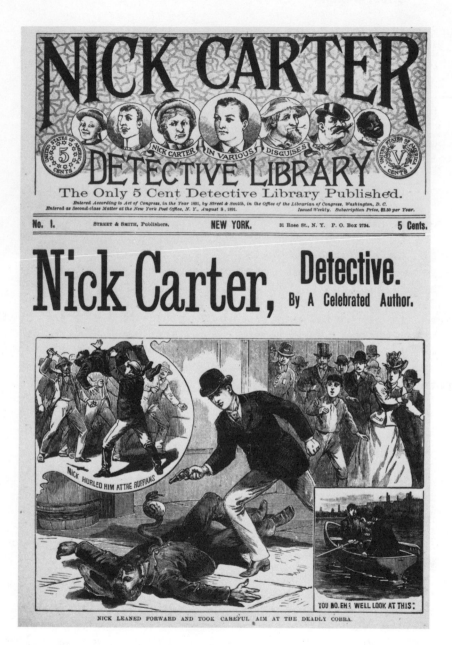

(Courtesy Edward T. LeBlanc, *Dime Novel Round-Up*)

liquidate their debt to him by paying such sums as seemed
reasonable out of profits.

By 1857 the Dispatch, "a journal of useful knowledge, romance, amusement, etc.," was sold at newsstands
for 4 cents a copy, or by subscription at $2.00 a year,
"invariably in advance." Smith was, during this period,
supplying most of the writing and on 10 October of that
year signed his own name to the first installment of a
serial, The Vestmaker's Apprentice; or, The Vampyres of
Society. The front page was illustrated with an engraving of the heroine, hands clasped piously to her bosom,
about to leap from the stern of a Hoboken-to-Manhattan
ferry, while the villain--hand outstretched--is attempt-
ing to clutch her. This story (according to Reynolds)
was an immediate success.

In March 1858, an editorial announced that, because
so many periodicals appeared under the title of Dispatch,
this word would be dropped and the periodical would henceforth be known as The New York Weekly. The following
year circulation had climbed past 80,000, and on 21
December 1863--with weekly sales of 150,000--Street &
Smith paid off the final installment of its debt.

The publishers knew what readers wanted: maidens
pursued--but never quite caught--by villains; poor lads
who overcame enormous obstacles to win fame and fortune.
It was a sentimental age. Religion was widely observed
in American homes and, from the pulpits, sin was pro-
foundly deplored. Temperance societies flourished and
the campaign for total abstinence was spreading. Unlike
competitors, The New York Weekly shunned lurid scenes of
violence and, during the Civil War, avoided tales of the
conflict. The only war story that appeared during that
period had the American Revolution as its setting. New
serials--usually in thirteen parts--commenced about every
three weeks. First installments, accompanied by a large
illustration, dominated the front page, moving to the
closely set inside columns as the story progressed.

Smith, who eventually became too busy to write these
serials, engaged top talent to delight readers. Ann S.
Stephens, whose Malaeska: the Indian Wife of the White
Hunter became the first Beadle dime novel in 1860, contributed several stories during the early 1860s. Horatio

281

Alger, Jr., who until then had been writing adult romances anonymously for the New York Sun, first appeared in The New York Weekly with Marie Bertrand; or, the Felon's Daughter, starting 7 January 1864. He returned in the 6 April 1871 number with Abner Holden's Bound Boy, a story for younger readers. Alger became a star contributor, writing an additional sixteen serials--all in the rags-to-riches pattern that had by then made him famous--between 1872 and 1889.

Alongside an increasing number of advertisements for patent medicines were romances of kidnapped English heiresses, noble schoolteachers, and courageous working girls. One early favorite was the often reprinted Bertha, the Sewing Machine Girl, by Francis S. Smith which, it was announced, "is not all romance, as many of the merciless cormorants who oppress and swindle our working girls will learn to their cost. Real characters and real incidents are jotted down which will send a thrill of horror through every sympathising heart." Introducing Out of the Dark, a temperance tale he had written, Edward Z. C. Judson--who as Ned Buntline also turned out the frontier adventures of Buffalo Bill--whetted readers' appetites for "a story in which I prove the fearful influence of that Serpent Coil which the demon of alcohol wraps about the soul, in which I portray temptation, ruin and a living death to all manhood, goodness and purity."

After the serials, advice columns were the most popular section of the publication. There appear to have been far more questions submitted by men than by women, and the widely scattered geographical scope of this correspondence must have impressed subscribers and advertisers alike. Besides the half-dozen or more serials that continued from week to week, pages were filled out with short stories, editorials, offers of premiums to enlist new subscribers, announcements of new and forthcoming features, puzzles, and jokes. There were occasional contests, items on astrology, dress patterns (usually a pull-out supplement), and inserted chromos or black-and-white portraits ("suitable for framing") of Weekly authors.

282

Another department offered technical information
on scientific, agricultural, mechanical and housekeeping
problems. The popular Henry Wheeler Shaw--writing as
Josh Billings--contributed a regular half-column of bu-
colic humor, for which he was paid $100.00 a week. As
any significant sort of organized professional athletics
was still in the future, sports stories as such rarely
appeared. There were, however, frequent articles dealing
with railroads and advice on how young men could apply
for railway employment.

The position The New York Weekly adopted toward
women's suffrage was that the respectable wife and daughter were better off close to the hearth. An 1871 editorial suggested that "the woman's movement, so-called,
is largely in the interest of religious infidelity."
Nevertheless, in serials, editorials, and a variety of
articles, women invariably were treated with respect.
Better working conditions and protection were sought for
those who toiled away from home. By the late 1860s--
aided by Buntline's frontier adventures in which his
female characters were as handy with the Winchester rifle
as they were with the needle--circulation had soared to
300,000, reaching its highest recorded sales, 350,000, in
1877.

The canny, farsighted Francis Street at this point
sensed that the popularity of his New York Weekly--as
well as of the story papers published by competitors--
would eventually wane, and the partners scanned the pos-
sibilities of the smaller-format dime novels, many of
which actually cost a nickel. These had proliferated
since Beadle first introduced them in 1860. Other publishers early joined the rush to provide this exciting,
action-filled, inexpensive literature to men who were
laying railroad tracks across the continent, to Union
soldiers who carried them in knapsacks to battlefields
in the South, to people who worked on farms or in teeming
cities, and to schoolboys.

Although by 1889 dime novels--perhaps the first
uniquely American form of literature--had already passed
their peak as fiction for mass entertainment, Street &
Smith did not join the competition until the year Ormond
Smith directed the publication of two series of dime

283

novels: the Log Cabin Library, priced at 10 cents, and
the Nugget Library, which sold for 5 cents. The Log
Cabin Library novels, which featured colored covers,
were mostly westerns and detective tales. Within a
year Street & Smith published sixty dime novels under
the Log Cabin Library heading and, according to Reynolds,
it became clear that revenues from this source were po-
tentially greater than The New York Weekly could ever
produce. The Nugget Library was aimed at younger readers,
with thirty-six numbers during the first year of
publication.

In format these were approximately 8 by 12 inches,
containing 16 to 32 pages. A partial list of the dime
novel series published by Street & Smith from 1889
through the turn of the century included Log Cabin Library (1889), Nugget Library (1889), Good News Library
(1890), Primrose Series (1890), Nick Carter Library
(1891), The New York Five Cent Library (1892), Diamond
Dick Library (1895), Flag Series (1895), Paris Series
(1895), Diamond Dick Jr. Weekly (1896), Tip Top Weekly
(1896), Red, White & Blue (1896), New Nick Carter Weekly
(1897), Army and Navy Weekly (1897), Adventure Weekly
(1897), Half Holiday (1898), True Blue Weekly (1898),
Klondike Kit Weekly Library (1898), and Starry Flag
Weekly Library (1898).

Beginning in 1897, series in smaller format--
approximately 5 by 7 inches, with the number of pages
varying but generally between 252 and 348--were introduced. Selling at 10 cents a copy, these included:
The Eagle Library Series (1897), The Daisy Library
(1897), The Arrow Library (1897), Magnet Library (1897),
Historical Series (1898), The Columbia Library (1898),
The Medal Library (1899), The Princess Series (1898),
Undine Library (1899), The Alliance Library (1899), and
The Alford Series (1899). Competition for these was
provided by Beadle, Norman L. Munro, and Frank Tousey.
Yet according to Albert Johannsen, author of The House
of Beadle and Adams, "While the Beadles were prolific,
they did not compare in productivity with Street & Smith,
who put out some fifty series of novels as well as many
story papers." Like other publishers, Street & Smith
capitalized upon the apparently inexhaustible supply of

adventure tales that originally appeared in various weeklies. It printed works of popular European authors and
hired armies of its own swift writers to produce sensational prose.

By the 1890s, publishers were profitably supplying
readers' demands for science fiction. Frank Tousey
signed up Luis Senarens to write Frank Reade Jr. stories
for Boys of New York and, according to John T. Dizer Jr.,
in his article, "Street & Smith Box M58," in Dime Novel
Round-Up (August 1977), Street & Smith was forced to compete. Tom Edison Jr., and His Air Yacht by Philip
Reade appeared in Good News 24 October 1891. Edward
Stratemeyer's Jack the Inventor followed on 23 January
1892. Also published were a number of Jules Verne-type
tales, all signed by the stock pseudonym Emerson Bell.
These included The Electric Air and Water Wizard (18
November 1893), In the Heart of the Earth (20 October
1894), and Lad Electric (2 May 1896). Several authors,
including Stratemeyer and Patten, contributed under the
Bell by-line.

Throughout the eighties and nineties the demand for
dime novels continued and, clearly, Street & Smith was
moving ahead of all competition. It had made national
heroes of Buffalo Bill and Nick Carter. Soon after the
Frank Merriwell stories first appeared in 1896 in Tip
Top Weekly, that publication approached a nationwide
circulation of a million copies weekly, with Diamond Dick
and Nick Carter not far behind. Street & Smith had over-
taken the venerable Beadle & Adams and--through the American News Company--was distributing more than a hundred
thousand different titles, old and new, in a variety of
weekly editions.

Readers were enthralled by story heroes whose names
have become American colloquialisms. And the lives of
some of the authors, if available facts are reliable,
were often as adventure-packed as those of their characters. Probably the most colorful of these writers was
Edward Zane Carroll Judson, better known by his pen name,
Ned Buntline, who gave the young hunter and army scout
William F. Cody the name Buffalo Bill. His first contribution to The New York Weekly, Buffalo Bill, King of
the Border Men, appeared in the number dated 23 December

285

1869. It covered the front page and was illustrated with
a large, three-column woodcut of Buffalo Bill with flowing mane, buckskin clothes, and moccasins. Besides the
long-barreled rifle he holds, a pistol and long-bladed
hunting knife are thrust into his belt. As this was the
garb Judson himself affected when touring the West in
search of stories, it is difficult to determine whether
he fashioned his story character after his own idea of
how a swashbuckling frontiersman should look, or whether
he was, in fact, copying Cody's attire. In any event,
that was the costume that Cody, after becoming a per-
former and operator of a traveling Wild West show, wore
during public appearances.

If stories told by and about Judson are to be believed, he led an extraordinary life. At eleven he ran
away to sea. Three years later he dove into New York
Harbor to rescue two children whose small craft had cap-
sized. The incident received so much publicity that it
came to the attention of President Van Buren, who commissioned Judson a midshipman. According to Reynolds,
Judson's fellow officers resented the upstart and refused
to let him dine in their mess, whereupon he took them on
in battle one by one.

At sixteen, Judson left the navy for the army and
took part in the Seminole War, emerging as a lieutenant.
Challenged to a duel some years later in Tennessee,
Judson put a bullet through his antagonist's head, kill-
ing him instantly. He was jailed and then dragged from
the jail by an incensed mob with lynching in mind.
Judson claims to have been shot three times, then hanged.
The mob, reports Reynolds, left the unconscious duelist
for dead, but he was later revived and returned to jail.
He eventually managed to escape, rejoin the army, and
fight in the Mexican War.

His writing career began after the war when, returning to New York, he began a weekly story paper,
Buntline's Own, which he filled with stories of piracy
on the high seas, the Wild West, and tales of the secret
organization known as the Know-Nothings. Becoming involved in a riot in which several persons were killed,
he spent a year in Blackwell's Island prison, from which
he continued to write and edit his publication. Upon

release he joined the Union Army, saw action in the Civil War, from which he is said to have emerged a colonel with no less tnan twenty bullet wounds. According to Reynolds, Judson once told Francis Smith, "I've got so much lead in me that if I ever fell in the water I'd sink from the weight of it."

Returning to the frontier, he roamed the plains with Texas Jack, Wild Bill Hickok, and the boastful young hunter William Frederick Cody, whose tales Judson recorded and further embellished. Buffalo Bill, King of the Border Men was an immediate sensation. It made Cody an all-American celebrity and--in a number of formats-- these stories remained for many years one of Street & Smith's most popular series.

When old wounds, overwork (Judson claimed he once wrote a 610-page book in sixty-two sleepless hours), and a bad heart caught up with him and he died, the publishers promptly turned over the assignment of continuing the Buffalo Bill tales to another real-life swashbuckler, Colonel Prentiss Ingraham. Similar in a number of ways to his predecessor, Ingraham--a Mississippian--was a southerner in the old tradition. He had fought with the Confederacy, becoming a lieutenant at eighteen. When Lee surrendered, he joined Juarez' army in Mexico and, a year later, was in the Austrian army, fighting against Prussia. Battle appealed to him, and he later fought the Turks, fought in Africa and Asia, and eventually joined the battle for Cuban independence. First a captain in Cuba's navy, he later was commissioned a colonel in its army. After a series of mishaps he headed for the West where, like Judson, he knew many of the colorful characters of the period. He met the scout Pawnee Bill, and stories about him that he sent back were nearly as popular as Judson's about Buffalo Bill. Ingraham was in the vicinity when General Custer and his troops were wiped out at Little Big Horn and, within a week of the slaughter, was writing the first dramatized account of the event.

A favorite during the period from post-Civil War days through the turn of the century was Horatio Alger, Jr., a Harvard-educated teacher, minister, and author of more than one hundred tales of impoverished lads who, with luck and pluck, strove and succeeded until they achieved fame and fortune. Between 1864 and 1889 he contributed eighteen serials to the New York Weekly, including Brave and Bold (5 August 1872), Dan the Detective (9 August 1880), The Errand Boy (10 September 1883), and Frank and Fearless (18 May 1885).

To obtain realistic material for his stories, Alger lived in the Newsboys Lodging House in New York, dashed westward with the homesteaders, traveled alone through wild Indian country, visited lawless mining camps in the California Sierras, and sailed around Cape Horn in a four-masted schooner. These exploits, which are fairly well documented, become more remarkable with the realization that Horatio Alger was barely five feet tall and suffered all his life from bronchial asthma. Because of these health problems he was three times rejected when volunteering for service in the Civil War.

Several Alger serials were reprinted in Good News, a new tabloid-sized story paper that Street & Smith introduced 15 May 1890, which--before its demise seven years later--reached a circulation of 200,000. As editor of this new periodical, the publishers hired Edward Stratemeyer, a young writer of adventure tales for boys. He had been brought up on Alger, worshipped the older man, and occasionally turned to him for literary advice. After Alger's death in 1899, Stratemeyer not only became the ghost who finished eleven tales Alger had in various stages of completion, but went on to write (or to have written by a team of eventually as many as fifty contract writers) such incredibly successful series as The Rover Boys, Tom Swift, Bomba the Jungle Boy, Bobbsey Twins, Hardy Boys, and others.

One of the two most successful character series published by Street & Smith was Nick Carter. The character was invented, almost unintentionally, by Ormond Smith's cousin, John Coryell. Proclaiming one day that he could write better detective yarns than any of the firm's established authors, he produced for the Weekly several that were well received. These included the first three in which Nick Carter appears as a character. But Coryell, who was equally adept at turning out sentimental romances, was--upon the death of popular contributor

Charlotte Mary Braeme--assigned to continue the popular series she had been writing under the by-line Bertha M. Clay. The breach was later filled by Frederick Van Rensselaer Dey, who joined the staff to write detective stories based upon his own experiences as a lawyer, newspaper reporter, and close friend of the famed Inspector Burns as well as New York's police commissioner and other ranking members of the force.

Ormond Smith liked the sound of "Nick Carter," even though the character had appeared only briefly in Coryell's stories, and Dey was willing to resurrect him. His first effort, Nick Carter, Detective: The Solution of a Remarkable Case, appeared as the first number of the Nick Carter Detective Library (after the first three numbers the name was shortened to Nick Carter Library), 8 August 1891. For the next seventeen years Dey turned out weekly 20,000-word tales of Nick Carter, the young detective who was the world's best marksman and could defeat thirty ruffians singlehanded, who could speak and read lips in a dozen languages and was a master of disguise, who always carried two revolvers and enough skeleton keys to open any lock. Needless to add, Nick neither drank nor smoked, swore nor lied. Some early titles included Nick Carter's Quick Work (15 August 1891), Nick Carter in Philadelphia (12 September 1891), and Nick Carter's Double Game (10 October 1891). Eventually there would be a dozen men writing these stories, which ultimately added up to 2,752 separate titles. J. Randolph Cox, in Dime Novel Round-Up (December 1975), describes Carter as "perhaps the first truly popular, immortal and thoroughly American series detective in American fiction. Poe's C. August Dupin preceded him, but Dupin was French. Old Sleuth and Old King Brady preceded him in the dime novel, but they have not found their way into the language the way Nick Carter has."

William G. Patten, who preferred to be called Gilbert Patten but was better known to millions of Street & Smith readers by his famous pseudonym, Burt L. Standish, was the creator of the long-running Frank Merriwell series. According to Ralph D. Gardner in The Princeton University Library Chronicle (Winter 1969), Patten was born in Maine toward the end of 1866. Inspired by a

dime novel pirate yarn by Colonel Prentiss Ingraham at
age fifteen, he quickly drafted two pieces and sent them
off to Beadle's. He received six dollars and was taken
on as a regular contributor. He was earning an average
$100.00 per novel when, in 1895, he moved to Street &
Smith for better wages.

Several months after Patten began working for the
firm, Ormond Smith approached him with a suggestion for
a new character. In a letter dated 16 December 1895
(quoted by Ralph D. Gardner in The Princeton University
Chronicle, Winter 1969), Smith outlined his need for

> a series of stories . . . in all of which will
> appear one prominent character surrounded by
> suitable satellites. The essential idea . . .
> is to interest readers in the career of a young
> man at a boarding school. . . . The stories
> should [be] American and thoroughly up to date.
> After the first twelve numbers, the hero is
> obliged to leave the academy, or he takes it
> upon himself to leave. . . . A little love
> element would not be amiss, though this is not
> particularly important.
>
> When the hero is once projected on his trav-
> els there is an infinite variety to choose
> from. . . . After we run through twenty or
> thirty numbers of this, we would bring him
> back and have him go to college--say, Yale
> University; thence we could take him on his
> travels again to the South Seas or anywhere.

Patten set to his task with gusto, giving considerable attention to another line in the memo: "It is important that the main character in the series should have
a catchy name." He finally came up with the name Frank
Merriwell, whose "face was frank, open and winning, and
a merry light usually dwelt in his eyes." Unlike most
fiction characters of that period, Frank Merriwell also
had a sense of humor. Scheduling Frank Merriwell; or,
First Days at Fardale for publication 18 April 1896 in

Tip Top Weekly No. 1, Smith signed Patten to a long-term
contract. A year later, Smith suggested to Patten that
he use a pen name and they agreed upon Burt L. Standish.
With few intermissions, Patten turned out a new 20,000-
word Merriwell weekly. His output totaled about 20 million words and included such titles as Frank Merriwell's
Tour of the Continent (Tip Top Weekly No. 13); Frank
Merriwell at Yale (Tip Top Weekly No. 40), and Frank
Merriwell on the Railroad (Tip Top Weekly No. 117), until
the eve of World War I, when he retired. George Jean
Nathan wrote in The American Mercury in 1925, "For one
who read Mark Twain's Huck Finn or Tom Sawyer, there were
ten thousand who read Standish's Frank Merriwell . . .
one of the most profitable publishing ventures, I am
told, that this country has ever known."

Two other writers who made satisfactory impressions
upon Street & Smith readers before establishing wider
ranging reputations for themselves were Upton Sinclair
and Theodore Dreiser. Shortly after Sinclair graduated
from New York's City College in 1897, and while he was
contributing to Munsey's Argosy and other publications,
he was hired to write for the short-lived (thirty-three
numbers) Army and Navy Weekly. Writing under the Street
& Smith stock pen name, Lieut. Frederick Garrison, United
States Army, Sinclair would write one week about the adventures of West Point Cadet Mark Mallory. On alternat-
ing weeks, writing as Ensign Clark Fitch, U.S. Navy, he
wrote about the progress of Annapolis Midshipman Clif
Faraday. When Army and Navy Weekly discontinued publication these tales ran in two other Street & Smith.
publications, Half-Holiday and True Blue. While neither
of these periodicals outlived Army and Navy Weekly by
much more than a year, there was sufficient time--once
the Spanish-American War started--to get both young
patriots out of their academies and up to the fighting
fronts. Ralph Admari in Dime Novel Round-Up (15 June
1956) reports that Upton Sinclair started at $40.00 per
week and by the turn of the century, when he had returned
to his studies, was receiving $70.00.

In 1898 twenty-seven-year-old Theodore Dreiser was
hired as a staff writer for the Street & Smith Ainslee's
at $15.00 a week. "He was a capable newspaper-trained

291

feature writer," wrote Quentin Reynolds, "and he allowed
none of the bitterness of his rebellious nature and tor-
tured soul to creep into the excellent articles he did
for Ainslee's." Ainslee's, the Magazine that Entertains,
was Street & Smith's first magazine venture. Dubious of
its potential, the firm published it not under its own
name, but under the name Howard, Ainslee & Company.
Street & Smith had created that firm name two years
earlier to publish The Yellow Kid, a short-lived weekly
publication that featured a comic strip character and
was the forerunner of today's comic books. According to
Reynolds, "no one knows to this day whether there actually was a Howard or an Ainslee." The first number
of Ainslee's appeared in February 1898, and for the next
thirty years it remained one of the most successful magazines published in the United States. At the initial
price of 5 cents, readers bought a literary potpourri
that featured some of the leading writers of that era.
Early numbers included stories by Bret Harte, A. Conan
Doyle, Lincoln Steffens, and Albert Bigelow Paine. It
was to Ainslee's that Sydney Porter (O. Henry) later
sold his first story for $50.00.

From its founding in 1855, and for the century
that followed, the house of Street & Smith--which remained family-held virtually until merging with Condé
Nast Publications in 1960--was conservatively innovative,
testing markets before plunging in. When a venture began to lose money, Ormond Smith would discontinue it
and immediately investigate other publishing ideas that
might prove more successful. The firm overtook and eventually outdistanced virtually all of its nineteenth-
century competitors, eliminating a number of them from
the field.

The New York Weekly--in format an amiable dino-
saur--although printed on rag content paper, is today
virtually extinct with the exception of the small number
of bound volumes that survive. The smaller-format dime
novels and pocket-sized volumes were printed on low quality pulp, and were read, reread, swapped, and borrowed
into early disintegration. Those that remain have become collectors' treasures.

Street & Smith

With its <u>New York Weekly</u> and its various dime novel
series, Street & Smith was among the most prolific publishers in a field that provided tons of entertaining
reading for the masses.[1] The firm's publications--like
its writers--were distinctively American, adding colorful
folk heroes to the dramatis personae of our national
literature.

Ralph D. Gardner

References and Note

Albert Johannsen, <u>The House of Beadle and Adams and Its
    Dime and Nickel Novels: The Story of a Vanished
    Literature</u> (Norman: University of Oklahoma Press,
    1950-1962).

Mary Noel, <u>Villains Galore . . . The Heyday of the Popu-
    lar Story Weekly</u> (New York: Macmillan Co., 1954).

Quentin Reynolds, <u>The Fiction Factory; or, From Pulp Row
    to Quality Street</u> (New York: Random House, 1955).

Edward T. LeBlanc with the aid of Ralph Admari, "A Check
    List of Street and Smith Dime Novel and Related
    Publications," <u>Dime Novel Round-Up</u>, 25
    (15 August 1957): 60-63.

Ralph D. Gardner, <u>Horatio Alger; or, The American Hero
    Era</u> (Mendota, Ill.: Wayside Press, 1964; reprinted,
    New York: Arco Publishing Company, 1978).

J. Randolph Cox, "Bibliographic Listing, Nick Carter
    Library," <u>Dime Novel Round-Up</u>, Supplement, 43
    (15 July 1974): 6, 23-38.

[1]There are archives of Street & Smith publications in the
    Hess Collection, 109 Walter Library, University of

293

Street & Smith

Minnesota. Mr. Gardner wishes to express deep appreciation to the University of Minnesota Libraries for awarding him a 1979 Hess Research Fellowship Grant in American Children's Literature, and to Hess Collection curator Dr. Karen Nelson Hoyle for her assistance during his research on the history of Street & Smith at the Walter Library. There is also a Street & Smith Collection in the George Arents Research Library, Syracuse University.

42   Frank Tousey

Frank Tousey (1876-1902), New York publisher of boys'
weekly story papers, cheap novels, jokebooks, songsters,
and other popular reading materials, published thousands
of titles upon every conceivable subject or character:
polar exploration, the Wild West show, circus life, crime
detection, humor, the Klondike gold rush, colonial America, the theatre, sports, outlaws, and all American wars.
With Street & Smith, Norman L. Munro, and Beadle & Adams,
the firm was a publishing giant of cheap popular literature during the last quarter of the nineteenth century.
From 1873 to 1876 Tousey was a partner of Norman L.
Munro, but in 1876 he broke away to found Tousey and
Small, located at 116 Nassau Street.   The partnership
was of brief duration and by 1879 Tousey was on his own
at 180 William Street.   From 1880 to 1882 the firm was
located at 18 Rose Street but by 1883 had moved to 34
North Moore Street, where it remained until well after
Tousey's death.
     Major Authors: Cecil Burleigh, Francis Worcester
Doughty, George W. Goode, Harrie Irving Hancock, John R.
Musick, Luis Philip Senarens, Harry K. Shackleford,
George G. Small, Edward Ten Eyck, Sinclair Tousey.
     Frank Tousey was born in Brooklyn, New York, on
24 May 1853 and died in New York City on 7 September 1902.
He was the nephew of Sinclair Tousey, president of the
American News Company.   After the establishment of his
own firm, he married Rosalie Andrews in 1879; she sur-
vived him by four years, dying on 28 December 1906.   He
resided in Brooklyn and New York City all his life.
     In 1876 Frank Tousey left the publishing firm of
Norman L. Munro and formed a partnership with George G.
Small, who had been Munro's editor as well as a prolific
author of serials written under various pseudonyms, including "Bricktop" and "Peter Pad."   The firm Tousey and
Small was of relatively short duration; Tousey became

295

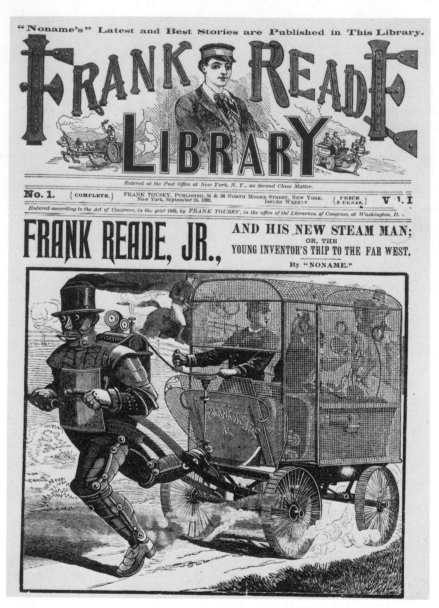

"Noname's" Latest and Best Stories are Published in This Library.

FRANK READE LIBRARY

Entered at the Post Office at New York, N. Y., as Second Class Matter.

No. 1. {COMPLETE.} FRANK TOUSEY, PUBLISHED, 34 & 36 NORTH MOORE STREET, NEW YORK. {PRICE 5 CENTS.} V¹. I
New York, September 24, 1892. ISSUED WEEKLY

Entered according to the Act of Congress, in the year 1892, by FRANK TOUSEY, in the office of the Librarian of Congress, at Washington, D. C.

FRANK READE, JR., AND HIS NEW STEAM MAN; OR, THE YOUNG INVENTOR'S TRIP TO THE FAR WEST.

By "NONAME."

(Courtesy Edward T. LeBlanc, *Dime Novel Round-Up*)

sole owner in January 1879, although Small remained with Tousey as a writer until his death in 1886. Tousey and Small however, gave serious competition to Munro's Boys of New York, the first story paper devoted solely to the boys of America, begun in August 1875.

On 17 March 1877, Tousey and Small published the first number of the New York Boys Weekly with a full-page action, black-and-white illustration, something Munro had never done. On 13 September 1877, the firm began to publish The Young Men of America, another story paper in the same sensational format. By June 1878 it was clearly the victor in this publishing battle, for it purchased from Munro most of his juvenile business including the story papers Boys of New York and Our Boys. Tousey's New York Boys Weekly was merged into Munro's Boys of New York with the latter title retained until 1894, when its name was changed to Happy Days, continuing until 1924. At the height of its popularity Happy Days is reported to have had a circulation of 500,000 copies a week.

Here appeared the famous Frank Reade Jr. and Jack Wright stories written by Luis Senarens under the pseudonym "Noname." Many of these stories had backgrounds and plots of a fantastic nature: strange machines flew to other planets, tunneled through this one, explored the depths of the ocean, battled Indians with robots. Each story had a believable background based upon the author's research into known scientific principles but applied to inventions (electric airships, submarines, helicopters) generated from his own fertile imagination.

Young Men of America absorbed Munro's Our Boys and ran until 6 November 1889 when its name changed to Golden Weekly, finally merging into Boys of New York in 1892. Adventure stories of the American Revolution, westerns with Kit Carson and the James Boys, detective stories, and the comic Muldoon stories created by Edward Ten Eyck were all regular features of this weekly. To keep these stories alive and before the public the Wide Awake Library was launched with reprints of complete stories previously published in other Tousey publications. This was a favorite technique of Tousey's, Wide Awake Library being the first of a series of similar Frank Tousey "libraries."

297

Frank Tousey

Tousey story papers and libraries include New York
Boys Weekly (70 numbers) 1877-1878; Young Men of America
(635 numbers) 1877-1889; Boys of New York (1,000 numbers)
1878-1894; Wide Awake Library (1,353) 1878-1893; Boys of
New York Pocket Library (224?) 1880-1885; Five Cent
Weekly Library (75?) 1882-1884; Wide Awake Library Special (43?) 1883-1885; New York Detective Library (801)
1883-1898; New York Comic Library (57?) 1884-1885; Boys
Star Library (379) 1887-1895; Golden Weekly (145) 1889-
1892; Frank Reade Library (191) 1892-1898; Young Sleuth
Library (143) 1892-1895; Comic Library (192) 1892-1898;
Happy Days (1,563) 1894-1924; White Elephant (16) 1896-
1897; Young Klondike (39) 1898-1899; Young Glory (19)
1898; Yankee Doodle (14) 1898; Pluck and Luck (1,605)
1898-1929; Work and Win (1,382) 1898-1924; Handsome Harry
(16) 1899; Secret Service Weekly (1,374) 1899-1927; Snaps
(72) 1899-1900; Three Chums Weekly (60) 1899-1900.   Ten
more weeklies were begun after the turn of the century,
most reprints of stories published earlier in other
Tousey papers.   The most notable ones include Liberty
Boys of "76" (1901-1928); Frank Reade Weekly Magazine
(1902-1904); Wild West Weekly (1902-1907); Fame and Fortune Weekly (1905-1928).

Like all publishers Tousey had a cadre of authors
who wrote for him on a regular basis. The authors of
popular serials were expected to produce thousands of
words regularly. Luis Philip Senarens (1865-1939) was
one of Tousey's most prolific and talented authors, his
editor-in-chief from 1895. He bagan writing for Tousey
at age fourteen, earning an average of $150.00 per week.
It is estimated that Senarens wrote some forty million
words in 1,500 individual stories under at least twenty
pseudonyms. He had a large personal library that was
used to provide accurate scientific data and background
information for his stories. A prolific author often
borrowed an idea or plot from another one. Jules Verne
published Robur the Conquerer; or, Clipper of the Clouds
(1886) with a helicopter as part of the story; Senarens
had written three similar stories with a helicopter that
had been reprinted in the Wide Awake Library in 1884 and
1885. Verne knew of Senarens's stories, for in 1881 he
had written to him congratulating him on one of them.

Senarens was aware of this borrowing, but did the same to Verne in Frank Reade Jr., and His Queen Clipper of the Clouds, in which he closely patterned his clipper after Verne's "Albatross" in Robur the Conquerer.

Although the story papers varied in size, they were generally 8 by 12 inches, containing two to four columns of print in 16 to 32 pages, selling for 5 cents each. The large size allowed for a bold, action-filled cover illustration. Each number usually had a complete action-packed story or an episode from a continuing serial with a popular character like Young Glory, Old King Brady, or Frank Reade Jr. In 1896 the first four-color-cover story paper appeared from Street & Smith, an innovation promptly imitated. Tousey's colored-cover weeklies included Pluck and Luck, Snaps, Yankee Doodle, Young Glory, and Young Klondike. Besides the bold cover illustrations that were always a part of Tousey's papers, many also had several smaller illustrations inside. Tousey used such artists as Thomas Worth, who did all the black-and-white illustrations for the New York Comic Library. A. Berghaus did colored covers for the short-lived Three Chums Weekly. The artist who did the wonderful black line drawings for the Frank Reade Library has yet to be identified.

Tousey's success as a publisher rests on his boys' story papers and reprint series. He did, however, make several serious attempts at publications for a strictly adult audience, many of which brought him grief and near ruin. In 1878 he began Under the Gaslight, the Great Illustrated Weekly, featuring stories of taverns, high and low life, divorce proceedings, and gossip with large sensational illustrations on both covers. The Illustrated American Life appeared in 1879 with much the same content, if less sensational. The Nightside Library (67 numbers?) circa 1879, with exposé-type stories reprinted from Under the Gaslight and Munro's The New Sensation also made a brief appearance. From 1881 to 1887, Tousey and the cartoonist James A. Wales published the magazine The Judge, which became a success only when they were no longer associated with it. It was the Brookside Library, however, that put Frank Tousey in jail and pushed him into bankruptcy, however short-lived. This library was devoted mainly to translations and reprints

Frank Tousey

of European literature (Zola, Daudet) but it was the publication in 1884 of stories of London court life that led
to his arrest and interrogation by Anthony Comstock,
postal inspector and secretary for the Society for the
Suppression of Vice. To get the prosecution dropped,
Tousey promised to destroy the offending plates. Comstock and his group regularly attacked publishers, authors, booksellers, and newsdealers in an attempt to
stop what they thought unwholesome literature. Tousey
yielded to this pressure in 1883 by abruptly stopping
all stories about outlaws (i.e., Jesse James). The los-
ses he incurred from Illustrated American Life, The
Judge, and the Brookside Library combined with labor
problems forced him into bankruptcy for a short time.

Tousey's career was punctuated by litigation. When
he left Norman L. Munro in 1876 a series of lawsuits followed. When George Munro began publishing the Old Sleuth
stories in the Fireside Companion, Tousey tried to capitalize on their success by publishing similarly named
stories. Munro brought a suit against him (one of a
number of suits against imitators) to prevent him from
using the word sleuth and won the case, but Tousey continued to use the word and in 1892 started the Young
Sleuth Library.

When Tousey died in 1902, the firm was publishing
many weekly story papers and preparing new ones, but the
great era of the boys' weekly was rapidly coming to an
end. Rising production and labor costs, changes in
postal rates, and a changing reading public all contributed to the steady decline in quality of the stories and
their popularity. Tousey's story papers, produced
quickly and cheaply, were created for mass entertainment.
They were eagerly read by thousands of young people who
were enthralled by these tales of adventure whose stilted
language, blatant sentimentality, outrageous characters,
and outlandish plots did not bother them at all. Not
until the advent of moving pictures and the radio would
these stories finally pass away, to become a fond memory
to some, a source of study for others, and highly sought-
after by bibliophiles and dime novel collectors.

Nathaniel H. Puffer

300

Frank Tousey

References

Dime Novel Round-Up (Fall River, Mass.: Edward T.
    LeBlanc, 1953-1976).

Mary Noel, Villains Galore . . . The Heyday of the
    Popular Story Weekly (New York: Macmillan Co.,
    1954).

Sam Moskowitz, Explorers of the Infinite: Shapers of
    Science Fiction (Cleveland: World Publishing Co.,
    1963).

Charles Bragin, Bibliography: Dime Novels, 1860-1964
    (Brooklyn, N.Y.: Dime Novel Club, 1964).

Ross Craufurd, Bibliographic Listing. OUR BOYS and
    NEW YORK BOYS WEEKLY: The Great Tousey-Munro
    Rivalry (Fall River, Mass.: Edward T. LeBlanc,
    1979).

301

43   Sinclair Tousey

Sinclair Tousey (1853-1887), wholesale distributor of
newspapers, books, and periodicals, was one of the principal founders of the American News Company and its first
president.   From 1853 to 1860 he was a partner in the New
York firm of Ross, Jones & Tousey, wholesale news agents
located at 103 and 121 Nassau Street, becoming sole proprietor in 1860.   In 1864 he was among the founders of the
American News Company and served as president until his
death in 1887.   The American News Company was first located in New York at 113 and 121 Nassau Street; 1865-1870
at 119 and 121 Nassau; 1871-1877 at 117, 119, and 121
Nassau, with a final move into a new building at 39 and
41 Chambers Street in April 1877.

The firm was primarily the distributor for all
publications of dozens of publishers, including Beadle &
Adams, Street & Smith, Frank Tousey, Norman L. Munro, as
well as Robert Bonner's New York Ledger.   In addition, a
certain number of books and series bear the imprint of
the American News Company alone, although publishing was
certainly not its principal activity.   Sinclair Tousey
did start a dime novel series in November 1863 entitled
American Tales or People's Ten-Cent Series.   In April
1867 it was announced that publication of the series
would be assumed by Beadle.   It is not clear whether
Tousey sold to Beadle or was simply acting on Beadle's
behalf from the beginning.   The American News Company did
publish the work of William H. Bushnell, Samuel L.
Clemens, Olive Logan, and Richard Grant White, among
others.   In 1865 it began a series entitled Railroad
Reading, with colored pictorial wrappers, of which probably only four numbers were published.

Sinclair Tousey was born on 18 July 1815 in New
Haven, Connecticut, and died in New York City on 16 June
1887.   As his parents died early, he received only a
rudimentary formal education.   At eighteen he became a

303

newspaper carrier for several New York papers. In 1836
he became general agent for a patent medicine company for
all states bordering the Mississippi. He is reputed to
have founded the first penny paper west of the Allegheny
Mountains--the Louisville Daily Times--although there is
no evidence to support this assertion. By 1840 he was
back in New York State working as a farmer, an occupation
that held him until 1853 when he joined the firm Ross,
Jones & Tousey, wholesale news agents in New York City.

From 1853 until his death in 1887, Tousey was in
the forefront of wholesale newspaper and periodical distribution in New York and the country at large. In addition to his business activities, he wrote three books:
Life in the Union Army (1864), recounting his adventures
in the army and his criticisms of the War Department, in
verse; Papers from Over the Waters (1869), a series of
letters recording a ten-month trip abroad in 1867-1868;
Indices of Public Opinion, 1860-1870, published privately,
reprinting his previously published letters. He was also
the principal contributor/compiler of the New York Comic
Library (1884-1885), a 5-cent weekly paper published by
his nephew, Frank Tousey. He was active in the Republican Party, the Union League, and was a leader in several
humanitarian societies including the New York Prison
Association. He married Mary Ann Goddard, circa 1836;
four sons survived him as well as his second wife,
Amanda Fay.

By 1860 Tousey's partners Ross and Jones had been
bought out and he was the sole proprietor of a news
agency handling 70,000 weekly New York Ledgers, nearly
half of Tousey's business, amounting to a million dollars annually. In 1864 Tousey joined with Dexter,
Hamilton, and Company, wholesale newspaper distributors,
to found the American News Company. The principal offi-
cers of the firm (Tousey was president) were Henry Dexter,
vice-president; John E. Tousey, secretary; Solomon W.
Johnson, treasurer; John Hamilton and Patrick Farrelly,
superintendents. By this merger of the two principal
news agencies into one firm, a virtual monopoly was
formed. It was further strengthened in 1872 when the
Union News Company, the leading newsstand owner, came
under the control of a subsidiary of the American News

Sinclair Tousey

Company. With the retail outlets secured few publishers dared stand against the rates charged by this agency. Actually, the only major publisher to challenge the company successfully was Frank Munsey.

The American News Company had thirty-two regional branches through which nearly all periodicals destined for newsstands passed. From the four-story building on Chambers Street hundreds of daily, weekly, semiweekly, monthly, and quarterly publications streamed forth, shipped express by rail and boat to regional agencies all over the country. By the early 1880s the house was doing an annual business of seventeen million dollars.

Sinclair Tousey directed the fortunes of the American News Company for the first twenty-three years of its life. He and his colleagues were the first news agents to handle successfully national distribution of newspapers and periodicals, which flowed through their offices by the millions. To a great extent, through its distribution of story papers, the American News Company made possible the mass entertainment of readers during the latter part of the nineteenth century.

Nathaniel H. Puffer

References

"Sinclair Tousey," Appleton's Annual Cyclopedia and Register of Important Events (New York: D. Appleton and Company, 1887).

Mary Noel, Villains Galore . . . The Heyday of the Popular Story Weekly (New York: Macmillan Co., 1954).

Frank Luther Mott, A History of American Magazines, Vol. 4 (Cambridge: Harvard University Press, 1957).

44 United States Book Company

United States Book Company (1890-1893), organized by
John W. Lovell, published paper-covered reprint editions
of standard writers on quality paper priced at 10 to 20
cents each. Organized in 1890, the publishing house de-
centralized in 1892 and formed several subsidiary
branches. Lack of investor confidence in 1893 forced
the company into receivership. Litigation and efforts
to reorganize continued into the next decade.

   <u>Major Authors</u>: Thomas Carlyle, James Fenimore
Cooper, Charles Dickens, Washington Irving, Rudyard
Kipling (in reprint editions).

   John Wurtele Lovell was born in Montreal in 1851
and died in 1932. He moved to Rouses Point, New York,
in 1873 and managed the publishing business of his father,
John Lovell. After a short period in the firm of Lovell,
Adam, Wesson and Company, Lovell became an independent
publisher in 1878 at 24 Bond Street, New York. He formed
the John W. Lovell Company in 1882 at 14 Vesey Street,
and served as president. In 1890 he organized the United
States Book Company. After its failure in 1893, Lovell
turned to real estate. He was one of the first members
of the American Theosophical Society and a friend of
Madame Blavatsky.

   In July 1890 the United States Book Company was
incorporated under New Jersey state law, Lovell serving
as vice-president and manager. He persuaded wealthy
Bostonian Horace K. Thurber to act as president and
Edward Lange of Trow Publishing as treasurer. The stock
prospectus preserved in the Bowker Library claimed:
"From the plates owned by this company are printed more
than three thousand different volumes, embracing, among
others, such standard works as those of Dickens,
Thackeray, Walter Scott, Carlyle, Cooper, Irving, George
Eliot, & etc., & c. More than twelve million copies of
the books printed from the plates now controlled by this

company were sold during 1889, the year preceding the
present organization."

According to the 12 July 1890 Publishers' Weekly,
arrangements were made with Hurst and Company, W. L.
Allison, Alden Book Company, G. W. Dillingham, Dodd,
Mead and Company, Empire Publishing, National Publishing, Estes and Lauriat, J. B. Lyon, Worthington, and
others to stop the publication of selected noncopyright
books. Lovell planned to buy or lease the book plates
of other firms, drawing them into the book trust. For
the rights he offered the houses a reasonable sum, half
in cash and the rest in United States Book Company stock.
He convinced several publishers that such a book trust
would end the destructive and self-defeating price war
that existed among paper-covered reprint companies.

Lovell's plan to provide protection and royalties
for British authors in the United States was used to promote his trust internationally. Through his English
agent, Wolcott Balestier, Lovell offered writers substantial payment for forthcoming books. In this way he
was able to introduce authorized editions of Rudyard
Kipling's works to America.

In addition to its standard sets, the United States
Book Company published several series: Canterbury,
Westminister, Metropolitan, Leather Clad, as well as
Lovell's Political and Scientific Series and Occult
Series. The size of the operation forced him to
decentralize in 1892, and to set up subsidiary companies
in New York City: Hovendon Company, 17 Waverly Place;
Lovell, Coryell & Company, 43 East 10th Street; Empire
Company, 142 Worth Street (Lovell's brother Frank serving
as president); National Book Company, International Book
Company, Seaside Publishing Company, all at 142 Worth;
and Lovell, Gestefeld and Company, East 23rd.

In 1893 the United States Book Company and its
numerous subsidiaries were reputed to possess assets of
over five million dollars, control no less than twenty
sets of plates of standard authors such as Dickens, and
have one million dollars worth of books in stock. The
firm's erratic payment of bills and the Panic of 1893,
however, created anxiety among its creditors, and legal
action against the trust began. Claims of various

308

creditors, including Trow Directory Printing and Book
Binding Company and Erastus N. Root, totaled approximately $300,000. The assets and books in stock seemed
more than adequate to cover the challenge, but on 27
January 1893 Lovell was fired. According to company
secretary James A. Taylor's press release, the action
was taken because he had missed directors' meetings and
failed to record financial transactions and to account
for $250,000. Without the money the company could not
meet its immediate obligations, and it was forced into
receivership. Lovell issued a prompt denial of the
charges from Boston, but his publishing career was at
an end.

More than an entrepreneur and "juggler of millions,"
Lovell actively published beliefs that reflected his own.
According to Madeleine B. Stern's Imprints on History,
"he was a pioneer socialist, laborite, and exponent of
women's rights, a man who gave the masses the cheap
paper-covered volumes that advanced their causes. At
least one side of his many-faceted career had been dominated by a social conscience."

When the United States Book Company dissolved, the
American Publishers Corporation was established. The new
company sued George Munro. The 19 June 1897 New York Law
Journal reported the final decision. Munro and his sons
signed a three-year contract with Lovell in January 1890
granting him the exclusive right to print the Seaside
Library. The contract was taken over by the United
States Book Company in September 1890. Munro recovered
his plates in October 1892 when United States Book Company defaulted on payments. After it failed in 1893,
American Publishers Corporation claimed the Seaside Library in a suit against Munro. The judge ruled that
Munro's right to the property was never questioned, and
dismissed the claim.

In January 1900 V. M. Coryell, J. N. Kenny, J. V.
Clark, and J. E. Hulshizer, Jr. formed the Publishers
Plate Renting Company. It was a continuation of the
old United States Book Company, but it published no new
titles. In June 1904 Coryell and Company, the largest
part of the remainder of the United States Book Company,
failed and was offered at public auction.

309

United States Book Company

Lovell's effort to establish a giant book trust made cheap editions available to millions of Americans. He addressed the need for copyright agreements with action. His United States Book Company was short-lived, but its impact on American publishing for mass consumption was great.

Michael B. Goodman

References

Arthur Waugh, One Man's Road (London: Chapman and Hall, 1931).

"J. W. Lovell Dead," The New York Times (22 April 1932): 7.

Madeleine B. Stern, Imprints on History: Book Publishers and American Frontiers (Bloomington: Indiana University Press, 1956; reprinted, New York: AMS Press, 1975).

45 Wiley and Putnam

Wiley and Putnam (1838 or 1840-1848) of New York is best
known for its Library of American Books, an attempt to
promote an indigenous national literature. It also provided valuable training for the two men who would later
go on to establish firms still in existence, John Wiley
and Sons and G. P. Putnam's Sons. The firm's New York
address was 161 Broadway; its London office was located
at 6 Waterloo Place.

Major Authors: Margaret Fuller, Nathaniel Hawthorne, Herman Melville, Edgar Allan Poe, William
Gilmore Simms.

The long foreground to the establishment of Wiley
and Putnam begins in 1807, when twenty-five-year-old
Charles Wiley opened his printing shop on Reade Street
in New York City. By 1815 Wiley had moved to 3 Wall
Street and was printing and selling books. The back
room of his store, called "The Den" by intimates, became
a meeting place for many of the authors of the day, and
in 1832 this group formally organized the famous Bread
and Cheese Club. Of the nearly sixty titles known to
have had Wiley's name in the imprint, two-thirds were by
foreign authors, including Byron, Goethe, James Hogg,
Thomas Moore, Scott, and Southey. In an age when reprints of English and continental authors formed nearly
all of a publisher's list, a surprising one-third of
Wiley's books were original works by American authors,
such as Richard Henry Dana, Sr., Fitz-Greene Halleck,
and James Kirke Paulding. Wiley also published James
Fenimore Cooper, although he lacked enough faith in
Cooper's first submission, The Spy, to purchase the copyright. (At this time, Cooper had written only the anonymously published Precaution.) When the book was
published in 1821, it was a success, and Cooper stayed
with Wiley, who subsequently handled his The Pioneers

(1823), <u>Tales for Fifteen</u> (1823), <u>The Pilot</u> (1824), and
<u>Lionel Lincoln</u> (1825). Charles Wiley died in 1826.

Charles's son, John, inherited the firm. John
Wiley, who was born in 1808 and died in 1891, worked in
his father's store as an apprentice. Following Charles's
death, John did little if any original publishing, preferring instead to act as agent for other firms, including the famous Carey & Lea of Philadelphia. In 1832 he
became an active publisher again, forming a partnership
with George Long as Wiley and Long. However, Long withdrew in 1838 or 1840 and Wiley took on a new partner,
George Putnam, and a new name, Wiley and Putnam.

George Palmer Putnam was born in Brunswick, Maine,
on 7 February 1814 and died in 1872. He was educated at
his mother's coeducational school. Although Putnam's
father had been educated at Harvard, family finances were
poor and Putnam moved to Boston in 1825 to board with his
uncle, John Gulliver, and work in his carpet store. But
the strict Puritan atmosphere of Gulliver's home soon
became oppressive to Putnam, and he moved on to New York
City in 1829. There, he applied for a job at the mercantile house of Phelps, Peck, and Company, but was
turned down. His next effort was more successful: he
was hired by George W. Bleecker to work in his bookstore.
After a few years, Putnam became general clerk at the
larger firm of Jonathan Leavitt, a leading theological
publisher and brother-in-law of Daniel Appleton, who
later founded D. Appleton & Company. During this period
Putnam read voraciously, and his reading formed the basis
for his first book: <u>Chronology: Or, an Introduction and
Index to Universal History</u> (1833). In 1833 Putnam joined
Wiley and Long, where he edited (anonymously) the <u>Pub-
lishers' Advertiser</u>, a book trade journal, from 1834 to
1837. He also kept active in book trade matters by serving, in 1837, as secretary to the first American association for the establishment of an international copyright
law. (Throughout his life, Putnam championed copyright
legislation, and refused to reprint foreign works without
payment to the author.) When Long left the firm in 1838
or 1840, Putnam became a full partner.

The history of Wiley and Putnam can be briefly
told. In 1840 Putnam went to London, where he saw the

possible advantages in opening a foreign branch. After
his marriage in 1841 to Victorine Haven, he returned to
London and established a branch of Wiley and Putnam on
Paternoster Row, the main booksellers' street. His home
became a literary meeting place for English authors and
American authors traveling abroad. Putnam also served
as correspondent to New York papers, including the Commercial Advertiser, the Evening Post, and the New World.
In 1845 he published his American Facts; Notes and Statistics Relative to the Government, Resources, Engage-
ments, Manufactures, Commerce, Religion, Education,
Literature, Fine Arts, Manners and Customs of the United
States of America, a defense of his homeland's literary
and political abilities. Putnam, his wife, and their
three children left London in June 1847. The following
year, Wiley and Putnam was dissolved amicably.

During the years of its existence, Wiley and Putnam
successfully published books in three areas: science,
history, and travel. John Wiley was responsible for the
solid list of scientific works published by the firm.
Both he and Putnam liked history and travel, and the
firm published a number of books dealing with the opening of the West in the 1840s. Two of the firm's best
publications in this area were George H. Colton's poem,
Tecumseh (1842), and Henry Rowe Schoolcraft's Oneota, or
. . . The Red Race of America (1844-1845). Most of Wiley
and Putnam's literary works appeared in two series, the
Library of American Books and the Library of Choice Reading. The latter was an omnibus series mainly of foreign
authors, and Carlyle, Coleridge, Dickens, Goethe,
Hazlitt, Hugo, Leigh Hunt, Charles Lamb, Thomas Love
Peacock, Ruskin, Schiller, and Thackeray were all published in its nearly one hundred volumes. But the real
jewel of the firm was its Library of American Books.

A driving force behind the Library of Choice Reading and the Library of American Books was Evert A.
Duyckinck, a native New Yorker and one of the most energetic members of the "Young America" movement, a campaign
for a truly national American literature. The Library of
American Books carried not only famous works, but also a
number of books popular in their time but not well known
today, such as George B. Cheever's Pilgrims in the Shadow

of <u>Mont Blanc and the Jungfrau</u> (1845) and <u>Journal of the</u>
<u>Pilgrims at Plymouth</u> (1848), Joel T. Headley's <u>Letters</u>
<u>from Italy</u> (1845) and <u>The Alps and the Rhine</u> (1846), and
Bayard Taylor's <u>Views a-Foot</u> (1847). More important
works were Margaret Fuller's <u>Papers on Literature and Art</u>
(1846), William Gilmore Simms's <u>The Wigwam and the Cabin</u>
(1845) and <u>Views and Reviews in American Literature, His-</u>
<u>tory, and Fiction</u> (1846-1847), and Whittier's <u>The Super-</u>
<u>naturalism of New England</u> (1847). But the most important
authors to appear in the Library of American Books were
Hawthorne, Melville, and Poe.

Hawthorne's first contribution to the Library of
American Books was also the first volume in the series,
his edition of his friend Horatio Bridge's <u>Journal of an</u>
<u>African Cruiser</u>. Published in mid-1845, the book sold
out its first printing of 2,000 copies and another 1,000
copies were printed before the end of the year. For the
impecunious Hawthorne, the royalties were welcome.
Hawthorne's <u>Mosses from an Old Manse</u> was published in
two volumes in 1846 and was even more successful: three
printings were called for during the year.

Melville's first book, <u>Typee</u>, appeared in the Library of American Books in March 1846. The book had
been rejected by Harpers in New York before Melville's
brother, Gansevoort, secretary of the American Legation
in London, placed it with John Murray. The book was
read in proofs by Washington Irving, who became so enthusiastic about the book's chances for success that he
introduced Gansevoort to his American publisher, George
Putnam. Almost immediately, Putnam offered a contract
for the book, and Wiley and Putnam became Melville's
first American publisher. Wiley and Putnam sold nearly
6,000 of the 6,500 copies of <u>Typee</u> it printed, and the
book earned Melville $732.75 in royalties.

Poe's <u>Tales</u> was published in June 1845 as the second volume in the Library of American Books. Apparently
1,500 copies were sold. Poe was disappointed with the
book, though, for Duyckinck had selected only twelve
tales from the seventy-two Poe had written, and Poe
wrote to a friend: "those chosen are <u>not</u> my best--nor
do they fairly represent me--in any respect." The book
made money for both Poe and Wiley and Putnam, and the

firm published Poe's next book, The Raven and Other Poems, in November 1845, with Poe making his own selections. A number of printings of this book, too, were done.

Even though Wiley and Putnam was commercially successful, the personalities of the two men were too dissimilar to allow them to continue working together in happy union. Wiley was conservative--both in person and in business--whereas Putnam was much more sociable and willing to take commercial risks. Too, Wiley was more interested in science, whereas Putnam's main concern was literature. The two agreed to friendly terms for the ending of the firm, with Putnam taking all the literature except Ruskin, Wiley's favorite. Both men then continued successful careers on their own.

During its brief existence the firm of Wiley and Putnam applied the series idea of publishing most innovatively in its Library of American Books, which introduced to a comparatively wide readership during the 1840s important specimens of a national American literature.

Joel Myerson

References

George Haven Putnam, A Memoir of George Palmer Putnam, Together with a Record of the Publishing House Founded by Him, 2 vols. (New York: Putnams, 1903); revised as George Palmer Putnam: A Memoir (New York: Putnams, 1912).

The First One Hundred and Fifty Years: A History of John Wiley and Sons, Incorporated 1807-1957 (New York: John Wiley & Sons, 1957).

Miriam N. Kotzin, "Putnam's Monthly and Its Place in American Literature," (Ph.D. dissertation, New York University, 1969).

46   R. W. Worthington & Company

R. W. Worthington & Company (1874-1893), publisher of
popular novels, children's literature, inexpensive (and
often unauthorized) reprints of European, English, and
American fiction, popular science and religion, published
nearly four hundred titles. Worthington began publishing
in Montreal and Boston and moved to New York City in
1874, where he established R. W. Worthington & Company
at 750 Broadway. After the first of several business
failures in 1876, he moved to 28 Lafayette Place and
then to 770 Broadway. In 1885 the firm became the
Worthington Company and relocated at 747 Broadway. Here
it remained until its final dissolution in 1893.

Major Authors: Abner Barnes, Bertha Behrens, Amy
Blanchard, C. Lever, Norm Macleod, Charlotte Yonge.

Richard Worthington was born in Preston, Lancashire,
England, in 1834 and died in Sea Cliff, Long Island, 7
October 1894. Some reports have him selling grain in
England until the 1870s, when he arrived in the United
States and began his career as a bookseller. However,
it seems likely that he emigrated to Canada when he was
nineteen and two years later, in 1855, established a publishing house in Montreal, which failed soon after. Between 1867 and 1869 Worthington moved to Boston, where he
again attempted to form a publishing house. In both
these enterprises, Worthington apparently published few
of his own editions, preferring to purchase entire runs
of English editions and market them under his own imprint.

By 1874 he had abandoned this venture and had settled in New York to begin R. W. Worthington & Company at
750 Broadway. A year later, in August 1875, he had sufficiently prospered to be the subject of an article in
the New York Evening Post, which reported that he "deals
largely in fine books." "Many of these elegant publications," the Post continues, "together with the works of
standard authors, have been bound under Mr. Worthington's

317

own supervision, and are as rich in appearance externally as their contents are entertaining and instructive."

Certainly, Worthington made his mark with such fine editions. He was especially noted for his ten-volume octavo edition of Chambers's Encyclopaedia, which sold for $25.00, a nine-volume set of the Arabian Nights ($5.00 per volume; $7.50 for vellum), and a two-volume edition of Greville's Memoirs ($9.50). He also brought out, among many others, an eight-volume set of Molière's Works, a seven-volume edition of the poems of Tennyson, and a twenty-volume edition of Thackeray's novels. Many of these editions were illustrated; many included maps, engravings, or portraits. Worthington likewise offered rather expensive editions ($7.50-$20.00) in science (such as Watts's seven-volume, $75.00 Dictionary of Chemistry), travel (for example S. Carter Hall's three-volume Ireland, with color illustrations), art (Llewellyn Jewitt's two-volume History of Ceramic Art in Great Britain; P. T. Sandhurst's Table-Book of Art), and natural science (such as H. G. Venor's Our Birds of Prey).

In the middle of the 1880s, however, after his second business failure in New York, Worthington by and large ceased to publish these deluxe editions in favor of less expensive books. He published children's literature (such as the twelve numbers of Aunt Charlotte's Picture Books by Charlotte Yonge, each priced at 25 cents, and the several volumes of tales by "Aunt May" [Ma. A. Lathbury], popular religious studies (books on Catholicism and on Freemasonry), Christmas gift books, and domestic craft guides.

In this same period, he turned much of his attention to cheap reprints of the standard classics (such as Bacon, Boccaccio, and Seneca) and of foreign novelists (he offered four works of George Sand for 50 cents each). Although many of these appeared in paperback editions selling for 50 cents and less, most of Worthington's books listed at $1.25 to $2.00. In this way, Worthington could offer a wide range of authors at minimal cost to himself and to his public, while avoiding most difficulties with copyright laws. He thus could publish translations of the novels of Bertha Behrens and Lola Kirschner, editions of Marcus Aurelius and the tales of Hoffmann, and

works by Macaulay, Swinburne, and W. B. Yeats (a 40-cent
edition of the Fairy and Folk Tales in 1888).

Many of these authors appeared in one or another of
Worthington's various special series, in particular the
International Library (paperback editions listed at 75
cents to $1.25) or the Camelot series edited by Ernest
Rhys (which Worthington sold for 40 cents). Worthington
also published the Banner Library (paperbacks, 25 cents
to 75 cents, including, for instance, George Eliot's Adam
Bede), the Household Library (paperback, 50 cents), the
Fair Library and the Rose Library (paperbacks, most sold
for 25 cents or 50 cents, which included Kirschner and
Leon de Tinseau), the Library of Select Romances
(twelvemo, $1.50, including works by C. Lever), and col-
lections such as the Romances of Fantasy and Humor (for
example, Hoffmann and Poe) and the five-volume Library of
Famous Fiction.

Worthington also attempted to market several annuals, two of which bore his name (the Worthington Album
and the Worthington Annual, 1891-1893) and one of which,
his Chatterbox series, earned him a troublesome lawsuit
and the enmity of at least one of his fellow publishers.

Worthington's firm was plagued by financial and
legal troubles throughout its course. The publisher's
first New York firm failed in 1876, two years after its
inception, with liabilities of $50,000. By collecting
additional capital he was able to begin again in that
same year, and in 1882 and again in 1884, Worthington
purchased stock from the John W. Lovell Company (over
115,000 clothbound books with a total price of nearly
$150,000). That purchase so depleted Worthington's
capital however, that an unforeseen decline in sales
and his failure to purchase Lovell's plates (which enabled competitors to publish and undersell Worthington's
books), forced him to declare bankruptcy again in 1885
with liabilities of $300,000. Once more Worthington
reorganized: again at a new location and on this occasion with a new name (the Worthington Company) and new
officers (Mrs. Worthington as president, Worthington
himself as secretary, treasurer, and general manager).
In 1890, when Lovell formed the United States Book Company to regulate the distribution and sale of cheap

editions, Worthington enthusiastically supported him.
Stung by his own recent failures and burdened by several
hundred thousand dollars of "dead property," as he called
it, Worthington saw Lovell's plan as a way to gain some
financial stability. The venture was short-lived, however, and Worthington soon reacquired his stock. By 1893,
Worthington had no further schemes to rescue his firm,
and he once again declared bankruptcy, for the final
time, with liabilities of $167,000.

Worthington's financial woes were exacerbated by
continual problems with the law. His most persistent
adversary was Anthony Comstock of the New York Society
for the Suppression of Vice. The two first fought over
Worthington's sale of Balzac's Droll Stories, which
Comstock attempted to have suppressed in 1877. A crimi-
nal charge brought against Worthington was resolved when
he agreed to sell the stock out of the country and promised not to traffic in such publications. Eight years
later Worthington tried to distribute Balzac and Payne's
translations of the Arabian Nights. Comstock found both
objectionable and once more threatened Worthington with
arrest. Finally, in 1894, after the dissolution of the
Worthington Company, Comstock instituted a suit to pro-
hibit the sale of much of the Worthington stock by his
creditors. A New York judge, however, ruled that neither
the Arabian Nights, Tom Jones, The Decameron, nor Ovid's
Art of Love was obscene.

Not all of Worthington's legal battles were with
the censors. Although in 1875 the Evening Post reported
that "as a dealer his views are respected, notwithstand-
ing the vigor with which he has competed with many of his
old and well-established contemporaries," by 1884 that
vigor resulted in a lawsuit brought by the Estes and
Lauriat firm over Worthington's use of the Chatterbox
trademark. A long and often bitter struggle ensued, and
in May 1887 Worthington lost the case, an important one
in the struggle for an international copyright law.

Eight years before the Chatterbox decision, after
he had acquired the plates to the 1860 edition of Leaves
of Grass, Worthington wrote to Whitman and offered him
an immediate payment of $250.00 for the rights to the
edition. Whitman refused, but nonetheless Worthington

ran off copies. In November 1880 Whitman received a copy
of the pirated edition and began proceedings against
"Holy Dick," as Whitman called him, to prevent the sale
of those "languid, surreptitious copies." Although
Whitman later denied receiving any royalties, he apparently was sent $143.50 by Worthington, who felt that
these payments entitled him to print hardbound copies.

Controversy followed Worthington even after the
final dissolution of his firm in 1893. In February 1894
a clerk in his firm was arrested for the theft of $2,000
worth of the company's stock. Two months later, Worthington himself was arrested on charges of perjury during the
settlement of creditors' claims. In June of that year,
he was again arrested--this time on the charge of misap-
propriating $20,000 of company funds and shipping $9,000
worth of books to Chicago on the premise that his wife
had bought them. He died the following year.

Worthington's claims as an important publisher rest
chiefly on the range of authors and series that his firm
presented in both expensive and cheap editions. He himself will perhaps be remembered more for his role in censorship and copyright proceedings than for his
contributions to American publishing.

Timothy K. Conley

References

"The Bookmakers: Reminiscences and Contemporary Sketches
     of American Publishers XXXIV--R. Worthington,"
     New York Evening Post (4 August 1875): 1.

"The Obituary Record--Richard Worthington," New York
     Times (9 October 1894): 3.

"Obituary--Richard Worthington," New York Tribune
     (9 October 1894): 5.

321

R. W. Worthington & Company

Raymond H. Shove, Cheap Book Production in the United States, 1870 to 1891 (Urbana: University of Illinois Library, 1937).

Madeleine B. Stern, Imprints on History: Book Publishers and American Frontiers (Bloomington: Indiana University Press, 1956; reprinted New York: AMS Press, 1975).

Raymond L. Kilour, Estes and Lauriat: A History 1872-1898; With a Brief Account of Dana Estes and Company (Ann Arbor: University of Michigan Press, 1957).

Edwin Haviland Miller, ed., Walt Whitman: The Correspondence, 5 vols. (New York: New York University Press, 1961-1969).

322

Author-Title Index

ABC Made Easy, 170
About, Edmond, 163
--Man with the Broken Ear,
   The, 159, 160, 162
Abridgement of the Debates
   of Congress for 1874-5,
   An, 162
Adams, Henry, 157
Adams, Samuel Hopkins, 68
Adams, William T., 44, 55
Admari, Ralph, 291
Agnew, Cora
--Peerless Cathleen, 85
Aguilar, Grace, 18
"Ah-Look, Commodore,"
   pseud. of Edward Greey,
   185
Aids to Object Teaching,
   257
Aiken, Albert W., 49
--Spotter-Detective, The,
   47
Aiken, George L.
--Uncle Tom's Cabin, 134
Aiken, Lucy, 273
Ainslee's, the Magazine
   that Entertains, 291,
   292
Ainsworth, William H.
--Don Bernardo's Daughter,
   111
Aladdin, 43
Alcott, A. Bronson, 267,
   273, 274
--Concord Days, 273
--New Connecticut, 273

--Sonnets and Canzonets,
   273
--Table Talk, 273
--Tablets, 173
Alcott, Louisa May, xvi,
   xix, 123, 125, 191,
   192, 195-196, 261,
   263-264, 267, 272
   274, 275
--"Abbot's Ghost, The,"
   126
--Aunt Kipp, 196
--"Behind a Mask," 126
--Hospital Sketches,
   263-264
--Kitty's Class Day, 196
--Little Men, 174
--Little Women, 126, 274
--"Marble Woman, A," 126
--Moods, 195
--Mysterious Key, The,
   126
--Old-Fashioned Girl, An,
   274
--On Picket Duty, and
   Other Tales, 264
--Proverb Stories, 196
--Psyche's Art, 196
--Rose Family, The, 265
--Skeleton in the Closet,
   The, 126
--V.V., 125
--Work, 274
Alden's Cyclopedia of Uni-
   versal Literature, 1, 6

Author-Title Index

Aldrich, Thomas Bailey, 82
--Course of True Love,
  The, 82
Alexander, Mrs., 163, 164
--Wooing O'T, 163
Alger, Horatio, Jr., xiv,
  xix, 27, 30, 32, 47,
  55, 65, 67, 85, 137,
  143, 191, 193-195, 197,
  245, 246, 247, 277,
  281-282, 187-288
--Abner Holden's Bound
  Boy, 282
--Ben, The Luggage Boy,
  194
--Bound To Rise, 194
--Brave and Bold, 195
  288
--Charlie Codman's Cruise,
  193
--Dan, The Detective, 86
  288
--Errand Boy, The, 288
--Fame and Fortune, 194
--Frank and Fearless, 288
--Frank's Campaign, 193
--Grand'ther Baldwin's
  Thanksgiving, 195
--Helen Ford, 193
--Herbert Carter's Legacy,
  194
--Jack's Ward, 195
--Joe's Luck, 67
--Julius, 194-195
--Luck and Pluck, 194
--Marie Bertrand, 282
--Mark, The Match Boy,
  194
--Paul Prescott's Charge,
  193
--Paul the Peddler, 194
--Phil, the Fiddler, 194

--Ragged Dick, 193-194
--Risen From the Ranks,
  194
--Rough and Ready, 194
--Rufus and Rose, 194
--Sam's Chance, 195
--Seeking His Fortune,
  195
--Shifting For Himself,
  195
--Sink or Swim, 194
--Slow and Sure, 194
--Strive and Succeed, 194
--Strong and Steady, 194
--Tattered Tom, 194
--Telegraph Boy, The, 195
--Timothy Crump's Ward,
  193
--Train Boy, The, 85-86
--Try and Trust, 194
--Wait and Hope, 195
--Western Boy, The, 85
--Young Adventurer, The,
  195
--Young Explorer, The,
  195
--Young Miner, The, 195
--Young Outlaw, The,
  195
Allen, Grant, 23
Allen, Joseph Henry, 273
Allen, Luman
--Lucia Lascar (A Romance
  of Passion), 119
Allison's Webster's
  Counting-House Dic-
  tionary of the Eng-
  lish Language, 9
American Annual
  Cyclopedia, 19
American Bookseller, The,
  3, 4, 171, 247

324

Author-Title Index

American Boy's Book of
  Sports and Games, 109
American Boys' Manual of
  Practical Mechanics,
  110
American Catalogue, 173
  247
American Cyclopedia, The,
  18-19
American Diamond Diction-
  ary of the English
  Language, 170
American Domestic
  Cyclopaedia, 217
American Housewife and
  Kitchen Directory,
  The, 109
American Literary Gazette
  and Publishers'
  Circular, 159
American Magazine, The,
  188
American Mercury, The,
  291
American Popular Dic-
  tionary, The, 170
American Publishers'
  Circular, 263, 265,
  271
American Quarterly Review,
  78
American Union, 28, 124
Appleton, Thomas Gold,
  272
Appletons' Journal, 19,
  20
Arabian Nights' Enter-
  tainment, xviii, 2, 169,
  318, 320
Argles, Margaret, 173,
  174

--Troublesome Girl, The,
  174
Argosy, 291
Arkansas Traveller's
  Songster, The, 107
Army and Navy Weekly, 291
Arnold, George
--Parlor Theatricals, 108
--Sociable, The, 103
Art and Etiquette of Mak-
  ing Love, The, 110
Art Instruction in The
  Primary School, 258
Arthur, T. S., 27, 32,
  143, 230, 231
--Ten Nights in a Bar-
  Room, 108, 143
Artistic Country Seats,
  20
Artistic Interiors, 20
Ashley, B. Freeman, 177
"Ashmore, Annie," pseud.
  of Mrs. J. M. Simpson,
  277
Atherton, Gertrude, 59,
  69
Athletic Sports for Boys,
  109
Atlantic Monthly, The, 45
Atlantic Souvenir, 77-78
Auerbach, Berthold, 163
"Aunt May," pseud. of
  Ma. A. Lathbury, 318
Aurelius, Marcus, 318
Austen, Jane, 73, 75,
  212, 274
Austin, Jane G.
--Kinah's Curse, 125
--Novice, The, 125
Automobile Joker, The,
  173

325

Author-Title Index

Bab Ballads
  (W. S. Gilbert), 247
Bacon, Francis, 11, 318
Badger, Joseph E.
--Dandy Darling,
  Detective, 47
Baker, Benjamin A.,
--Glance at New York, A,
  134
Ballantyne, R. M., 245
Ballou, Maturin Murray,
  27-34, 123, 124, 131,
  137, 139, 141, 142,
  143
--Child of the Sea, The,
  125
--Duke's Prize, The, 125
--Fanny Campbell, 28, 139
--Naval Officer, The, 28,
  139
--Red Rupert, 28, 139
--"Rosalette," 140-141
--Turkish Slave, The, 125
Ballou's Dollar Monthly
  Magazine, xii, 30, 31,
  124
Ballou's Magazine, 33
Ball-Room Companion, The,
  170
Balzac, Honoré de, xviii,
  275, 320
--Droll Stories, 320
--Vendetta, 264
Bancroft, George, 78
Bangs, John Kendrick, 149
Banner Weekly, 44
Barber, Joseph
--American Book of Ready-
  Made Speeches, 105
Baring-Gould, S., 23

"Barnard, A. M.," pseud.
  of Louisa May Alcott,
  125
Barnard, Charles, 197
--Gardening for Money,
  197
--Simple Flower Garden
  for Every Home, A, 197
Barnes, Abner, 317
Barrie, James M., 69, 199,
  204, 208, 211, 212
--Little Minister, 204
Barringer, Maria Massay
--Dixie Cookery, 197
Barritt, Mrs. Francis F.
--Land Claim, The, 42
Bartol, Cyrus A., 273
Barton, Jerome
--Comic Recitations and
  Humorous Dialogues,
  105
Bayly, Ada Ellen, 173,
  174
Beach, Rex, 69, 153
Beadle's Dime Drill Book
  for Squad and Company,
  48
Beadle's Dime Songbook,
  40
Beadle's Monthly, 46
Beadle's Weekly, 44
Beadle's, Irwin P., Comic
  and Sentimental Song
  Book for the People,
  51
Beadle's, Irwin P., New
  No.1 Comic & Senti-
  mental Song Book, 54
Beale, Anne
--Simplicity and
  Fascination, 196

326

Author-Title Index

Bean, Fannie
--Dr. Mortimer's Patient, 86
Beard, James Carter
--Painting on China, 110-111
Beard, John R.
--Toussaint L'Ouverture, 263
Beckett, Cecil Griffith
--Victory Deane, 196
Beecher, Alvah C.
--Recitations and Readings, 105
Beecher, Henry Ward, 13
Behind the Bars, 226
Behrens, Bertha, 317, 318
Belford's Monthly Magazine, 59, 60
"Belknap, Boynton," pseud. of Edward Sylvester Ellis, 56
"Bell, Emerson," pseud., 285
--Electric Air and Water Wizard, The, 285
--In the Heart of the Earth, 285
--Lad Electric, 285
Bellah, James Warner, 69
Benchley, Robert, 69
Benjamin, Park, 142
Bennett, Emerson, 215, 230, 231
Benson, E. F.
--Dodo, 23
Berry's Laugh-and-Grow-Fat Songster, 107
Besant, Walter
--French Humorists, The, 274

Bible, 11, 12, 151, 154-155, xiv, 81, 83
"Billings, Josh," pseud. of Henry Wheeler Shaw, 277, 283
Birch, William
--Ethiopian Melodist, 107
Bird, Robert Montgomery, 73
--Calavar, 77
--Hawks of Hawk Hollow, 77
--Infidel, The, 77
--Nick of the Woods, 77
Bishop, George
--Every Woman Her Own Lawyer, 110
Bishop, W. H., 213
Bjornson, Bjornstjerne, 163
Black, William
--In Silk Attire, 186
Black Avenger of the Spanish Main, The, 34
Blackbridge, John
--Complete Poker-Player, The, 106
Black Indies, The, 222
Blackmore, R. D.
--Lorna Doone, 149
Blakelee, George E., 237, 239
--Rainbow, 238
Blanchard, Amy, 317
Bob Hart's Plantation Songster, 107
Boccaccio, Giovanni, 318
--Decameron, The, 320
Book of Household Pets, 111
Bookseller and Stationer, 5
Booth, the Assassin, 91

327

Boston Almanac, 263
Boston Budget, 33
Boston Globe, 33
Boston Harbor, 98
Boston Illustrated, 98
Boston: What to See and
    How to See It, 98
Bottle Nose Ben, the
    Indian Hater, 89
Boucicault, Dion, 134
--Poor of New York, The,
    134
Bowen, James L.
--Red-Skin's Pledge, The,
    42
Bowen, Seranus
--Dyspepsia, 197
Boys of New York, 226,
    285, 297, 298
Boys Own Story Teller,
    The, 225-226
Bradbury, Osgood, 27, 93
--Belle of the Bowery,
    The, 111
Braddon, Mary Elizabeth,
    101, 181, 183
--Aurora Floyd, 183
--Eleanor's Victory, 183-
    184
--Lady Audley's Secret,
    112, 183
Braeme, Charlotte Mary,
    119, 173, 174, 199,
    203, 277, 289
--Diana's Discipline, 203
--Lord Lisle's Daughter,
    174
--Love's Warfare, 203
--Love Works Wonders, 203
--My Sister Kate, 218
--Wife in Name Only, 185

--See also "Clay,
    Bertha M."
Bragin, Charles, 174
--Bibliography of Dime
    Novel Publications,
    239
Brand, Max, 69
"Bricktop," pseud. of
    George G. Small, 295
Bridge, Horatio
--Journal of an African
    Cruiser, 314
Bright Side Stories, 1
Brisbane, William D.
--Golden Ready Reckoner,
    110
Brocier, Marco
--Jovel Fortunat, A
    Roumanian Romance, 120
Brontë, Charlotte, 120,
    212
--Jane Eyre, 222
Brooks, Charles T., 273
Brooks, Phillips, 13
Brougham, John, 134
Broughton, Rhoda
--Good-by, Sweetheart!,
    186
Brown, T. Allston
--History of the American
    Stage, 108
Brown, William Wells, 261
--Black Man, The, 261,
    263
--Clotelle, 264
Browne, Charles Farrar,
    xiv, 81, 83
--Artemus Ward; His Book,
    83
--Artemus Ward; His
    Travels, 83

Author-Title Index

--Artemus Ward in London,
  83
--Artemus Ward's Panorama,
  83
--Complete Works of
  Artemus Ward, 83
Browne, George Waldo,
  136, 137, 142
Browning, Robert, 2
Bryant, William Cullen,
  13, 19, 77, 233,
Buchan, John, 69, 157
Buel, J. W., 59
Buell, E. C.
--Ku-Klux-Klan Songster,
  107
Buffon, George Louis, 167
--Natural History, 170
Bulletin de la Société
  d'Études Töpfsériennes,
  112
Bulwer-Lytton, Sir Edward,
  75, 99, 186, 230
--Last Days of Pompeii,
  The, 222
Bunce, Oliver B., 19
--Love in '76, 134
"Buntline, Ned," pseud.
  of Edward Z. C. Judson,
  xiv, 31
Buntline's Own, 286
Bunyan, John
--Pilgrim's Progress, 2,
  13, 169, 203, 254
Burbank, Alfred
--Collection of Humorous,
  Dramatic and Dialect
  Selections, A, 105
"Burdick, Austin C.,"
  pseud. of Sylvanus
  Cobb, Jr., 142
Burleigh, Cecil, 295

Burnett, Frances Hodgson,
  215
--Little Lord Fauntleroy,
  133
Burnett, W. R., 69
Burns, Robert, 2
--Complete Works, The,
  169
Burroughs, Edgar Rice,
  65, 68
--Return of Tarzan, The,
  68
Bury, Lady Charlotte
--Divorced, The, 230
--Ensnared, 230
Bushnell, William H.,
  123, 303
--Hack, The Trailer,
  126-127
Butler, Henry D.
--Family Aquarium, The,
  111
Butler, Nicholas Murray,
  161
Butler, William Allen
--Nothing to Wear, 82
Byrn, M. Lafayette, 167,
  171
--Art of Beautifying...
  the Hair, The, 171
--Common Complaints, 171
--How to Live a Hundred
  Years, 171
--Scientific Treatise on
  Stammering, A, 171
--Secret Beauty, The, 171
Byron, George Gordon,
  Lord, 2, 13, 311

Cabin Boy, The, 169
Caine, Hall, 18, 23, 213
Camille, 218

Author-Title Index

Campaign Sketches, 253
Camp-Fire Songster, The, 107
Cape Cod Folks, 98
Captain Doe, 169
Care of Children, The, 13
Carey, Henry C., 73-80
--Principles of Political Economy, 79
--Principles of Social Science, 79
Carey, Rosa Nouchette, 174
--Wee Wife, 174
"Carleton, Capt. Lathan G.," pseud. of Edward S. Ellis, 222
Carleton, George Washington, 81-88
--Our Artist in Cuba, 87
--Our Artist in Cuba, Peru, Spain and Algiers, 87
--Our Artist in Peru, 87
Carleton's Condensed Classical Dictionary, 86
Carleton's Hand-Book of Popular Quotations, 86
Carleton's Household Encyclopaedia, 86
Carleton's New Hand-Book of Popular Quotations, 86
Carlyle, Thomas, 99, 213, 307, 313
--Life of Robert Burns, 2
--Sartor Resartus, 13
Carroll, Lewis
--Alice's Adventures in Wonderland, 13

Carter, Grace
--Plant Forms Ornamentally Treated, 257
Castle, Edgerton, 23
Castlemon, Edward, 67
"Castlemon, Harry," pseud. of C. A. Fosdick, 247
"Cavendish, Harry," pseud. of Charles Jacobs Peterson, 41
"Caxton, Laura," pseud. of Elizabeth B. Comins, 196
Century Dictionary, 62
Chadwick, Henry, 48
--Base-Ball Guide, 48
Chadwick, John White, 273
Chamberlain, N. H., 97
Chambers, Robert
--Cyclopaedia of English Literature, 1, 2, 9, 18-19
Chambers, Robert W., 147, 69, 153
Chamber's Encyclopaedia, 2, 318
Chamber's Information for the Millions, 170
Channing, Ellery, 273
Channing, William Ellery, 273
--Perfect Life, The, 273
Channing, William Henry, 273
Chatterbox, 310, 319, 320
Cheatham, 89
Cheever, George B.
--Journal of the Pilgrims at Plymouth, 314
--Pilgrims in the Shadow of Mont Blanc and the Jungfrau, 313-314
Cheney, Ednah D., 274

Cheney, Olive Augusta,
    195
Chesterfield, Ruth
--New Version of Old
    Mother Hubbard, A, 255
Chew, Samuel, ed.
--Fruit Among the Leaves,
    24
Chicago City Directory,
    117
Child, Lydia Maria, 272
Chips from Uncle Sam's
    Jack-Knife, 105
Choice Literature, 3, 5
Christy's Bones and Banjo
    Melodist, 107
Cinderella, 255
Clarissa, the Conscript's
    Bride, 91
Clark, Georgiana C.
--Dinner Napkins and How
    to Fold Them, 111
Clark, Sir James
--Ladies' Guide to Beauty,
    The, 110
Clarke, James Freeman,
    273
"Clay, Bertha M.," pseud.
    of Charlotte Mary
    Braeme, 119
--Claribel's Love Story,
    120
--Her Only Sin, 120
--Lord Lynne's Choice,
    120
--Thorns and Orange
    Blossoms, 120
Clemens, Samuel Langhorne.
    See Twain, Mark
Clerk Barton's Crime, 169
Coates, Henry Troth, 246

Cobb, Irvin S.
--Plea for Old Cap
    Collier, A, 226
Cobb, Sylvanus, Jr., 27,
    29, 30, 31, 32, 111,
    123, 131, 137, 141-
    142, 143
--Bravo's Secret, The,
    125
--Ducal Coronet, The,
    125
--Golden Eagle, The,
    124, 126
--Gunmaker of Moscow,
    The, 31, 33
--Patriot Cruiser, The,
    126
--Yankee Champion, The,
    125
Cochin, Augustin
--Results of Emancipation,
    263
Coleridge, Samuel Taylor,
    201, 313
--Rime of the Ancient
    Mariner, The, 12
College Joker, The, 173
Collins, Mabel
--Blossom And The Fruit,
    The, 206
--Idyll of the White
    Lotus, The, 206
Collins, Wilkie, 120,
    149, 186, 230
Colton, George H.
--Tecumseh, 313
Comins, Elizabeth B.
--Hartwell Farm, The, 196
--Marion Berkley, 196
Commercial Advertiser,
    37, 313
Commonwealth, The, 263

Author-Title Index

Comstock, Augustus, 37, 44, 300, 320
--On the Deep, 42
Conklin's Handy Manual, 178
Conrad, Joseph, 23
"Constellano, Illion," pseud. of Julius Warren "Leon" Lewis, 56
Conversation and Table Talk (Hand-Book), 170
Converse, Frank B.
--Banjo Instructor, Without a Master, 107
Converse, Frank H., 44
Convivial Songster, The, 107
Conyngham, Dane, 213
Cooper, James Fenimore, 2, 18, 23, 54, 55, 73, 76, 78, 116, 213, 233, 307, 311-312
--Last of the Mohicans, The, 76
--Lionel Lincoln, 312
--O-i-chee: A Tale of the Mohawk, 55
--Pilot, The, 312
--Pioneers, The, 311-312
--Precaution, 311
--Spy, The, 311
--Tales for Fifteen, 312
Corelli, Marie, 120, 173-174, 211
--Romance of Two Worlds, A, 174
--Thelma, 174
Coryell, John, 288-289
"Cousin Virginia," pseud. of Virginia Wales Johnson, 170

Cowley, J. E.
--Crawford's Claim, 108
Cox, J. Randolph, 289
Crabb's Handy Cyclopedia, 170-171
Craik, Dinah. See Mulock, Dinah Maria
Cranch, Christopher Pearse, 273
Craufurd, Ross, 225, 226
Cricket on the Hearth, 215
Critic: an Illustrated Monthly Review, 3
Crowen, Mrs. T. J.
--American Lady's Cookery, Book, 109
Cruden, George
--Calisthenic Training and Musical Drill, 109
Curtis, George William, 148
Curtis, Newton Mallory, 44
--Matricide's Daughter, The, 111
Cushing, Caleb, 78
Cushing, Luther
--Manual of Parliamentary Practice, 173
Cutler, Bradley D., 211-212

Dale, Horace C.
--Josiah's Courtship, 108
Dana, Charles A., 19
Dana, Richard Henry, Sr., 311
Dana, Richard Henry, Jr.
--Two Years before the Mast, 147

332

Dante Alighieri, 2
--Inferno, 12, 169, 242
--Purgatory and Paradise,
    12
Dare-Devil Dick, 169
"Darrell, Dyke," pseud.
    of A. F. Pinkerton,
    178
Darwin, Charles, 69, 212
Daudet, Alphonse, xviii,
    120, 300
Davis, Jefferson, 59
Davis, Richard Harding,
    149
Deadwood Dick, the Prince
    of the Road (Wheeler),
    xiii
De Amicis, Edmondo
--Heart of a Boy, The,
    178
Defoe, Daniel
--Robinson Crusoe, 2, 13,
    43, 169, 255
De la Ramée, Marie Louise
--Granville de Vigne, 186
Delisser, George P.
--Horseman's Guide, 109
Dell, Ethel M., 69
Denier, Tony
--Amateur Hand-book and
    Guide to Home or Draw-
    ing Room Theatricals,
    The, 135
Denison, Mary A., 37, 44
De Walden, Emile
--Ball-Room Companion,
    107
Dewey, John, 157
Dewey, Orville, 273
Dey, Frederick Van
    Rensselaer, 44, 277,
    289

--Nick Carter, Detective,
    289
--Nick Carter in Phila-
    delphia, 289
--Nick Carter's Double
    Game, 289
--Nick Carter's Quick
    Work, 289
Dial, 273
Dick, Harris B., 101, 112,
    113
Dick, William B., 101-114
--American Card-Player,
    The, 106
--American Hoyle, The,
    105-106
--Commercial Letter
    Writer, 110
--Dick's Art of Gym-
    nastics, 109
--Dick's Book of Toasts,
    105
--Dick's Comic and Dia-
    lect Recitations, 105
--Dick's Comic Dialogues,
    105
--Dick's Dialogues and
    Monologues, 105
--Dick's Diverting Dia-
    logues, 105
--Dick's Dutch, French
    and Yankee Dialect
    Recitations, 105
--Dick's Festival Reciter,
    105
--Dick's Irish Dialect
    Recitations, 105
--Dick's Stump Speeches
    and Minstrel Jokes,
    105

--Encyclopedia of Prac-
  tical Receipts and
  Processes, 110
--Society Letter Writer,
  110
--Uncle Josh's Trunk-Full
  of Fun, 103
--What Shall We Do To-
  Night?, 105
Dick & Fitzgerald's Cata-
  logue for 1881, 113
Dick & Fitzgerald's
  Descriptive Book
  Catalogue, 113
Dickens, Charles, 1, 2,
  18, 22, 23, 62, 69,
  73, 75-76, 99, 116,
  120, 148, 201, 212,
  213, 218, 227, 229,
  230, 231, 307, 308,
  313
--Mystery of Edwin Drood,
  The, 22
--Posthumous Papers of
  the Pickwick Club, The,
  75
Dickinson, Emily, 272,
  273-274
--Letters, 274
--Poems, 273
--Poems, Second Series,
  274
--Poems, Third Series,
  274
Dick's Art of Bowling,
  109
Dick's Art of Wrestling,
  109
Dick's Descriptive Cata-
  logue of Dramas, Come-
  dies, Farces, 113

Dick's Dumb-Bell and
  Indian-Club Exercises,
  109
Dick's Ethiopian Scenes,
  108
Dick's Games of Patience,
  106
Dick's Hand-Book of
  Cribbage, 106
Dick's Home Made Candies,
  109
Dick's Mysteries of the
  Hand, 106
Dick's Parlor Exhibitions,
  108
Dick's Quadrille Call-
  Book, 107
Dick's Theatrical Make-Up
  Book, 108
Dime Novel Round-Up, xxi,
  89, 225, 285, 289, 291
Dime Song-Book, The, 53
Disraeli, Isaac, 75
Dizer, John T., Jr., 285
"Doesticks, Q. K.
  Philander," pseud. of
  Mortimer Thomson, 82
Dostoievsky, Feodor
--Buried Alive, 164
Doughty, Francis
  Worcester, 195
Doyle, A. Conan, 65, 149,
  211, 218, 292
Dreiser, Theodore, 277
  291-292
Drummond, Henry, 13
"Duchess, The," pseud.
  of Margaret Wolfe
  Hungerford, 203
Due South; or Cuba, Past
  and Present, 33

Author-Title Index

Duganne, A. J. H., 27,
44, 131, 137
Dumas, Alexandre, 211,
213, 230
Dumas, Alexandre, Jr.,
174
--Annette, 183
Du Maurier, George
--Trilby, 149
Dunlap, George T., 212
--Fleeting Years, The,
212
Dunn, Henry Arthur C.
--Fencing Instructor, 109
Duponceau, Peter, 78
Dupuy, Eliza Ann, 218,
229, 230, 233
Durivage, Francis A., 31
Duyckinck, Evert A., 313,
314

East Lynne (Wood, Mrs.
Henry), 111-112, 222
Eclectic Magazine, 3
Edge Tools of Speech, 33
Educational Review, The,
161
Edwards, Annie
--Vagabond Heroine, A,
186
"Eflor, Colonel Oram,"
pseud. of Maro Rolfe,
239
Egan, Pierce
--Imogene, 112
Eichendorff, J. von
--Memoirs of a Good-for-
Nothing, 161
Eliot, George, 2, 99, 120,
148, 206, 227, 307
--Adam Bede, 222, 319
--Daniel Deronda, 147

Elliott, W. J.
--Art of Attack and
Defence, 109
Ellis, Edward Sylvester,
37, 44, 51, 55-56, 67,
221-222
--Hunters, The, 222
--Seth Jones, 42, 45, 55
Ellis, Sarah Stickney
--Pique, 193
Emerson, Ralph Waldo,
12, 195, 272, 273
--Essays, 14
Encyclopaedia Americana,
78
Encyclopedia Britannica,
59, 61, 167
English, Thomas Dunn
--Mormons, The, 134
Epictetus
--Morals, The, 265
Etiquette, 98
Everett, Edward, 78
Ewing, Edwin Evans, 51,
56
Exman, Eugene
--House of Harper, The,
155
Eyster, William R.
--Sport in Velvet, The,
48

Fame and Fortune Weekly,
298
Fargus, Frederick John,
181
--Living or Dead, 184,
185
Farmer's Almanac, 83
Farnol, Jeffrey, 69
Fawcett, Edgar, 59, 272
Fern, Fanny, 30

335

Author-Title Index

Feval, Paul
--White Wolf, The, 111
Fielding, A., 69
Fielding, Henry, 213
--Tom Jones, 320
Fireside and Home, 217
Fireside Companion, 300
Fiske, John, 157
"Fitch, Ensign Clark,"
    pseud. of Upton
    Sinclair, 291
595 Pulpit Pungencies, 86
Flag of the Free, 28
Flag of Our Union, The,
    xi, 28, 30, 31, 34,
    124, 125, 126, 131,
    139, 140, 141, 142,
    143
Flagg, Jared, Jr.
--How to Take Money Out
    of Wall Street, 111
Fleischman, Joseph
--Art of Blending and
    Compounding Liquors
    and Wines, 111
Fleming, May Agnes, 277
--Mad Marriage, A, 85
--Midnight Queen, The,
    111
--Terrible Secret, A, 85
--Wonderful Woman, A, 85
Fletcher, J. S., 69
Flowers from Fairy Land,
    170
Footprints of Travel; or
    Journeyings in Many
    Lands, 33
Ford, Paul Leicester, 157
Fortnightly Review, The,
    59, 60
Forum, The, 160
Fosdick, C. A., 245, 247

Foster, George G.
--New York by Gas-Light,
    95
--New York Naked, 95
Francatelli
--Modern Cook, 233
Frank Leslie's Atlantic
    Telegraph Cable Pic-
    torial, 184
Frank Leslie's Boy's &
    Girl's Weekly, 183
Frank Leslie's Bubbles
    and Butterflies, 187
Frank Leslie's Budget of
    Fun, 183
Frank Leslie's Children's
    Friend, 183
Frank Leslie's Chimney
    Corner, 182, 183, 185
Frank Leslie's Chimney
    Corner Cookery Book,
    184
Frank Leslie's Christmas
    Pictorial, 183
Frank Leslie's Comic
    Almanac, 184
Frank Leslie's Holiday
    Book, 187
Frank Leslie's Illustrated
    Famous Leaders...of the
    Civil War, 188
Frank Leslie's Illustrated
    History of the Great
    National Peace Jubilee,
    184
Frank Leslie's Illustrated
    Newspaper, 32, 144,
    182, 184, 187, 279
Frank Leslie's Illustrirte
    Zeitung, 183
Frank Leslie's Ladies
    Gazette of Fashion, 182

Frank Leslie's Lady's
[Illustrated] Almanac,
184
Frank Leslie's Lady's
Journal, 182, 183, 188
Frank Leslie's Lady's
Magazine, 182, 188
Frank Leslie's New Eng-
land Almanac, 184
Frank Leslie's Pictorial
History of the Amer-
ican Civil War, 183
Frank Leslie's Pictorial
Life of Abraham
Lincoln, 184
Frank Leslie's Pictorials
of Union Victories,
183
Frank Leslie's Pleasant
Hours, 183
Frank Leslie's Popular
Monthly, 183, 188
Frank Leslie's Sunday
Magazine, 183
Frank Leslie's Ten Cent
Monthly, 183
Franklin, Benjamin
--Works, 269
Frank Reade Weekly
Magazine, 198
Freedley, Edwin T.
--Philadelphia and its
Manufactures, 231
Freitag, Gustave, 163
Fremont, John C., 162
French's Costumes, 135
Frikell, Wiljalba
--Fireside Games, 103
--Parlor Tricks with
Cards, 106
Frobisher, J. E.
--Acting and Oratory, 135

--System of ... Voice and
Action, A, 135
Fuller, Margaret, 273,
311
--Memoirs of Margaret
Fuller Ossoli, 273
--Papers on Literature
and Art, 314

Gallatin, Albert, 78
Gannett, Ezra Stiles,
273
Ganthony, Robert
--Ventriloquism Self-
Taught, 106
Gardner, Ralph D., 188,
289, 290
--Horatio Alger, 86
"Garrison, Lieut.
Frederick," pseud. of
Upton Sinclair, 291
Gautier, Théophile, 120,
161
Gayler, Charles, 181
--Fritz, The Emigrant,
185
--Montague, 185
George, Henry, 199, 205
--Progress and Poverty,
204-206
George, Henry, Jr.
--Life of Henry George,
The, 205
German Self-Instructor,
173
Gerstäcker, Friedrich W. C.
--Hunter's Trail, The, 112
Gibbon, Edward
--History of the Decline
and Fall of the Roman
Empire, 2
Gilpin, Henry D., 78

Gissing, George, 23
Glasgow, Ellen
--Voice of the People,
    The, 67
Gleason's Home Circle,
    144
Gleason's Literary
    Companion, 144
Gleason's Magazine, 20
Gleason's Monthly
    Companion, 144
Gleason's Pictorial Draw-
    ing Room Companion,
    xii, 29, 30, 31, 32,
    33, 141, 142-143,
    144, 253
Godey's Lady's Book, 208,
    233
Godin, Jean Baptiste
    André
--Social Solutions, 203
Goethe, Johann Wolfgang
    von, 275, 311, 313
Golden Weekly, 297, 298
Goldsmith, Oliver, 12
--Vicar of Wakefield, The,
    2
Goode, George W., 295
Goodholme's Domestic
    Cyclopedia, 162
Good Literature, 1, 3, 5,
    217
Good News, 285, 288
Goodrich, Samuel
    Griswold, 78
--Token, 78
Goody Two-Shoes, 255
Gosse, Edmund, 204
Gourary, Marianne C., 112
Graham's Magazine, 27,
    233

Granite State Magazine,
    137, 142
"Grant, Major A. F.,"
    pseud. of T. C.
    Harbaugh, 238
Gray, Zane, 65, 67-68,
    153
--Spirit of the Border,
    The, 68
Great Eastern Steamship
    Pictorial, 183
Greeley, Horace, 261
Green, Jonathan
    Harrington
--Gamblers' Tricks with
    Cards, Exposed and
    Explained, 106
Greenwood, Grace, 212-213
Greey, Edward
--Three Yankee Boys, 185
Greville, Charles
    Cavendish Fulke
--Memoirs, 318
Grimm, Jacob Ludwig and
    Wilhelm Karl, 247
Gundy, H. Pearson, 60
Guyon, Jeanne Marie de la
    Motte
--Spiritual Torrents, 265
Gynaecological Case Book,
    98

Habberton, John, 191, 215
--Helen's Babies, 116,
    196, 197
Habits of Good Society,
    The, 86
Haco, Dion, 91
Haggard, H. Rider, 120,
    173, 174
--King Solomon's Mines,
    149

Hale, Edward Everett, 272
--Old and New, 271
Hale, Mrs., 233
Half-Holiday, 291
Hall, S. Carter
--Ireland, 318
Hall, William Jared
--Slave Sculptor, The, 42
Halleck, Fitz-Greene, 77
  311
Halpine, Charles G., xiv,
  81, 84
--Baked Meats of the
  Funeral, 84
--Life and Adventures ...
  of Private Miles
  O'Reilly, The, 84
Halsey, Harlan P., 221
--Old Sleuth Detective,
  222
Hamerton, Philip G., 267,
  274
Hancock, Harrie Irving,
  295
Handbook of Etiquette for
  Ladies, A, 169
Handford, Thomas W., 119
Handsome Harry, 298
Happy Days, 297, 298
Harbaugh, Thomas C., 225,
  237, 238
--Lincoln's Spy, 239
--Old Frosty, the Guide,
  47
Harding, Stanley
--Amateur Trapper and
  Trap-Maker's Guide,
  109
Harding, William Edgar
--Athlete's Guide, The,
  109

Hardy, Thomas, 157, 163,
  164, 174
--Far From the Madding
  Crowd, 163, 164
--Pair of Blue Eyes, A,
  163, 164
--Under the Greenwood
  Tree, 164
"Harland, Marion," pseud.
  of Mary Virginia
  Hawes Terhune, 85
Harper's Bazar, 153
Harper's New Monthly
  Magazine, 46, 148, 153
Harper's Weekly, 32, 82,
  144, 148, 149, 153, 182
Harper's Young People, 153
Harris, Miriam Coles, 85
--Frank Warrington, 85
--Happy-Go-Lucky, 85
--Missy, 85
--Perfect Adonis, A, 85
--Rutledge, 85
Harris, William T., 273
Hart, M. C.
--Amateur Printer, The,
  110
Harte, Francis Brett
  [Bret Harte], 96
--Mliss, 96, 292
Hartmann, Franz
--Magic White and Black,
  206
--Talking Image of Urur,
  The, 206
Harvard: The First Amer-
  ican University, 98
Harvey, Charles M., 45
Hawks, the Conscript, 91
Hawthorne, Julian, 59

Author-Title Index

Hawthorne, Nathaniel,
xiii, 2, 12, 28, 77,
272, 311, 314
--Mosses from an Old
Manse, 314
--See Bridge, Horatio
Hay, Mery Cecil
--Reaping the Whirlwind,
185
"Hazel, Harry," pseud. of
Justin Jones, 28, 139
Hazlitt, William, 313
Headley, Joel T.
--Alps and the Rhine, The,
314
--Letters from Italy, 314
Hearn, Lafcadio
--Some Chinese Ghosts,
272
Hearth and Home, 1
Hector, Annie, 173, 174
Hedge, Frederic Henry,
267, 273
Heine, Heinrich, 161
Hemens, Felicia, 167
Hemyng, Samuel
Bracebridge, 181, 185
--Jack Harkaway and his
Friends, 185
--Jack Harkaway and the
Secret of Wealth, 185
--Jack Harkaway in
America, 185
--Jack Harkaway out West,
185
--Red Dog, Blue Horse,
185
Henty, G. A., 65, 67
Hentz, Caroline Lee, 215
229, 230, 233
Higginson, Thomas
Wentworth, 273

Hill, Georgiana
--How to Cook Potatoes,
Apples, Eggs, and Fish
400 Different Ways,
109
Hill, John B.
--Proceedings at the Cen-
tennial Celebration ...
of Mason, N.H., 127
Hillgrove, Thomas
--Complete Practical
Guide to the Art of
Dancing, 106-107
Hints to Young Men on the
True Relations of the
Sexes, 98
Historical Register of
the United States Cen-
tennial Exposition, 187
History of Yule, 162
Hoffman, J. Milton, 221
Hoffman, E. T. A., 318,
319
Hogg, James, 311
Helberton, Wakeman
--Art of Angling, The,
109
Holmes, Mary J., 84, 277
--Cameron Pride, The, 84
--Cousin Maude, and
Rosamund, 84
--Darkness and Daylight,
85
--Ethelyn's Mistake, 85
Holmes, Oliver Wendell,
171, 272
--Autocrat, The, 171
Holt, Henry, 157-166
--Calmire-Man and Nature,
160
--Garrulities of an Octo-
genarian, 160

340

Author-Title Index

--On the Cosmic Relations, 160

--Sturmsee-Man and Man, 160

--Talks on Civics, 160

Home, The, 40

Home Circle, The, 103

Homer, Winslow

--Life in Camp, 253

Home Weekly, The, 5

Hook, Theodore, 73, 75

Hope, Anthony, 23, 157, 161

--Prisoner of Zenda, The, 165

--Rupert of Hentzau, 161

Hosmer, Margaret, 245, 247

House and Garden, 248

Howard, Jane

--Zelda. A Tale of the Massachusetts Colony, 126

Howells, William Dean, 149

Howland, Edward, 203

Howland, Marie, 203

--Papa's Own Girl, 206

How to Cook and How to Carve, 109

How to Write a Letter, 170

How to Write the History of a Family, 98

Hudson, Frances

--Private Theatricals for Home Performance, 108

Hughes, Rupert

--Unpardonable Sin, The, 68

Hugo, Victor, 186, 313

--Battle of Waterloo, 264

--Miserables, Les, 86

Hungerford, Margaret Wolfe, 203

--Airy Fairy Lilian, 203

--Dick's Sweetheart, 203

Hunt, Leigh, 313

Hunters' and Trappers' Guide, 170

Ibanez, V. B., 69

Ibsen, Henrik, 212

Illuminated Western World, 132

Illustrated American Life, 299, 300

Illustrated Literary Monthly, The, 237

Illustrated London News, The, 29, 142, 181

Illustrated News (New York), 29, 143, 182

Incidents of Camp Life, 89

Incidents of the Civil War in America, 183

In-Door and Out, 237

Inez, The Forest Bride, 169

Ingelow, Jean, 267, 274

Ingraham, Joseph Holt, 27, 28, 32, 93, 94, 111, 137, 139, 272

Ingraham, Prentiss, xiv, 37, 44, 277, 287, 290

--Wild Bill, the Pistol Dead Shot, 47

In His Steps (Sheldon), 13

Insane: Handbook for Attendants, 98

341

Author-Title Index

Ireland, Joseph N.
--Fifty Years of a Play-
    Goer's Journal, 135
Irving, Henry, 212
Irving, Washington, 2,
    73, 77, 116, 120, 242,
    307, 314
--Alhambra, The, 77
--Astoria, 77
--Conquest of Granada, 77
--Crayon Miscellany, 77
--Irving's Works, 242
--Sketch Book, 160
--Tales of a Traveller,
    77

Jack Johnson's Jokes for
    the Jolly, 105
Jackson, Helen Hunt, 267,
    272
--Ramona, 272
Jack the Joker, 226
James, G. P. R., 230
James, Henry, 149
James, W. I.
--Old Cap Collier, 226
James, William, 157, 165
--Briefer Course, 165
--Psychology, 165
Jeffries, Richard
--Story of My Heart, The,
    274
Jenkins, Mrs. C., 163
Jerome, Jerome K., 157
Jewitt, Llewellyn
--History of Ceramic Art
    in Great Britain, 318
"Jinks, Joshua Jedidiah,"
    pseud. of William B.
    Dick, 105
Johannsen, Albert, 41,
    174

--House of Beadle and
    Adams, The, 184
Johnson, Eastman
--Barefoot Boy, The, 255
--Boyhood of Lincoln,
    The, 255
Johnson, Samuel
--Rasselas, 2
Johnson, Virginia Wales,
    167
--Christmas Stocking, The,
    170
Jolly Joker, 183
Jones, Henry
--American Leads at Whist,
    106
Jones, Justin, 27, 28,
    137, 139
Jones, L. Augustus, 221
Judd, Sylvester
--Margaret, 273
Judge, The, 299, 300
Judson, Edward Zane
    Carroll, xiv, 27, 31,
    32, 37, 44, 93, 123,
    137, 141, 277, 282,
    283, 285-287
--Buffalo Bill, King of
    the Border Men, 285-286,
    287
--G'Hals of New York, The,
    94
--"King of the Sea, The,"
    141
--Out of the Dark, 282
--"Red Revenger, The," 141
--Volunteer, The, 125,
    126, 141
--White Cruiser, The, 111
Justina, the Avenger, 89
Juvenile Gems, 6

342

"Keene, Lieutenant,"
    pseud. of St. George
    Rathborne, 238
Kellogg, Edward
--Labor and Capital, 206
Kemble, Fanny, 157
--Memoirs, 165
Kempis, Thomas A., 12, 13
Kennedy, John Pendleton,
    73
--Horseshoe Robinson, 77
--Swallow Barn, 77
Kennedy, the Incendiary
    Spy, 91
Kilgour, Raymond, 273
--Messrs. Roberts
    Brothers Publishers,
    275
Killdare, the Black
    Scout, 89
Kingsford, Anna B.
--Clothed With the Sun,
    206
Kingsley, Charles, 161
King Winter, 255
Kipling, Rudyard, 199,
    204, 208, 211, 218,
    307, 308
--Soldiers Three, 204
Kirschner, Lola, 318, 319
Kiss Me While I'm Dream-
    ing, 48
Knight, Charles, 247
--Popular History of
    England, 201
Knox, Isa Craig, 181
--Half Sisters, The, 184,
    185
Knox, Thomas W., 149
Koehler, S. R.
--Architecture, Sculpture
    Industrial Arts, 258

--Theory of Color in its
    Relation to Art, The
    (with Pickering), 257-
    258
Konversations-Lexikon
    (Brockhaus), 78

Ladies Companion, The, 41
    233
Ladies' World, 217
Lamartine, Alphonse
--Life of Christopher
    Columbus, 2
--Life of Oliver
    Cromwell, 2
--Mary Queen of Scots, 2
Lamb, Charles, 12, 313
Lamb, Mary, 12
Landor, Walter Savage
--Imaginary Conversations,
    274
--Pericles and Aspasia,
    274
Lantern, The, 81
Larry, the Army Dog
    Robber, 89
Lathbury, Ma. A., 318
Lathrop, George Parsons,
    272
Lawrence, George Alfred
--Sword and Gown, 186
LeBlanc, Edward T., xxi,
    89
"Lee, Holm," pseud. of
    Harriet Parr, 245
Legends of the Infancy and
    Boyhood of Jesus Christ,
    264
Lehmann-Haupt, Hellmut, 67
Leithead, J. Edward, 89

Leland, Charles Godfrey
--Art of Conversation,
    The, 86
Leslie, Miriam Florence
    Follin (Mrs. Frank
    Leslie), 181-189
--California: A Pleasure
    Trip, 182
Leslie, Miss, 233
Lessons in Pencil Draw-
    ings from Nature, 258
Lester, C. Edward
--Lives and Public Ser-
    vices of Samuel J.
    Tilden and Thomas A.
    Hendricks, 184
Lever, Charles, 317, 319
Lewis, Charles Bertrand,
    44
Lewis, Julius Warren
    "Leon," 44, 51, 56
Leypoldt, Frederick, 157,
    159, 160, 161, 162
Liberty Boys of "76",
    298
Library Magazine of Select
    Foreign Literature, 1,
    3, 5, 6
Lieber, Francis, 78
Life and Adventures of
    Claude Duval, The, 111
Life and Adventures of
    Dick Clinton, 111
Lincoln, Joseph C., 65,
    68
Line of Battle Ship
    (Gleason's), 28, 144
Lingard, William Horace
--William Lingard's On the
    Beach at Long Branch
    Song Book, 107

Linton, Elizabeth Lynn
--From Dreams to Waking,
    186
Lippard, George, 230, 231
Literary Bulletin and
    Trade Circular, 159
Littell's Living Age, 3
Little Lord Fauntleroy
    (Burnett), 133
Little Red Riding Hood,
    255
Locke, William J., 23
Lockwood, Ralph Ingersoll
--Insurgents, 77
--Rosine Laval, 77
Logan, Olive, 303
London Society, 59, 60
Longfellow, Henry
    Wadsworth, 13, 233,
    272
--Poems, 203
--Psalm of Life, 208
--Voices of the Night, 203
Loti, Pierre, 120
Louisville Daily Times,
    304
Lover's Companion, 170
Lowell, James Russell,
    272
Lyall, Edna
--Donovan, 23
Lyell, Henry
--Amusing Adventures,
    Afloat and Ashore, 187

"M. Quad," pseud. of
    Charles Bertrand Lewis,
    44
Macaulay, Thomas Babington,
    214, 319
--Frederick the Great, 2
--History of England, 2
--William Pitt, 2

Author-Title Index

Macdonald, George
--David Elginbred, 196
--Robert Falconer, 196
Machen, Arthur
--Great God Pan, The, 174
MacLeod, Norm, 317
Madame Le Marchand's
    Fortune-Teller, 106
Madame Le Normand's Un-
    erring Fortune-Teller,
    106
Mad Bard, The, 89
Madison, Charles A., 163,
    164
Maine, Henry S., 157
"Manly, Marline," pseud.
    of St. George
    Rathborne, 238
Manning, William H., 237,
    238
Maretzek, Max
--Crotchets and Quavers,
    135
Marriage Looking Glass,
    The, 169-170
Marryat, Frederick, 111,
    230
Marshall, Edison, 69
Martin, H. Newell
--Human Body, The, 165
Martine, Arthur
--Hand-Book of Etiquette,
    110
Marx, Karl
--Kapital, Das, 22
Masque of Poets, A, 272
Master Mouse's Supper
    Party, 184
Mathews, Carnelius, 93
May, Samuel Joseph, 273
"Mayne, Leger D.," pseud.
    of William B. Dick, 105

McBride, H. Elliott
--All Kinds of Dialogues,
    105
McCarthy, Justin, 23, 214
McCutcheon, George Barr,
    69
McLean, Sally Pratt, 97
Meehan, Thomas
--Native Flowers and Ferns
    of the United States,
    258
Melville, Hermann, xiii,
    149, 311, 314
--Typee, 314
Mercedes, the Outlaw's
    Child, 89, 169
Mercier, Jerome J.
--Mountains and Lakes of
    Switzerland and Italy,
    184
"Meredith, C. Leon," pseud.
    of George Blakelee, 238
Meredith, George, 274
Merrick, Leonard, 23
Merrill, James Milford,
    237, 238
--Girl Guerilla, The, 239
Merron, Eleanor, 213
Michelet, Jules
--Femme, La, 86
--Woman, 86
Mill, John Stuart, 157,
    162
--Autobiography, 162
--Dissertations and Dis-
    cussions, 165
"Millbank, H. R.," pseud.
    of Edward Sylvester
    Ellis, 56
Miller, Joaquin, 272
Milnes, Richard Monckton
--Poetical Works, 274

345

Milton, John, 2, 167, 201
--Paradise Lost, 12
Mitchell, C.
--Art of Boxing, 110
Mitchell, Edward
--$5000 A Year, 197
Molière, Jean-Baptiste
   Poquelin
--Works, 318
Montez, Lola
--Arts of Beauty, The,
   110
Mooney, James
--Two Women in Black, 119
Moore, Thomas, 13, 73,
   311
Morgan, Lewis H., 157
Morley, John, 211
Morris, Charles
--Dark Paul, the Tiger
   King, 47
Morris, William
--Earthly Paradise, The,
   274
Mosby, the Guerrilla, 89
Mother and Son, 133
Mother Shipton's Fortune
   Teller, 106
Mott, Ed., 44
Mott, Frank Luther, xiv,
   68
--Golden Multitudes, 62
   84, 112
Moulton, Louise Chandler,
   272
Mrs. Beeton's Book of
   Household Management,
   184
Mühlback, Louisa, 18, 23
Muldoon, James
--Wrestling, 109-110
Mulock, Dinah Maria, 186

--Hannah, 186
--John Halifax, Gentleman,
   149, 186, 222
Munro's Pocket Magazine,
   226
"Murray, Lieutenant,"
   pseud. of Maturin M.
   Ballou, 28, 139, 141
Murray, W. H. H., 97, 98
--Adventure in the Wilder-
   ness, 98
Musick, John R., 295
Myers, P. Hamilton, 51, 56
Mystery of Pain, The, 98

Nathan, George Jean, 291
National Era, 232
National Farmer's and
   Housekeeper's Cyclo-
   paedia, 217
National Standard Diction-
   ary, The, 65
Neal, John, 76
--Logan, 76
--Wandering Recollections
   of a Somewhat Busy Life,
   272
Newcomb, Simon and
   Edward J. Holden, 157
--Astronomy, 165
New Sensation, The, 299
New World, The, 27, 313
New York Boys Weekly, 226,
   297, 298
New York Comic Library,
   298, 299, 304
New York Evening Post,
   234, 256, 313, 317, 320
New York Family Story
   Paper, The, 225, 226
New York Fireside Compan-
   ion, The, 222

New York Jack Shephard,
The, 226
New York Journal of
Romance, General Lit-
erature, Science and
Art, The, 135
New York Law Journal, 309
New York Ledger, 27, 30,
31, 32, 142, 143, 144,
232, 279, 303, 304
New York Public Library
Bulletin, The, 40
New York Sun, The, 60,
187, 282
New York Times, The, 6,
148
New York Tribune, 19, 42
95, 163, 261, 265, 279
New York Weekly, The, xii,
27, 31, 32, 56, 84,
86, 144, 281, 282, 283,
284, 285, 288, 292,
293
New York Weekly Dispatch,
The, 279-281
Noel, Mary
--Villains Galore, 279
"Noname," pseud. of Luis
Senarens, 297
Norma Danton, 89
Norris, Charles, 69
Norris Kathleen, 69
Norris, William, 211
North, Ingoldsby
--Book of Love Letters,
110
North American Review,
The, 78, 265
Notable Thoughts About
Women, 33
Novelette, 124
Novelist, The, 6

Nursery Picture-Gallery,
The, 184
Nye, Bill, 59

O. Henry (Sydney Porter),
292
Ohio Farmer, 237
Old Arm Chair, The, 48
Oliphant, Margaret, 211
Olive Branch, The, 27, 141
Once a Week, 183
Oppenheim, E. Phillips,
65, 68, 69
--Great Impersonation,
The, 69
"Optic, Oliver," pseud.
of William Taylor
Adams, 44
Orczy, Baroness, 69
"O'Reilly, Private Miles,"
pseud. of Charles G.
Halpine, xiv, 81, 84
Ormsby, George F.
--Madonna of Pass Chris-
tian, The, 119-120
Osgood, Frances Sargent,
142
Osgood, the Demon Refugee,
89
Otis, James, 67
--Toby Tyler, 149
"Ouida," pseud. of Marie
Louise de la Ramée, 186
Our Boys of New York, 225,
226, 297
Our New States and Terri-
tories, 46
Ovid
--Art of Love, 320
Owen, Albert K.
--Integral Co-Operation,
206

"Pad, Peter," pseud. of George G. Small, 295

Paine, Albert Bigelow, 292

Palmer, Julius, Jr.

--Mushrooms of America, 258

Paper World, The, 257

Parker, Gilbert, 23

Parker, Perley

--Foundling, The, 126

Parker, Theodore, 273

Parlor Library, The, 237

Parlor Pastimes, 170

Parr, Harriet, 245

"Patten, Gilbert," pseud. of William G. Patten, 277, 289

Patten, William G., xix, 277, 285, 289-291

--Frank Merriwell at Yale, 291

--Frank Merriwell on the Railroad, 291

--Frank Merriwell; or, First Days at Fardale, 290-291

--Frank Merriwell's Tour of the Continent, 291

Paulding, James Kirke, 77, 78, 311

Pauline, the Female Spy, 89

Payn, James

--Murphy's Master, 186

Payne, John, xviii, 320

Peabody, Elizabeth Palmer, 273

--Record of a School, 273

--Record of Mr. Alcott's School, 273

Peacock, Thomas Love, 313

Pearson, Edmund

--Dime Novels, 226

Peck, G. W., 59

People's Home Journal, 211

Perdita, the Demon Refugee's Daughter, 89

Perfect Gentleman, The, 110

Personal Beauty, 170

Peterson, Charles Jacobs, 230, 233

--Privateer's Cruise, The, 41

Peterson's Magazine, 233

Philadelphia Dollar Newspaper, 56

Phillips, Wendell, 261

--Speeches, Lectures, and Letters, The, 261-263

Picayune, The, 81

Picton, Thomas

--Fireside Magician, The, 106

Pictorial History of President Garfield's Career, 188

Pictorial History of the Harpers Ferry Insurrection, 183

Pictorial History of the Life of James G. Blaine, 188

Pictorial History of The War of 1861, 183

Picturesque America, 19, 22

Picturesque Europe, 19

Picturesque Palestine, 19

Pierce, Etta W.

--Prince Lucifer, 187

Pine and Palm, 261

Pinkerton, A. F., 172

Author-Title Index

--$5,000 Reward, The, 178
--Life for a Life, 178
--Saved at the Scaffold, 178
Pluck and Luck, 298, 299
Plutarch, 214
--Lives of Illustrious Men, 2
Pocket Lawyer, 247
Poe, Edgar Allan, xiii, 2, 13, 27, 33, 77, 137, 142, 233, 289, 311, 314-315, 319
--Raven, The, and Other Poems, 315
--Tales, 314
Pole, William
--Theory of the Modern Scientific Game of Whist, The, 106
Poole, John F.
--Champagne Charley Songster, 107
Poore, Ben Perley, 27, 123, 137
--Mameluke, 125
--Scout, The, 125, 126
Pope, Alexander, 167
Portland Magazine, The, 233
Practical Magician, 170
Prang's Chromo, 254, 255
Prang's Natural History Series for Children, 258
Prang's Standard Alphabets, 258
Prescott, William Hickling, 214
Price, Edmund E.
--Science of Self-Defense, The, 109

Princeton University Library Chronicle, The, 289, 290
Proctor, Richard A.
--Poker Principles and Chance Laws, 106
Progressive Studies in Water Color Painting, 258
Publishers' Advertiser, 312
Publishers' Trade List Annual, 68, 69, 212, 217
Publishers' Weekly, xxi, xxii, 4, 5, 6, 12, 21, 22, 63, 68, 99, 159, 160, 157, 165, 171, 214, 234, 241, 308
Puffer, Nathaniel H., 112
Pullan, Matilda M. C.
--Lady's Manual of Family Work, 109
Putnam, Alfred P.
--Singers and Songs of the Liberal Faith, 273
Putnam, George Palmer, 160, 311-315
--American Facts, 313
--Chronology, 312
"Pylodet, L.," pseud. of Frederick Leypoldt, 159

Quantrell, the Terror of the West, 91
Queen Titania's Book of Fairy Tales, 187
Quo Vadis (Sinkiewicz), 13

Author-Title Index

Raife, Raymond, 213
"Randolph, Lt. J. H.,"
    pseud. of Edward
    Sylvester Ellis, 56
Rathborne, St. George,
    237, 238
--Black Cudjo, 238
--Fighting Joe Hooker,
    238
--Young Gold Hunters,
    The, 238
Read, Opie, 177
--Jucklins, The, 178
--Kentucky Colonel, A,
    178
--Tennessee Judge, A,
    178
Reade, Charles, 99, 116,
    186
Reade, Philip
--Tom Edison Jr., and His
    Air Yacht, 285
Ready Remedies for Common
    Complaints, 45
Rebellion Record, The
    (ed. Frank Moore),
    160
Rede, L. T.
--Guide to the Stage, The,
    135
Redpath, James, 261-266
--Echoes of Harper's
    Ferry, 261
--Guide to Hayti, A (ed.),
    261
--Public Life and Auto-
    biography of John
    Browne, The, 261, 263
--Public Life of Capt.
    John Brown, The, 261
--Talks About Ireland,
    265

Redpath's Weekly, 265
"Redwing, Morris," pseud.
    of James Milford
    Merrill, 238
Reed, Isaac George, Jr.
--Erring, Yet Noble, 196
Reid, Christian
    (Frances C. Tiernan),
    18
Reid, Mayne, 46-47, 85, 93,
    94, 95-95
--Croquet, 265
--Onward, 85
--Rifle Rangers, The, 85
--Scalp Hunters, The, 85
--White Squaw, The, 47
Reynolds, Quentin, 281,
    284, 286, 287, 292
--Fiction Factory, The,
    279
Richardson, Samuel
--Clarissa Harlowe, 163
Rinehart, Mary Roberts,
    69
Ripley, George, 19
Rippard, the Outlaw, 89
Rives, Amelia, 213
"Robins, Seelin," pseud.
    of Edward Sylvester
    Ellis, 56
Robinson, John Hovey,
    44, 131
--White Rover, The, 126
Robinson, Solon, 93
--Hot Corn, 94, 95
Robinson Crusoe (Defoe),
    2, 13, 43, 169, 255
"Rodman, Emerson," pseud.
    of Edward Sylvester
    Ellis, 56
Roe, Azel Stevens, 81, 85

--Cloud on the Heart, The, 85

--How Could He Help It?, 85

--James Montjoy, 85

--Like and Unlike, 85

--Star and the Cloud, The, 85

Rogers, Denis R., 221

Rogers, Will, 69-70

Rolfe, Maro

--Libby Prison, 238-239

--Sky Scouts, The, 239

Rollin, Charles

--Ancient History, 2

Rossetti, Christina

--Poems, 274

Rosetti, Dante Gabriel

--Dante and His Circle, 274

--Poems, 274

Rowson, Susannah

--Charlotte Temple, 218

Ruskin, John, 1, 12, 212, 313, 315

--Works, 6

Russian Bullet, A, 185

St. Pierre, Jacques Henri Bernardin de

--Paul and Virginia, 2

Sainte-Beuve, Charles Augustin, 275

"St. George, Harry," pseud. of St. George Rathborne, 238

Sala, George Augustus Henry

--Breakfast in Bed, 265

Saltus, Edgar, 59

Sanborn, Franklin B., 273

Sand, George, 161, 230, 275, 318

Sandhurst, P. T.

--Table-Book of Art, 318

Sangster, Margaret E., 44

Sargent, Epes, 272

--Peculiar, 85

Saturday Evening Post, 230, 232

Saturday Journal, The, 44, 46

Saturday Star Journal, 44

Scenes for Amateurs, 135

Schiller, Johann Christoph Friedrich von, 161, 313

Schmucker

--Arctic Explorations and Discoveries During the Nineteenth Century, 9

Schoolcraft, Henry Rowe

--Oneota, 313

Schreiner, Olive

--Story of an African Farm, The, 274

Schwartz, Marie S., 246

Scott, Sir Walter, 1, 2, 13, 18, 22, 69, 73, 74, 75, 76, 167, 212, 230, 307, 311

--Waverley Novels, xvi, 23, 74, 75, 98, 246,

Scribner's Magazine, 144

Secret Service Weekly, 298

Semmes, the Pirate, 89

Senarens, Luis Philip 285, 295, 297, 298-299

--Frank Reade Jr., and His Queen Clipper, 299

Seneca, 318

--Seneca's Morals, 147

Shackleford, Harry K., 295

Author-Title Index

Shakespeare, William,
  xvii, 1, 2, 4, 9, 163,
  170, 218
Shall We Suffocate Ed.
  Green?, 263
Shamrock, The, 107
Shaw, Henry Wheeler, xiv,
  81, 83, 277, 283
--Josh Billings' Farmer's
  Allminax, 83-84
--Josh Billings: His
  Works, Complete, 84
--Josh Billings, Hiz
  Sayings, 83
--Josh Billings' Old
  Probability, 84
--Josh Billings on Ice,
  83
Sheldon, Charles M.
--In His Steps, 2, 68
Shelley, Mary
--Frankenstein, 75
--Last Man, 75
--Perkin Warbeck, 75
Shelley, Percy Bysshe, 2
Shields, Sarah Anne
  Frost, 101
--Amateur Theatricals and
  Fairy-Tale Dramas, 108
--Art of Dressing Well,
  The, 110
--Book of Tableaux and
  Shadow Pantomimes, 108
--Humorous and Exhibition
  Dialogues, 105
--Parlor Acting Charades,
  108
Shove, Raymond H., 9, 23
Sigourney, Lydia H., 27,
  77, 139, 142
Silver King, The, 133

Simms, William Gilmore,
  120, 311
--Views and Reviews, 314
--"Voltmeier," 132
--Wigwam and the Cabin,
  The, 314
Simpson, Mrs. J. M., 277
--Faithful Margaret, 85
Sinbad the Sailor, 43
Sinclair, Upton, 279, 291
Six Penny Cooking Book, 45
Slate Pictures, 255
Small, George G., 221,
  225, 295
Smedley, Menella Bute
--Linnet's Trial, 196
--Twice Lost, 193
Smith, C. W.
--Art of Acting, The, 135
Smith, Francis S., 277-294
--Bertha, the Sewing
  Machine Girl, 282
--Vestmaker's Apprentice,
  The, 281
Smith, Henry Nash, 140
Smith, Julie P., 85
--Blossom-Bud and Her
  Genteel Friends, 85
--His Young Wife, 85
--Kiss, and Be Friends, 85
--Lucy, 85
--Widow Goldsmith's
  Daughter, 85
"Smith, S. Le Compton,"
  pseud. of Sylvanus
  Cobb, Jr., 142
Snaps, 298, 299
Soldiers' Directory to
  Pensions and Bounties,
  48
Southey, Robert, 167, 311

352

Author-Title Index

Southworth, Mrs. E. D.
E. N., 173, 174, 215,
229, 230, 232-233
--Hidden Hand, The, 232
--Lost Heiress, The, 232
--Retribution, 232
Sparks, Jared, 269
Spencer, Herbert, 212
Spirit Eye, 169
Spyri, Johanna, 97
Squier, Ephraim George,
182, 183
Standard American Poultry
Book, The, 217
Stand by the Flag, 48
"Standish, Burt L.,"
pseud. of William G.
Patten, 277, 289, 291
Stanley, H. A., 177
"Starbuck, Roger," pseud.
of Augustus Comstock,
36, 42
Starkweather, A. J. and
S. Robert Wilson
--Socialism, 206
Star Spangled Banner, 28
Stead, William T.
--If Christ Came To
Chicago, 178
Stedman, Edmund Clarence
--Prince's Ball, The, 82
Steffens, Lincoln, 292
Stephens, Ann Sophia, 27,
28, 37, 41, 44, 137,
139, 142, 182, 215,
229, 230, 232, 233,
277, 281
--Malaeska: the Indian
Wife of the White
Hunter, xiii, 41, 124-
125, 281
--Myra, the Child of
Adoption, 42

Stern, Madeleine B.
--Imprints on History, —
171, 309
Stevenson, Robert Louis,
163, 173, 174
--Travels with a Donkey,
274
--Treasure Island, 274
Stoddard, W. O., 149
--Elinor's Chase, 185
--Lone Wolf, 185
Stopes, Marie C.
--Married Love, 70
Story, Joseph, 78
Stowe, Harriet Beecher
--Uncle Tom's Cabin, 45
Stratemeyer, Edward,
277, 285, 288
--Bobbsey Twins, 288
--Bomba the Jungle Boy,
288
--Hardy Boys, 288
--Jack the Inventor, 285
--Rover Boys, The, 288
--Tom Swift, 288
Street Scenes in New York,
254
Student and Schoolmate,
193
Studies in Composition and
Color, 258
Sue, Eugène, 230
Sue Munday, the Guerrilla
Spy, 89
Sullivan, Matt
--"Coon Yarns", 173
Sumner, William G., 157
Sunday Dispatch, The, 277,
279
Swift, Jonathan
--Gulliver's Travels, 2,
43, 264

353

Author-Title Index

Swinburne, Algernon
    Charles, 319
--Songs Before Sunrise,
    274
Swiss Family Robinson,
    The, 147
Symonds, John Addington,
    157

Taine, Hippolyte A., 157,
    161-162
--French Revolution, 161
--History of English
    Literature, 161
--Tour Through the
    Pyrenees, A, 161-162
Tait, A. F.
--Group of Chickens, 255
--Group of Ducklings, 255
Tale of New York Life, A,
    169
Tarkington, Booth, 153
Tayleure, Clifton W.
--Horseshoe Robinson, 134
Taylor, Bayard, 19
--Views a-Foot, 314
Teacher's Manual for the
    Prang Course in Draw-
    ing, A, 258
Tebbel, John, 169
--History of Book Pub-
    lishing in the United
    States, A, 67
--Rags to Riches, 67
Ten Eyck, Edward, 225,
    295, 297
Tennyson, Alfred Lord, 2,
    13, 318
Tent and Forecastle Song-
    ster, The, 197
Terhune, Mary Virginia
    Hawes, 85

--Alone, 85
--At Last, 85
--Empty Heart, The, 85
--Helen Gardner's Wedding-
    Day, 85
--Jessamine, 85
--My Little Love, 85
--Phemie's Temptation, 85
Textbook of Art Education,
    The, 258
Thackeray, William
    Makepeace, 2, 69, 99,
    148, 161, 201, 212
    218, 307, 313, 318
--Vanity Fair, 203
Theuriet, André
--Dangerous Delights, 120
Thimm, Franz
--French Self-Taught, 110
This Book-Collecting Adven-
    ture Presented by The
    Delaware Bibliophiles,
    112
Thomas, Jerry
--How to Mix Drinks, 111
Thomes, William Henry,
    124-129
--Belle of Australia, The,
    128
--Bushrangers, The, 128
--Gold Hunters' Adven-
    tures, The, 128
--Gold Hungers in Europe,
    The, 128
--Life in the East Indies,
    128
--Ocean Rovers, The, 128
--On Land and Sea, 128
--Running the Blockade,
    128
--Slaver's Adventures, A,
    128

--Whaleman's Adventures
in the Sandwich Islands
and California, The,
128
Thompson, Roy
--Respectable Family, A,
119
Thomson, Mortimer, 82
--Nothing to Say, 82
Thoreau, Henry David, 272
Three Chums Weekly, 298,
399
Ticknor, George, 78
Tid-Bits, 204
Timayensis, Telemachus,
173
Tinseau, Leon de, 319
Tip Top Weekly, 285, 291
Tony Pastor's "444" Com-
bination Songster, 107
Tony Pastor's 201 Bowery
Songster, 107
Tony Pastor's Waterfall
Songster, 107
Töpffer, Rodolphe
--Adventures of Mr.
Obadiah Oldbuck, The,
112
Tousey, Sinclair, 295,
303-305
--Indices of Public
Opinion, 304
--Life in the Union Army,
304
--Papers from Over the
Waters, 304
Townsend, Charles
--Darkey Wood Dealer, 108
Townsend, Edward W., 213
Townsend, Virginia
Frances, 191, 196

--Boy from Bramby, The,
196
--Hope Darrow, 196
--Joanna Darling, 196
--Max Meredith's Millen-
nium, 196
Tricks and Diversions with
Cards, 170
Trollope, Anthony, 116
True Blue, 291
True Flag, 28, 123
True Politeness, 169
"Trumps," pseud. of
William B. Dick, 105
"Trumps, Jr.," pseud. of
Harris Brisbane Dick,
113
Turgeneve, Ivan, 161, 163,
164
--Fathers and Sons, 162
--Smoke, 162
Turner, Ned
--Clown Joke Book, 105
Turner, William Mason, 44
Twain, Mark, 59, 60, 61,
149, 153, 291, 303
--Jim Smiley's Frog, 46
--"Jumping Frog of
Calaveras County, The,"
46, 87
--Notebook, 87
--Prince and the Pauper,
The, 60-61
--Tom Sawyer, 34

Uncle Jeremiah and His
Family, 178
"Uncle Remus," pseud. of
Joel Chandler Harris,
44
Uncle Sam, 28
Under the Gaslight, 299

Author-Title Index

Unpartizan Review, The,
161
Unpopular Review, The,
161
Use of Models, The, 258

Van Zile, E. S., 213
Venor, H. G.
--Our Birds of Prey, 318
Ventriloquists' Guide,
170
Verne, Jules, 116, 120,
174, 285, 298-299
--Michael Strogoff, 185
--Robur the Conquerer,
298, 299
Victor, Metta V., 37, 39,
44
--"Dead Letter, The," 132
--Dime Cook-Book, 40
--Dime Recipe Book, 40-41
--Maum Guinea and Her
Plantation Children,
45
Victor, Orville J., 39-40,
132
--Life of Joseph
Garibaldi, 39
Views in Central Park, 254
Views of Niagara Falls,
254
Vincent, Louis, 221
Visit from St. Nicholas,
A, 255
Von Falke, Jacob
--Art in The House, 258
Voynich, E. L., 157

Walker, Francis A.
--Political Economy, 165
Wallace, Edgar, 65, 69

Wallace, Lew
--Ben Hur, 149
Walters, A. T., Collection
of Oriental Ceramic
Art, 258
"Ward, Artemus," pseud. of
Charles Farrar Browne,
81, 83
Ward, Mrs. Humphry, 173,
199, 204
--Robert Elsmere, 204
Warfield, Mrs. C. A., 218
Warne, Philip S.
--Hard Crowd, A, 47
Warner, Anna B., 98
Warner, Susan, 97
Warren, Eliza
--How I Managed My House
on £200 A Year, 197
Watts, Dictionary of
Chemistry, 318
Webb, Charles H., 84
--St. Twel'mo, 84
Webber, Charles W., 93
--Gold Mines of the Gila,
The, 94
Webster, Noah, xvii
--Dictionary, 81-82
--Elementary Spelling
Book, xiv, 21, 24
Weekly Novelist, The, 237
Weekly Sun, The, 279
Welcome Guest, The, 33
Weldon's Fancy Costumes,
108
Wells, Carolyn, 69
Wells, H. G., 157
--Time Machine, The, 165
Western World, 127
What Next? Favorite
Poems, 1
Wheeler, Edward L., 37,
44, 49, 174

Author-Title Index

--Deadwood Dick, the
Prince of the Road,
xiii, 47
--Fritz, the Bound-Boy
Detective, 47
Whistler, James M., 212
White, Richard Grant, 303
White Elephant, 298
White Lies, 133
White Mountain Scenery,
254
Whitman, Walt, 320-321
--After All, Not to
Create Only, 272-273
--Leaves of Grass, xix-
xx, 320-321
Whitney, Mrs. A. D. T.,
191, 196
--Faith Gartney's Girl-
hood, 192, 193
--Hitherto, 196
--Mother Goose for Grown
Folks, 196
--Patience Strong's Out-
ings, 196
Whittier, John Greenleaf,
272
--Supernaturalism of New
England, The, 314
Wide World, 132
Widow Machree Song Book,
48
"Wigwam Edition." The
Life . . . of Abraham
Lincoln, 82
Wilcox, Ella Wheeler, 59
Wilde, Oscar, 188
--Poems, 274
Wild West Weekly, 298
Williams, Henry L., 93
Wilson, Augusta Evans,
81, 84

--Macaria, 84
--St. Elmo, xiv, 84
--Vashti, 84
Wilson, Floyd Baker
--Book of Recitations and
Dialogues, 105
"Wilton, Capt. Mark,"
pseud. of William H.
Manning, 238
Winthrop, Theodore, 163
Wister, Owen
--Virginian, The, 149
Wodehouse, P. G., 69
--Jeeves, 69
Woman-Hater, A, 222
Women's Work in the House,
13
Wood, Mrs. Henry (Ellen),
101, 229, 230, 233
--East Lynne, 111-112,
222, 233
Wood, Norman D., 119
--White Side of a Black
Subject, The, 120
Wood, William
--Laws of Athletics, The,
109
Work and Win, 298
World's Fair Viewbook,
The, 178
Worthington Album, 319
Worthington Annual, 319
Wright, A. S.
--Book of Three Thousand
American Receipts, 109
Wright, Harold Bell, 65,
68
--Calling of Don Matthews,
The, 68
--Shepherd of the Hills,
The, 68

357

Author-Title Index

--Winning of Barbara
  Worth, The, 68
Wright, Lyle
--American Fiction, 62

Yankee, 28
Yankee Doodle, 298, 299
Yankee Nation, 28
Yankee Privateer, 28
Yates, Edmund
--Broken to Harness, 196
--Forlorn Hope, 196
--Running the Gauntlet,
  196
Yeats, William Butler,
  319

--Fairy and Folk Tales,
  319
Yellow Kid, The, 292
Yonge, Charlotte, 317
--Aunt Charlotte's Pic-
  ture Books, 318
Young Glory, 298, 299
Young Klondike, 298, 299
Young Men of America, The,
  226, 297, 298
Youth's Casket, The, 40

Zola, Emile, xviii, 177,
  178, 230, 300
--Dream, 178